Mastering Mobile Forensics

Develop the capacity to dig deeper into mobile device
data acquisition

Soufiane Tahiri

PUBLISHING

BIRMINGHAM - MUMBAI

Mastering Mobile Forensics

First published: May 2016

Production reference: 1250516

Published by Packt Publishing Ltd.
Livery Place
35 Livery Street
Birmingham B3 2PB, UK.

ISBN 978-1-78528-781-7

www.packtpub.com

Credits

Author
Soufiane Tahiri

Reviewer
Michael Yasumoto

Commissioning Editor
Julian Ursell

Acquisition Editor
Rahul Nair

Content Development Editor
Trusha Shriyan

Technical Editor
Taabish Khan

Copy Editors
Sonia Mathur

Sneha Singh

Project Coordinator
Shweta H Birwatkar

Proofreader
Safis Editing

Indexer
Hemangini Bari

Graphics
Kirk D'Penha

Disha Haria

Jason Monteiro

Production Coordinator
Aparna Bhagat

Cover Work
Aparna Bhagat

About the Author

Soufiane Tahiri is an independent computer security researcher and science enthusiast from Morocco, who specializes in .NET reverse code engineering and software security. He has an interest in low-level techniques and in recent years he has developed an interest in computer and smartphone forensics. He has been involved in IT security for more than 10 years and has dozen of publications and a lot of research in different computer security fields under his name.

I owe my deepest gratitude to a lot of people, including my family and my friends.

This book is for my dad, Abdelkebir; I know how proud you are of me but I want you to know how proud I am of you; you've always been an engine for me, I love you. My mom, Halima; thank you for your unconditional love and support, I love you, and this book is for you. My sisters Soundous, Kaoutar, and Souad for always supporting and telling me that they are proud of me, I love you.

I would also like to thank all my friends, especially Mounir, who does not miss a chance to encourage me and to tell me that I can achieve this and who bought me candies so I'd have sufficient energy while I was writing this book, thank you brother, you are the best. Also a big thank you to Youssef for his daily encouragement and for giving me all the support I needed, you are my big bro. I also want to thank Simohamed Ghannam, Ayoub Faouzi, Kamal, Abdelouahed, and all the others whom I have not have listed here.

I want to tell all of you that I feel proud of this achievement because of your help, support, and love. Thank you all.

About the Reviewer

Michael Yasumoto is the CEO at Deadbolt Forensics, a digital forensics consulting company located in Portland, Oregon. He is a digital forensics examiner for attorneys and private companies and has testified as an expert witness in court. He is also an instructor for AccessData, teaching mobile forensics to law enforcement, both domestically and abroad.

Michael holds a bachelor's degree in chemistry from the University of Washington and a master's degree in computer science from the George Washington University. Some of his forensic credentials include Certified Computer Examiner (CCE), X-Ways Professional in Evidence Recovery Techniques (X-PERT), EnCase Certified Examiner (EnCE), AccessData Certified Examiner (ACE), Cellebrite Certified Mobile Examiner (CCME), and AccessData Mobile Examiner (AME).

www.PacktPub.com

eBooks, discount offers, and more

Did you know that Packt offers eBook versions of every book published, with PDF and ePub files available? You can upgrade to the eBook version at www.PacktPub.com and as a print book customer, you are entitled to a discount on the eBook copy. Get in touch with us at customercare@packtpub.com for more details.

At www.PacktPub.com, you can also read a collection of free technical articles, sign up for a range of free newsletters and receive exclusive discounts and offers on Packt books and eBooks.

https://www2.packtpub.com/books/subscription/packtlib

Do you need instant solutions to your IT questions? PacktLib is Packt's online digital book library. Here, you can search, access, and read Packt's entire library of books.

Why subscribe?

- Fully searchable across every book published by Packt
- Copy and paste, print, and bookmark content
- On demand and accessible via a web browser

Table of Contents

Preface

It's not a secret that mobile devices have evolved dramatically from being those fateful boxes to extremely advanced brains; their names have also changed from phones to smartphones.

Mobile devices are getting as powerful as personal computers and they can do almost any task that we might need on a daily basis, such as taking and sharing photos and videos, sending and receiving e-mails, checking your bank balance and making bank transactions, social networking, managing tasks and reminders, and so on. Any mobile phone is a huge repository of sensitive data related to its owner and given the pace at which mobile development is progressing, there is no doubt that the need for forensic examination of these devices is on the rise too.

Mobile forensics is a set of scientific methodologies with the goal of extracting digital evidence in a legal context. Extracting digital evidence means recovering, gathering, and analyzing data stored within the internal memory of a mobile phone. Mobile forensics is a continuously evolving science, which involves permanently evolving techniques and presents a real challenge to the forensic community and law enforcement due to the fast and unstoppable changes in technology.

There are a huge number of mobile device models that are in use today and new models are manufactured every five months, and most of them use closed operating systems, thus making the forensic process much more difficult. This book gives the forensic community an in-depth look at mobile forensic techniques by detailing methods of gathering evidence from mobile devices running on Android, iOS, and Windows Phone.

What this book covers

Chapter 1, Mobile Forensics and the Investigation Process Model, talks about the importance of smartphone forensics in our continually growing digital world. We will then describe smartphone forensic models and how they have evolved with time. We will also point out challenges that today's investigators face in the smartphone forensics evidence acquisition process.

Chapter 2, Do It Yourself – Low-Level Techniques, covers the techniques used to carve files and to manually extract GPS data, and explains how things are in there at a low level. This chapter will also cover some techniques that extract strings from different objects (for example, smartphone images) and it will also describe the basics of reverse engineering smartphone applications.

Chapter 3, iDevices from a Forensic Point of View, provides an overview of the forensic approach of an iOS device. We will introduce iOS architecture components and filesystems. This chapter will indicate the methodologies, techniques, and tools used to acquire evidence from iOS devices. It will also point out the difference between different modes (DFU and recovery), introduce the jailbreaking concept, and discuss the biometric aspect of iOS devices.

Chapter 4, Android Forensics, brings to light some important points about Android OS internals, filesystem, data structures, and security models. It will also discuss how it is possible to logically and physically acquire an Android device. We will also take a look at the JTAG and chip-off techniques; this chapter will also explain how to bypass lock screens, security, and encryption. In this chapter, we will discuss a real case of forensic analysis of a third-party application.

Chapter 5, Windows Phone 8 Forensics, introduces Windows Phone 8. In the first part of this chapter we will see the main difference between WP7 and WP8 and then, in the upcoming section, we will go through Windows 8 internals and describe WP8 security models and their implementation. This chapter also describes the WP filesystem, and then we will go through the steps to logically acquire a Windows Phone 8 device; we will also describe WP PINs and hardware encryption. Finally, we will cover evidence location in the Windows Phone registry and analyze Windows Phone PINs.

Chapter 6, Mobile Forensics – Best Practices, will go beyond the technical aspects of smartphone device forensics and introduce you to some of the best practices of recovering digital evidence from a mobile device under forensically sound conditions. This chapter will describe the methodology of the forensic process used for mobile devices and will present guidelines for specific activities in the handling of digital evidence.

Appendix, Preparing a Mobile Forensic Workstation, will show you how to prepare a mobile forensics workstation based on Santoku Linux.

What you need for this book

This book is designed to help the reader use different operating systems (Windows and Linux) and also covers various forensic approaches and techniques on iOS, Android, and Windows Phone through freeware, open source, and commercial software. The content is organized to let any reader perform a forensic investigation on most popular smartphone operating systems. Most topics are introduced from basic or intermediate level to in-depth. Across the chapters, the reader is always linked to the software used and, if needed, to the webpages that have more details about a given topic. This book is not in any way meant to be a form of advertising for the commercial tools used.

Who this book is for

This book is for mobile forensics professionals who have experience of handling forensics tools and methods. This book is designed for skilled digital forensic examiners, mobile forensic investigators, and law enforcement officers.

Conventions

In this book, you will find a number of text styles that distinguish between different kinds of information. Here are some examples of these styles and an explanation of their meaning.

Code words in text, database table names, folder names, filenames, file extensions, pathnames, dummy URLs, user input, and Twitter handles are shown as follows: "The res directory is the directory used to store application resources."

A block of code is set as follows:

```
for i = 1 to Nr-1 stepsize 1 do
   SubBytes(state);
   ShiftRows(state);
   MixColumns(state);
   AddRoundKey(state,round_key[i]);
end for
```

Any command-line input or output is written as follows:

```
adb shell pm path com.facebook.lite
```

New terms and **important words** are shown in bold. Words that you see on the screen, for example, in menus or dialog boxes, appear in the text like this: "After opening the software, click on **Open File**."

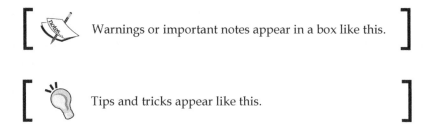

[Warnings or important notes appear in a box like this.]

[Tips and tricks appear like this.]

Reader feedback

Feedback from our readers is always welcome. Let us know what you think about this book—what you liked or disliked. Reader feedback is important for us as it helps us develop titles that you will really get the most out of.

To send us general feedback, simply e-mail feedback@packtpub.com, and mention the book's title in the subject of your message.

If there is a topic that you have expertise in and you are interested in either writing or contributing to a book, see our author guide at www.packtpub.com/authors.

Customer support

Now that you are the proud owner of a Packt book, we have a number of things to help you to get the most from your purchase.

Downloading the color images of this book

We also provide you with a PDF file that has color images of the screenshots/diagrams used in this book. The color images will help you better understand the changes in the output. You can download this file from https://www.packtpub.com/sites/default/files/downloads/MasteringMobileForensics_ColorImages.pdf.

Errata

Although we have taken every care to ensure the accuracy of our content, mistakes do happen. If you find a mistake in one of our books—maybe a mistake in the text or the code—we would be grateful if you could report this to us. By doing so, you can save other readers from frustration and help us improve subsequent versions of this book. If you find any errata, please report them by visiting `http://www.packtpub.com/submit-errata`, selecting your book, clicking on the **Errata Submission Form** link, and entering the details of your errata. Once your errata are verified, your submission will be accepted and the errata will be uploaded to our website or added to any list of existing errata under the Errata section of that title.

To view the previously submitted errata, go to `https://www.packtpub.com/books/content/support` and enter the name of the book in the search field. The required information will appear under the **Errata** section.

Piracy

Piracy of copyrighted material on the Internet is an ongoing problem across all media. At Packt, we take the protection of our copyright and licenses very seriously. If you come across any illegal copies of our works in any form on the Internet, please provide us with the location address or website name immediately so that we can pursue a remedy.

Please contact us at `copyright@packtpub.com` with a link to the suspected pirated material.

We appreciate your help in protecting our authors and our ability to bring you valuable content.

Questions

If you have a problem with any aspect of this book, you can contact us at `questions@packtpub.com`, and we will do our best to address the problem.

1
Mobile Forensics and the Investigation Process Model

Smartphone forensics is a relatively new and quickly emerging field of interest within the digital forensic and law enforcement community. Today's mobile devices are getting smarter, cheaper, and easily available to the common man for daily use.

Mobile forensics are a set of scientific methodologies with the goal of extracting digital evidence (in general) in a legal context. Extracting digital evidence means recovering, gathering, and analyzing the data stored within the internal memory of a mobile phone. Mobile forensics is a continuously evolving science, which involves permanently evolving techniques; it presents a real challenge to the forensic community and law enforcement due to the fast and unstoppable changes in technology.

To investigate the growing number of digital crimes and complaints, researchers have put in a lot of effort to develop the most affordable investigative model; in this chapter, we will place emphasis on the importance of paying real attention to the growing market of smartphones and the effort put in this area from a digital forensic point of view in order to bring about the most comprehensive investigation process.

This chapter will be oriented towards the importance of smartphone forensics in our continuously growing digital world; then, we will describe some smartphone forensic models and how they evolved through history. We will also be pointing out the challenges that today's investigators face in the smartphone forensics evidence acquisition process.

This chapter will cover the following topics:

- Why mobile forensics?
- Smartphone forensics models
- Smartphone forensics challenges

Why mobile forensics?

The promptly evolving mobile phone industry has reached an unimaginable peak and smartphones will definitely replace computers, since a lot of those tiny devices are becoming as powerful as personal computers.

On a daily use basis, each smartphone is a huge repository of sensitive data related to its owner. Nowadays, smartphones are used to perform almost any task that we need to do, starting from the "traditional" tasks involving sending and receiving of calls, short text messages, and e-mails to more complex ones, such as geolocation, balance checking, making bank transactions, and managing tasks and reminders. Given the pace at which development is progressing, the need for forensic examination is as well. Data contained within modern devices is continuously becoming richer and more relevant, which is partly due to the exploding growth and the use of mobile applications and social networks. In addition to this, all mobile phones are now capable of storing all kinds of personal information and usually even unintentionally.

According to ABI research (`https://www.abiresearch.com/market-research/ product/1004938-smartphone-technologies-and-markets/`), which is a technology market intelligence company, at the time of writing this book there are more than 1.4 billion smartphones that are in use; more than 798 million of them are running on Android, more than 294 million are running Apple's iOS, and more than 45 million are running Windows Phone, which represents a growth rate of 44% for 2013 according to the same source.

In its report, Cisco states (`http://www.cisco.com/c/en/us/solutions/ collateral/service-provider/visual-networking-index-vni/white_paper_ c11-520862.html`) that an average smartphone user will make five video calls and download 15 applications each month.

If we refer to data given by Nielsen Informate Mobile Insights, (`http://www. nielsen.com/us/en/insights/news/2014/smartphones-so-many-apps--so- much-time.html`) in the US, Android and iPhone users spent 30 hours and 15 minutes using apps on their smartphones in Q4 2013, and this amount of time is not decreasing, as shown in the following chart:

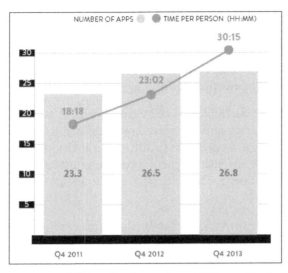

NUMBER OF APPS   TIME PER PERSON (HH:MM)

In the Q4 2013, users used 28.8 applications and spent 30 hours, 15 minutes on them.

All this advancement has a lot of benefits for sure, but without any doubt it represents new challenges to law enforcement as cybercrime and digital complaints continue to grow. This issue was raised by the Federal Bureau of Investigation (FBI) and the Internet Crime Complain Center (`http://www.ic3.gov/media/ annualreport/2014_IC3Report.pdf`). In 2014, the total number of complaints received is 269,244 and all statistics are huge, as shown here:

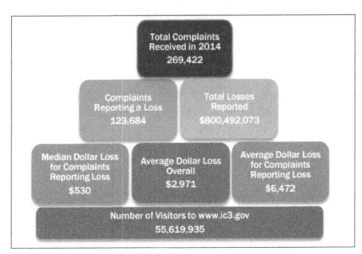

Total digital complaints and digital complaints loss as given by the FBI Internet Crime Complaint Center

So, why is mobile forensics important? Simply because acquiring a smartphone means acquiring a person's everyday life in terms of data. Some proactive acquisition approaches are gaining place in a criminal context not only after a crime, but also when people violate regulations and laws, such as preventing terrorist attempts, crimes against states, and pedophilia.

Today's smartphones contain all kinds of evidence stored as heterogeneous data generated from the hardware and the software constituting the device. Categorizing this data is quite important; in order to produce some kind of evidence classification, only a well-driven mobile forensic approach can help us make the correct correlation between data, data type, and evidence type. (refer to *Chapter 6, Mobile Forensics – Best Practices*, for more details)

The importance of mobile forensics is established and cannot be denied in this age of information where every single byte matters.

Smartphone forensics models

Given the pace at which mobile technology is growing and the variety of complexities that are produced by today's mobile data, forensics examiners face serious adaptation problems, so developing and adopting standards makes sense.

The reliability of evidence depends directly on the adopted investigative processes; choosing to bypass or bypassing a step accidentally may (and will certainly) lead to incomplete evidence and increases the risk of rejection in the court of law.

Today, there is no standard or unified model adapted to acquire evidence from smartphones. The dramatic development of smart devices suggests that any forensic examiner will have to apply as many independent models as necessary in order to collect and preserve data. There are a lot of proposed forensic models and reviewing each one of them will be a colossal task. In the following paragraphs, I'll be presenting some of them without pretending that the selected models are the best. The following models are sorted chronologically, starting from the earliest model established.

Computer Forensic Investigation Process

Historically, back in 1984, the FBI and many other law enforcement agencies began modeling the examination of digital evidences based on the earlier versions of computers, and the first digital forensic process model was **Computer Forensic Investigation Process (CFIP)**. CFIP was first presented in 1995 by M. M. Pollitt (M. M. Pollitt. (1995). *Computer Forensics: An Approach to Evidence in Cyberspace*), and this model focuses exclusively on the result, in other words the model focuses principally on data acquisition and how reliable and legally acceptable this data is.

The Computer Forensic Investigation Process model is conducted in 4 stages:

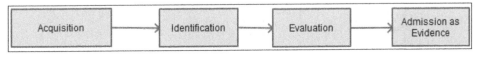

CFIP model

Acquisition is a technical problem, which is not free from the legal aspect, and data acquired must answer three main questions: what can be sized, from whom, and from where can it be sized. This means that digital evidence must be acquired in an acceptable manner with the necessary approvals from concerned authorities. This stage is followed by the **Identification** phase; as in this model, this phase is subdivided in to a three step process: defining the physical form of data, defining the data's logical position, and then placing this data (evidence) in its correct context. Digital evidence follows the path shown here:

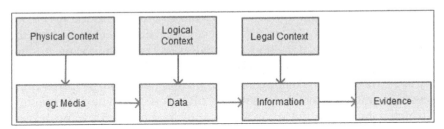

Digital evidence Identification process

The **Evaluation** stage consists of placing the gathered data in its proper context and this is as legal as a technical task. At this point of the forensic process, we can determine if the acquired information is relevant and can be described as legitimate evidence in the case being investigated or not. Finally, the **Admitting** process includes admitting the extracted data as legal evidence and presenting it in the court of law.

Digital Forensic Research Workshop

In 2001, the first **Digital Forensic Research Workshop (DFRWS)** (http://www.dfrws.org/2001/dfrws-rm-final.pdf) was held to produce and define a scientific methodology to drive digital forensics to produce a reliable framework (it's dubbed as Investigative Process for Digital Forensic Science) to drive the majority of digital investigation cases, and the result was a six stage linear process. Each step or stage is defined as a category or class and each class has candidate methods belonging to that category.

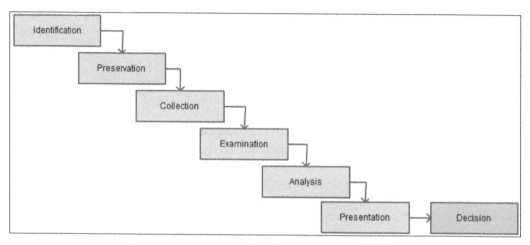

Investigative Process for Digital Forensic Science (DFRWS)

As seen in the preceding diagram, the DFRWS model starts with the **Identification** stage, which is subdivided to tasks such as event detection, signature resolving, profile detection, anomalous detection, complaints, system monitoring, and audit analysis. This stage is followed by **Preservation**, which is a candidate for four tasks; they are setting up case management, managing technologies, ensuring a chain of custody, and time synchronization. **Collection** comes next, as the third phase in which data is collected according to approved methods, using approved software/hardware and under legal authority; this phase is also based on lossless compression, sampling, data reduction, and data recovery techniques. After collection, comes **Examination**, which is directly followed by the **Analysis** phase, where very important tasks are performed and evidences are traced, validated, and filtered. Data mining and timeline analyses are done as well. At this stage, the hidden and encrypted data is discovered and extracted. The stage that comes after this is **Presentation,** in which documentation, clarification, expert testimony, mission impact statement, and recommended countermeasures are presented. However, this model is open to criticism regarding the use of the collection and preservation stages and if one is an actual subcategory of the other.

Abstract Digital Forensics Model

Being a more generic framework, DFRWS inspired researchers in the US Air Force in 2002 to present the Abstract Model of the Digital Forensic Process (M. Reith, C. Carr & G. Gunsh. 2002. *An Examination of Digital Forensics Models*) or **Abstract Digital Forensics Model (ADFM)**, which is meant to be an enhanced DFRWS model with adding three more stages added to the existing process: **Preparation**, **Approach Strategy**, and **Returning Evidence**, leading to the following nine phases:

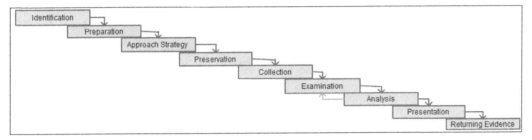

Abstract Digital Forensics Model

The actual added value of this model is the introduction of the pre/post-investigation approaches, before any exercise and after identifying the type of the incident: preparing tools, techniques and searching warrants, and securing management support, followed by the approach strategy, which is meant to dynamically establish an approach to collect the maximum amount of evidence without impacting the victim. However, this phase is criticized for being a duplicate of the second stage, since preparing to respond to an incident will likely end with preparing for an "approach strategy". Lastly, returning evidence shows the importance of safely storing evidence removed from the scene in order to return it back to the owner.

The Abstract Digital Forensics Model ignored the importance of chain of custody, but authors of this model assumed that a chain of custody is obviously maintained through an investigation process and is implied in any forensic model.

Integrated Digital Investigation Process

In 2003, Brian Carrier and Eugene H. Spafford (Carrier, B., & Spafford, E. H. 2003. *Getting Physical with the Digital Investigation Process*. The International Journal of Digital Evidence) introduced an **Integrated Digital Investigation Process (IDIP)**, which is an integration of digital forensics to physical investigation; it's a framework based on the available processes of physical crime scene investigation.

The main idea of this model is to consider a digital crime scene as a "virtual crime scene" and to apply adapted crime scene investigation techniques. This model is macroscopically composed of five stages, consisting microscopically of 17 stages.

The following diagram shows the five macroscopic stages of an IDIP model:

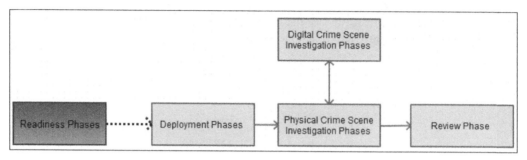

The five macroscopic stage of IDIP model

Physical and digital crime scenes are processed together and digital forensics are fed into a physical investigation.

The **Readiness Phase** ensures that human competences and technical infrastructures are able to fully carry the whole investigation process; this stage is subdivided into two phases:

- **Operation Readiness**: This involves the preparation of adequate training and equipment for the personnel who will investigate the crime scene.

- **Infrastructure Readiness**: This phase aims to ensure data stability and integrity, for as long as the investigation process takes. This phase may include, for example, hashing files, securely storing evidence, and maintaining a change management database.

The first stage is followed by **Deployment phase**, the goal of this stage is to provide a mechanism to detect and confirm an incident, and this stage is also subdivided in to two phases:

- **Detection and notification**: Concretely, this phase triggers the start of the investigation process where the incident is detected and the appropriate people are notified.

- **Confirmation and authorization**: Once a crime or incident is confirmed, in this phase, authorization must be received to fully investigate the digital crime scene.

The **Physical Crime Scene Investigation Phase** which come after the first phase, is when the investigation itself begins with the goal of collecting and analyzing the physical evidences to reconstruct actions that first took place. This stage is subdivided into six phases that are typical to real cases' post-physical crime investigation process and are described in the following diagram:

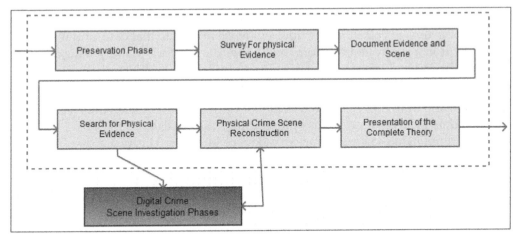

Physical Crime Scene Investigation

This stage is followed by a similar stage of a digital context focusing on digital evidence within a "virtual" digital environment. The **Digital Crime Scene Investigation Phases** follows the previously presented path by considering any smartphone (or other digital device) as a separate crime scene.

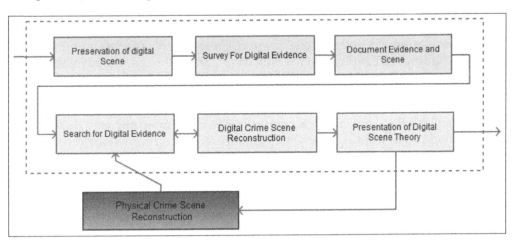

Digital Crime Scene Investigation

It is subdivided into the following phases:

- **Preservation of Digital Scene**: In this phase, the investigator must pay attention to maintaining data integrity, meaning that at this level, the digital scene must be secured in order to avoid any external interference that could alter the evidence.

- **Survey For Digital Evidence**: Depending on the case being investigated, this phase aims to collect the obvious evidence related to that case, and it should occur in a controlled environment (a forensic lab, for instance) using a replica of the original crime scene.

- **Document Evidence and Scene**: The documentation phase involves documenting every acquired evidence during the conducted analysis, and using cryptographic hashing techniques such as MD5 or SHA-1 is recommended to keep a trace of evidence integrity. This phase does not substitute the final forensic report.

- **Search for Digital Evidence**: The collection phase involves a deeper digging and more in-depth analysis of what was found in the previous phase and focuses on a more specific and low-level analysis of the digital device activities. Deleted file recovering, file carving, reverse engineering, and encrypted file analysis are some examples of techniques that can be applied at this stage.

- **Digital Crime Scene Reconstruction**: All digital evidence acquired is put together in order to define at what point we can trust or reject the collected evidence and to determine if further analysis is required and if a search for digital evidence should be resumed in the case of any missing parts of the whole puzzle.

- **Presentation of Digital Scene Theory**: This phase documents and presents the findings of the physical investigation team in the case the investigation was not performed by the same team.

The final stage of the whole model is the **Review Phase**, and it is a kind of self-criticism in which the whole process is reviewed to determine how well the investigation process went right or wrong and to detect the improvement points.

This model presents many similarities with the previously presented models and can easily be considered as an enhanced model of both; nevertheless, the IDIP model is way too abstract and the interaction between physical and digital investigations may not be applicable in many cases.

End-to-end digital investigation process

By the same year, that is, 2003, Peter Stephenson (Stephenson, P. 2003. *A Comprehensive Approach to Digital Incident Investigation*) reviewed the DFRWS framework and translated it into a "more" practical investigative process dubbed as the **End-To-End Digital Investigation** (**EEDI**) process by extending the existing process into nine stages. It's called end-to-end because in his model, Stephenson considers that "every digital crime has a source point, a destination point, and a path between those two points".

The model itself is schematized as follows:

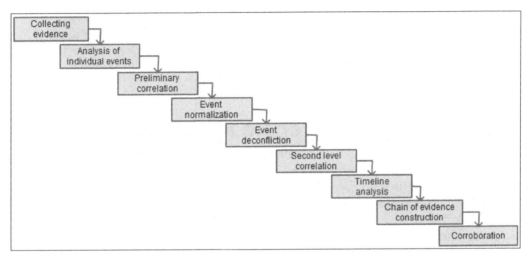

The basic End-to-End Digital Investigation process

EEDI can be considered as a layer applied to the DFRWS model. Depending on the cases, the whole EEDI process is applied to each class of the DRFWS model (refer to the diagram in the *Digital Forensic Research Workshop* section). This model defines the critical steps to be performed in order to correctly preserve, collect, and analyze digital evidence. In the **Collecting Evidence** phase, primary and secondary evidence is collected and taken in their respective contexts. The context here is related to an event's time sensitivity, which brings us to the second step of this process, **Analysis of Individual events**, where each individual event is isolated and analyzed separately to determine how it can be tied with other events and to consider the potential value it can add, or they can add, to the overall investigation. This is followed by the **Preliminary Correlation** step, in which individual events are linked with each other to determinate a primary chain of evidence in order to determine what happened, when, and which devices were involved.

Event normalization is a step that mainly aims to remove redundancy in evidentiary data assuming that the same events can be reported separately from different sources using multiple vocabularies. As an extension to the normalization, irrespective of how and from where they were reported, the same evidentiary events are combined into one evidentiary event in the **Event deconfliction** step; at this stage, all the events and evidentiary events are refined and a **Second level correlation** can be performed. The previously outlined steps result in a timeline, which is defined in the **Timeline analysis** step. The timeline analysis is an iterative task, which lasts as long as the investigation lasts. The **Chain of evidence construction** can begin based on the result of the timeline of events; theoretically, a coherent chain is developed when each evident will lead to the other and this is what is meant to be done in this step. The last phase of this model is **Corroboration**, where digital investigators support, strengthen, and confirm each evidence, within the chain of evidences previously developed, with other independent or traditional events and evidence collected in the case of a digital forensic investigation being conducted with the support of a group of investigators outside the digital forensic unit.

Systemic Digital Forensic Investigation

In 2004, four models were developed: the **Enhanced Integrated Digital Investigation Process**, invented by Baryamureeba and Tushabe containing 21 phases; Séamus Ó Ciardhuáin presented an **Extended Model of Cybercrime Investigation** with 13 activities to follow; followed by a six phase **Hierarchical, Objective-based Framework** that was invented by Beebe and Clark. The same year, Carrier and Spafford announced the **Event-based Digital Forensic Investigation Framework** and detailed the 16 phases to follow.

Approximately each year, at least one new forensic model is developed and according to the pace at which the digital world rises, researchers keep trying to give birth to "the perfect" forensic model.

Considering the space allocated to this chapter, I will jump directly to 2011; A. Agarwal, M. Gupta, S. Gupta, and S. C. Gupta came up with the **Systemic Digital Forensic Investigation (SRDIFM)** model (A. Agarwal, M. Gupta, S. Gupta, and S. C. Gupta. *Systematic digital forensic investigation model*). This model is similar to most of the previously presented models; it has common phases and some specific phases adapted to the model requirement. SRDIFM is composed of 11 phases: preparation, securing the scene, survey and recognition, documentation of the scene, shielding, volatile and non-volatile evidence collection, preservation, examination, analysis, presentation, result, and review.

The following diagram schematizes the model:

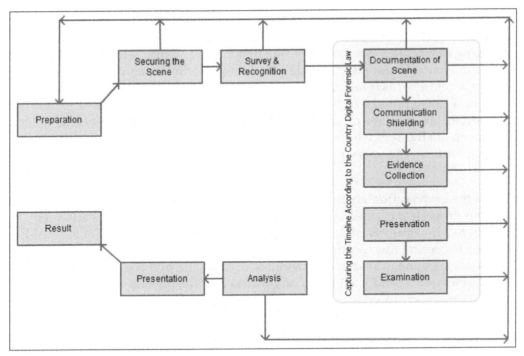

Phases of Systematic Digital Forensic Investigation Model (SRDFIM)

The first step of this model is **Preparation,** which is before the process of investigation and involves obtaining prior legal authorization. An initial understanding of the case will be investigated in order to prepare the adequate human and technical resources before going any further in the process of investigation. It's followed by **Securing the Scene** this phase aims principally to keep data integrity intact and to minimize possible data corruption. The **Survey and Recognition** phase comprises of tasks to elaborate an initial plan to collect and analyze evidence where, potential sources of evidences must be identified, including sources other than the main smart device itself; for example the presence of a personal computer in the scene means that there is a chance to find smartphone related data synchronized with it.

The next phase is known as **Documentation of Scene**, in which crime scene mapping is done and every electronic device within the scene is documented; this includes the device itself, its power adaptor, external memory cards, cradle, and everything else related to the device. Before starting evidence collection, **Communication Shielding** is important in order to be sure that there is no risk of damaging the current evidence; RF isolation, Faraday shielding, or cellular jammers are usually used to isolate devices from interacting with the environment. Now **Evidence Collection** comes into the picture; differentiating volatile and non-volatile collection is important and requires proper guidelines. At this phase, for example, investigators must maintain the device if it's turned on and running out of battery, otherwise imaging the device memory must be done quickly and properly using appropriate tools.

Next is the **Preservation** phase, wherein the evidence is securely stored and the device is properly packaged and transported. The collected evidence is analyzed and filtered; the integrity of data must also be guaranteed and the use of the hashing function to confirm this is conducted in the **Examination** step. The **Analysis** phase comes just after and is kind of an examination extension. In this phase, a more technical review is conducted based on the results of the previous phase; at this stage, the more advanced research is done, such as hidden data analysis, data recovery, and file decryption. The results of this phase must be documented to help in the achievement of the final reports that will summarize the whole process in the **Presentation** phase. Finally, the **Result** phase, just like in the IDIP model, is meant to be an open door to review the result of the whole process in order to find any points for improvements.

The SRDIFM model is interesting as it's more practical and presents some flexibility, which is not necessarily found within the other models; however, by adding more phases, the model increases the timeline of the process and its complexities.

Smartphone forensics challenges

Unlike a traditional computer forensics investigation, mobile forensics skills become much solicited in today's investigations because of many facts that make gathering digital evidence from a smartphone a painful task. This can be due to the changes occurring in mobile-based operating systems, the diversity of standards, technology of data storage, and procedures of data protection. In contrast to a computer investigation, a mobile investigation can hardly be standardized. Per each single device model, and according to services it makes available to its owner, a very big range of evidence categories is distinguished in mobile forensics.

Storage and the wide range of daily growing functionalities make today's smartphones a rapidly changing and challenging environment for forensic investigators.

The most challenging aspects of smartphone forensics are discussed in the following sections.

Operating systems' variety and changeability

In contrast to computers, major smartphone operating systems can vary significantly from one smartphone to another; each Android, iOS, WP, or Blackberry version can be found in any smartphone and tablet on the market. Operating system updates are very frequent among vendors and major updates are usually released every quarter. The main issue regarding this is keeping up with these environment changes; this issue is accentuated by the fact that major OS and forensic tools developers consider their respective developments trade secret and do not release information regarding the low-level working of their codes.

In addition to this, the growth of "less common" operating systems, such as Windows Phone requires lot of forensic experience.

Important hardware variations

By definition, a smartphone is a portable device and is meant to have a wide set of functionalities. The hardware architecture of smartphones is significantly different from computers and it also varies from one mobile manufacturer to another.

A smartphone device is typically composed of a microprocessor, main board, ROM and RAM memories, touch screen and/or keyboard, radio module and/or antenna, display unit, microphone and speakers, digital camera, and GPS device. The operating system is stored in general in a ROM and can be flashed or updated according to the hardware or operating system.

The same manufacturer usually produces highly customized operating systems to fit hardware specifications. Depending on phone providers, manufacturers may customize the same device to suit the demand. The replacement cycle for smartphones and customers' smartphone upgrades are the shortest relative to other devices, thus forensic examiners must have hundreds of adapters and power cords based on the type of hardware.

Different filesystems

Different operating systems and different hardware means different ways of storing data and running different filesystems. The same application running under Android, for example, is way different from its similar application running under iOS.

A variety of file formats and data structures are adopted depending on the manufacturer; this fact significantly complicates the decoding, parsing, and carving of information.

This difference in filesystems means that forensic tools are not able to process some files and must be updated very frequently in order to assume OS updates, otherwise forensic examiners might have to process data and device images manually.

Built-in security

A smartphone's built-in security features are present at many levels to protect user data and privacy. User locks in today's smartphones can vary from simple four-digit PINs to more complex and long passcodes, as it may consist of pattern-locks; the newest smartphone models can even have fingerprint locks and use biometrics to identify the user. It's true that some commercially available tools offer password extraction or lock screen bypassing, but this is not available for every device. Some smartphones (with or without the help of third-party applications) can offer password protection to individual files, file types, or directories; in this case, sensitive data such as SMS, e-mails, and photos can be individually protected. Newer OS versions offer full-disk encryption, which can be a real pain to decrypt in a scenario of data acquisition. Smartphone operating systems also offer application sandboxing, meaning that every individual application cannot directly access the space allocated to another application or to system resources, thus each application is installed in its own sandbox directory; this way, data within the sandbox is guaranteed some level of protection.

Encrypted data wiping

Data wiping is not data deletion; wiped data cannot be recovered or be recovered easily. Encrypted data can be wiped with a variety of methods depending on the smartphone configuration; data can be wiped via desktop managers or after entering a wrong password for a predefined number of times. Encrypted data can be wiped remotely in most modern smartphones: Blackberry devices can be remotely wiped via BlackBerry Enterprise Server, iPhone devices via iCloud, Android devices can be wiped via Google Sync, and Windows Phone devices via the Find My Phone service. At this point, the isolation phase of mobile forensics is important.

Data volatility

A lot of important evidentiary data resides within a smartphone in a volatile way, which adds an important consideration while seizing a device. Smartphones add this constraint to forensic examiners; seized devices must be kept turned on and isolated to prevent data loss or overwriting present data.

The cloud

For the sake of memory, storage space saving, or for back-up purposes, today's devices store lot of important data on the cloud; e-mails, photos, videos, files, notes, and so on are not necessarily preserved within the internal memory of the device, especially relatively old data.

Most vendors offer some GBs free of charge in order to achieve this and data, in most cases, is automatically synchronized with some account in the cloud. Android data is sent to Google, iPhone data is sent to iCloud, and Windows Phone data is synchronized with OneDrive. In addition to this, some third-party services are also offered to a certain point free of charge, such as Dropbox. In some cases, gathering evidence is not necessarily a technical task but also, and above all, a legal one, as demands must be addressed by cloud storage services for us to receive the desired data.

Today's climbing necessity of advanced smartphone forensic skills is indisputable, and smartphone investigation has become more challenging, tools are rapidly outdated, and the scope they cover in each case is smaller. Analysis, coding, and understanding and handling low level techniques are now "must have" skills for today's smartphone investigators and are, nowadays, more important than ever.

Summary

There are a huge number of mobile device models in use today, and almost every five months new models are manufactured, and most of them use closed operating systems, making forensic process difficult. Our goal is to bridge the gap by giving to the forensic community an in-depth look at mobile forensics techniques by detailing methods on how to gather evidence from mobile devices with different operating systems and how to use the appropriate model.

Seeing the daily increase in the use of smartphone, the unwilling-to-stop development of today's smartphone capabilities, and given the pace at which this development occurs, the forensics professionals, law enforcement, and researchers were and still are in need of producing a standardized framework to follow to assure a well driven investigation. Researches in this scope are not yet done, thus improvement is continually done to keep responding to permanent challenges offered by smartphone manufacturers and mobile operating systems vendors. In this chapter, we showed the importance of smartphone forensic field and discussed some models and frameworks applied in order to correctly lead forensic investigation cases. This chapter also discussed major smartphone forensic challenges, in an effort to help bypass some of the previously presented challenges when commercially available forensic tools cannot deal with some files or file types.

In the next chapter, we will see some low-level techniques that can be applied to gather forensically important evidences independently of the available forensics tools, operating systems, or device subjects of the eventual investigation.

2
Do It Yourself – Low-Level Techniques

In the continuously evolving environment of the mobile world, digital forensic examiners can neither always nor exclusively rely on commercially available tools. The ability to handle low-level techniques is a must. In this chapter, we will go deep into some commonly used techniques to carve files, manually extract GPS data, and explain how things are at a lower level. This chapter will also cover some techniques for extracting strings from different objects (for example, smartphone images), and will describe the basics of applying reverse engineering on smartphone applications.

We will look at the following topics in this chapter:

- Getting acquainted with file carving
- Extracting metadata – GPS analysis
- String dump and analysis
- Encryption versus encoding versus hashing
- Decompiling and disassembling

So let's get started with file carving!

Getting acquainted with file carving

Digital Forensic Research Workshop (DFRWS) defined data carving as the process of extracting a collection of data from a larger dataset. Applied to a digital investigation case, file carving is the process of extracting "data" from unallocated filesystem space using the file type inner structure, and not filesystem structure, which means that the extraction process is principally based on file types' headers and trailers.

Basically, all data gathered from a smartphone is always in the form of a file. In the digital world, each file is a block of stored binary digits, and each file type is defined depending on how these digits are stored — the use of extensions in file names is meant to easily and precisely determine the file's generic type. This is not a reliable approach since eyes, and even computers, can be fooled just by renaming the files. This leads us to a more advanced approach based on an analysis of the inner file structure in order to determine the actual file type. Each file type contains a kind of unique signature — constants within their inner file structures that constitute what we call **magic numbers**. Thus, we will take advantage of magic numbers to extract valuable files from smartphone ROMs or unallocated space.

In the scope of smartphone forensics, some file types are more valuable than others, and we will focus on some of the obvious ones like photos, videos, and audios.

One of the most famous file type for images is **JPEG**; the acronym stands for **Joint Photographic Experts Group**. Technically, JPEG is not a file type but a file compression algorithm, the resulting stream of which is stored and exchanged using a number of file format standards. The most important and widely used file formats are **JFIF**, which stands for **JPEG File Interchange Format** (it is now being replaced by SPIFF) and which is commonly used to exchange JPEG compressed streams over the web, and the **Exif (Exchangeable image file format)**, the format commonly used by digital cameras and smartphones today.

[JPG and JPEG represent the same type of file format for storing digital images. There is no actual difference between a `.jpeg` file and a `.jpg` file.]

Carving the JPEG format

Just like a file and any other digital object, every JPEG file has a header and a trailer, which are binary values equal to `0xFF\0xD8` and `0xFF\0xD9` respectively. A JPEG file contains several bits of binaries data translated as `0xFFXX`, which are called **markers**.

The marker `0xFF\0xD8` means **Start of Image (SOI)**, and `0xFF\0xD9` means **End of Image (EOI)**; these are the only markers that are not followed by data. All other markers are followed by 1 byte representing the marker number, 2 bytes representing the data size, and *n* bytes representing the data itself. Technically, each marker has the following binary format:

0xFF + 1 byte + 2 bytes + n bytes

Sometimes, a start of stream marker is placed after data description markers in order to start an image stream.

The following is a basic/generic JPEG file format:

Start of Image (SOI) Marker FFD8		
Marker Number FF??	**Data size** ????	**DATA** ????...??
Marker Number FF??	**Data size** ????	**DATA** ????...??
....		
Start of Stram (SOS) Marker FFDA	**Data size** ????	**DATA** ????...??
Image Stream **??????...????**		
End of Image (EOI) Marker FFD9		

Figure 1: Basic JPEG file format structure

In our forensic context, the marker that interests us, in addition to the SOI and EOI markers, is the **application marker (APP?)** used to embed information, such as the device used to take the photo, the device configuration, thumbnails, and GPS data, if present. There are many APP markers; JFIF uses the APP0 binary equivalent to `0xFF\0xE0`, and to avoid conflicts, Exif uses the APP1 marker, equivalent to `0xFF\0xE1`. The APP1 marker is present in the binary form within a JPEG file, as follows:

SOI FFD8	APP1 Marker FFE1	APP1 Data XXXX 457869660000...

Figure 2: Exif marker location

So, as seen in the preceding diagram, Exif data comes directly before the start of image marker, which shows that the current file is actually a JPEG one. Please note that XXXX represents the Exif data size followed by `0x45\0x78\0x69\0x66`, which is the ASCII form of *Exif*, then 2 bytes of `x00`, and then the actual Exif data. Exif data is a real repository of forensically important data. It contains the original file thumbnail, characteristics of the device used to take the picture, GPS locations, and so on.

Based on what we've learned till now, let's try to extract a valid image from an Android ROM (which can be downloaded from `https://sourceforge.net/projects/namelessrom/files/n-2.1/n7100/nameless-5.1.1-20151107-n7100-NIGHTLY.zip/download`) file. At this stage, all we need is a hexadecimal editor — you can use whichever one you like, I'll be using WinHex.

In the following steps, we will open a compressed system partition (`system.new.dat`) with our hexadecimal editor, and try to carve a valid JPEG file:

1. In the opened file, we will look for the sequence SOI APP1 marker (*Figure 2*), which is `FFD8FFE1`, as you can see in the following screenshot:

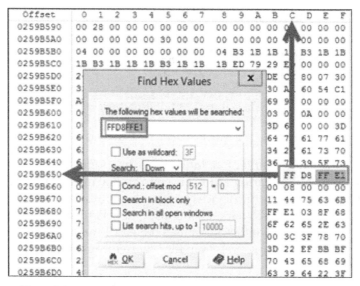

Figure 3: Location of SOI and APP1 markers inside a system partition

2. The image starts from the offset `0x259B65C`. Starting from this offset, let's search downwards for the trailer of the image `0xFFD9`:

Offset	0	1	2	3	4	5	6	7	8	9
025A1660	DA	9E	2A	57	3C	1E	E4	07	D0	D4
025A1670	27	34	DD	00	B6	36	B6	16	36	C1
025A1680	01	F5	E3	19	9A	C0	DB	82	86	F9
025A1690	D6	24	A0	42	50	21	7F	FF	D9	50
025A16A0	08	00	00	80	34	22	44	4A	68	A5

Figure 4: Location of EOI marker

3. The image ends in the offset `0x25A1697`; a simple offset subtraction ($0x25A1697 - 0x259B65C = 0x603B$) gives us the file size (in decimal, 24,635 bytes).

4. Now let's define and extract the block containing your file. From the WinHex menu, navigate to **Edit | Define Block | Edit,** and then copy the block into a new file. Give your carved file a name with extension `.jpg`, and note that it's actually 24 KB in size:

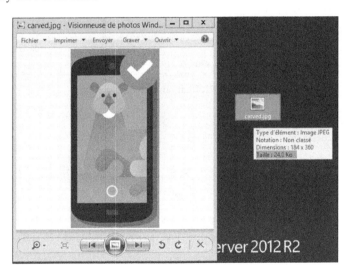

Figure 5: Carved image

Carving the ZIP format

The previous example was a demonstration when the conditions are perfect, in which the file was easily identified and was contiguously allocated.

In the forensics investigation context, there are some common file type targets of file carving, such as: pictures (JPG, PNG, BMP, and so on), videos(MP4, AVI, MOV, 3GP, and so on), audio files (MP3, WAV, WMA, and so on), office documents (DOC, DOCX, XLS, XLSX, PPT, PPTX, PDF, and so on), application databases and web content (HTML, SQLite, and so on), compressed archives (ZIP, 7z, RAR, and so on), execs, logs, and more. To successfully and completely carve a valid file, uniquely identifiable start and final data blocks are required, and the file must be contiguously and sequentially allocated. But this is not the case in several practical cases, especially when we are willing to manually recover wiped files, which is beyond the scope of this section.

If you paid enough attention to *Figure 3*, you might have noticed an interesting entry named **PK**:

Figure 6: PK location from Figure 3

Location of the PK entry

Figure 6a: PK location from Figure 3

The sequence `0x50/0x4B/0x03/0x04` is, in fact, the header of a ZIP file, which is quite interesting. Each ZIP file (also known as PKZIP file) is structured in the following manner:

Local File Header	File Data 1	Data Descriptor 1	Archive Decryption Header	Archive Extra Data Record	Central Directory

Figure 7: General structure of a ZIP file

 PK refers to the initials of the co-creator of the ZIP file format, Phil Katz.

Each ZIP file can contain as many local file descriptors as the actual content of the compressed archive. The local file header has its own structure, as shown here:

	0x0	0x1	0x2	0x3	0x4	0x5	0x6	0x7	0x8	0x9	0xa	0xb	0xc	0xd	0xe	0xf
0x0000	Signature				Version		Flags		Compression		Mod time		Mode date		Crc-32	
0x0010	Crc-32		Compressed size				Uncompressed size				File name len		Extra field len			
0x0020	File name (variable size)															
0x0030	Extra field (variable size)															

Figure 8: ZIP local file header structure

What is important to note is that the signature of a ZIP file (its header) is always `0x50\0x4b\0x03\0x04`, followed by two bytes describing the PKZIP version needed to extract the archive, then two bytes containing general purpose bit flags describing if the file is encrypted, compression option used, data descriptors' language encoding, and more. After these flags come two bytes defining the compression method. If it is 0, for example, it means that no compression is used, if it equals 4, it means that it is reduced with a compression factor of 3, and if 14 then the **Lempel-Ziv-Markov chain algorithm (LZMA)** is used to compress the data. After the compression method bytes, there are four bytes that hold modification time and modification date respectively. Both are stored in standard MS-DOS format. Further information is available at `https://pkware.cachefly.net/webdocs/casestudies/APPNOTE.TXT`.

The case we are facing here is as follows:

```
0259B5F0  A8 02 38 00 00 1D A7 01  76 9F FA 69 90 00 00 00   " 8   § vŸúi
0259B600  00 49 45 4E 44 AE 42 60  82 50 4B 03 04 0A 00 00    IEND®B`‚PK
0259B610  08 00 00 80 34 22 44 D3  4E 43 3A 3D 60 00 00 3D    €4"DÓNC:=` =
0259B620  60 00 00 34 00 01 00 72  65 73 2F 64 72 61 77 61   `  4   res/drawa
0259B630  62 6C 65 2D 78 68 64 70  69 2D 76 34 2F 61 73 70   ble-xhdpi-v4/asp
0259B640  65 63 74 5F 72 61 74 69  6F 5F 31 36 78 39 5F 73   ect_ratio_16x9_s
0259B650  65 6C 65 63 74 65 64 2E  6A 70 67 00 FF D8 FF E1   elected.jpg ÿØÿá
0259B660  00 18 45 78 69 66 00 00  49 49 2A 00 08 00 00 00    Exif  II*
0259B670  00 00 00 00 00 00 00 00  FF EC 00 11 44 75 63 6B          ÿì  Duck
0259B680  79 00 01 00 04 00 00 00  49 00 00 FF E1 03 8F 68   y       I ÿá  h
0259B690  74 74 70 3A 2F 2F 6E 73  2E 61 64 6F 62 65 2E 63   ttp://ns.adobe.c
```

Figure 9: ZIP file structure

Magic number (ZIP header)	0x50\0x4B\0x03\0x04
Version	0x0A\0x00
Flags	0x00\0x08
Compression method	0x00\0x00
File modification time	0x80\0x34
File modification date	0x22\0x44
CRC-32 checksum	0xD3\0x4E\0x43\0x3A
Compressed size	0x3D\0x60\0x00\0x00
Uncompressed size	0x3D\0x60\0x00\0x00
File name length	0x34\0x00
Extra field length	0x01\0x00
File name	From 0x72\...\0x67

We can see that the compressed file size and uncompressed file size are equal, and this is clear since Compression Method is set to 0, which means the file is not compressed.

According to the official ZIP file format specification, each ZIP file end is marked with 0x50\0x4B\0x05\0x06, also called **End of Central Directory Record,** followed by 18 bytes (describing the number of the disk, total number of central directory records, size of central directory, and so on) + *n* bytes that hold comment (if any). So we will export bytes from the offset of our ZIP header to the offset of the End of Central Directory Record (data from 0x259B609 to 0x283BCC5), and see what is inside:

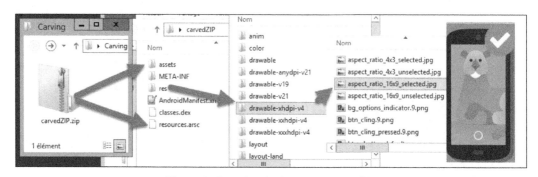

Figure 10: Carved and uncompressed ZIP file

The previously carved JPEG file was inside a ZIP file! We carved a valid JPEG file from a compressed ZIP archive, which itself resides within an Android ROM; at this stage, we can see clearly the original file name of the JPEG file.

One important point to note is that deleted files in smartphones are just "marked" as such, and are not permanently deleted until they are overwritten. This is because smartphones use a kind of nonvolatile/solid state memory to store data like: SMS, all kind of records, pictures, and videos. The problem here is that every device manufacturer has developed its own way of storing data. Thus, in order to recover/ carve data, understanding the target's device model/OS is a must. For example, for extracting SMS messages from a physical dump, it's important to know how SMS messages are usually compressed — what is the PDU format, and what encoding is used. There is no unified or standardized "how to" way applicable for carving data from a smartphone. Once a snapshot of the content of a smartphone is taken, many of the commercially available forensic tools work just like official backup utilities, and cannot always dig into the deleted items. This is why manual investigation is sometimes the only way to recover valuable evidence.

Please keep in mind that till now we have been using a basic data carving technique, since the beginning of the searched image is not overwritten, and the file is neither fragmented nor compressed. Relying on advanced and deep knowledge of a file's structure is, in some cases, a must in order to extract more readable data. This is because sometimes, even if we can extract/carve files based on their respective headers and trailers, they are not readable since this technique does not consider the file's data, meaning that the deleted, moved, or missing sectors (sequential or not sequential), or even missing fragments, are not at all considered within this method.

Extracting metadata – GPS analysis

What is metadata? Well, this is quite an embarrassing question! In an ambiguous way, metadata is data that describes data or information about information. In general, metadata is extra hidden information generated and embedded automatically in a digital file. The definition of metadata differs depending on the context in which it's used and the community that refers to it. It can be considered as machine-understandable information, or can be referred to as records that describe digital records. In fact, metadata can be subdivided into three important types: **descriptive** (including elements like author, title, abstract, and keywords), **structural** (describing how an object is constituted, and how elements are arranged), and **administrative** (including elements like date and time of creation, data type, and other technical details).

For example, camera settings (like camera marker, camera model, exposure time, ISO speed, focal length, shutter speed, and so on) are stored in a lot of metadata. Multimedia objects like photographs and videos, Microsoft Office, and PDF documents use metadata to store name of author, computer name, total editing time, and creation and modification date-time. Media like MP3 and MP4 files can hold metadata that describes the artist and album name, cover picture, encoding information, and so on. Metadata is very important in a forensic context. We will see how metadata within JPEG files can hold GPS information, and how this data (which describes data) is binary stored.

Further to what was said in the previous part of this chapter, every JPEG file that holds Exif data starts with the SOI marker (`0xFF\0xD8`) followed by the APP1 marker (`0xFF\0xE1`), then the APP1 data composed of two bytes and describing the Exif data size. This is followed by the Exif header (`0x45\0x78\0x69\0x66\0x00\0x00`), then eight bytes describing the TIFF format (`0x4D\0x4D\0x00\0x2A\0x00\0x00\0x00\0x08`); the important thing to note about the TIFF format is that the first two bytes of the TIFF header define byte alignment of the TIFF data depending on the CPU of the device producing the file. If the TIFF header starts with `0x49\0x49` (ASCII = II), it means that data is aligned following the **Intel** type data alignment (little endian). If it starts with `0x4D\0x4D` (ASCII = MM), it means that the **Motorola** type byte alignment has been adopted (big endian).

The TIFF header structure can be either of the two following ways:

0x4D\0x4D = MM	0x00\0x2A	0x00\0x00\0x00\0x08

or

0x49\0x49 = II	0x2A\0x00	0x08\0x00\0x00\0x00

This detail is very important in order to correctly extract the values of Exif data. Next to the byte alignment field is always `0x00\0x2A` bytes, followed by the last four bytes of the TIFF header, indicating an offset to the first **Image File Directory (IFD0)**, which has the value `0x00\0x00\0x00\0x08`.

The important parts (in our context) of the structure of the APP1 marker (Exif data) is described in the following table (for more information about TIFF format and TIFF 6.0 Specification, visit `http://partners.adobe.com/asn/developer/PDFS/TN/TIFF6.pdf`):

APP1 Marker		FFE1			
APP1 Data	APP1 data size	2 bytes			
	Exif header	0x45\0x78\0x69\0x66\0x00\0x00			
	TIFF header	0x4D\0x4D\0x00\0x2A\0x00\0x00\0x00\0x08			
	Image file directory0 (IFD0 containing main image)	2 bytes	Number of fields in directory		
		12 bytes	Directory	Image width	
		12 bytes		Image height	
		... n x 12 bytes		...	
		12 bytes		Exif offset	
		12 bytes		GPS offset	
		8 bytes	Next image file directory offset (IFD1)		
		n bytes	Data area of IFD0		
	EXIF image file directory	2 bytes	Number of fields in directory		
		12 bytes	Directory	EXIF version	
		... n x 12 bytes		....	
		0x00\0x00\0x00\0x00	No next IFD		
		n bytes	Data area of Exif IFD		
	GPS image file directory	2 bytes	Number of fields in directory		
		12 bytes	Directory		GPS version
		n x 12 bytes			
		0x00\0x00\0x00\0x00	No next Image File Directory		
		n bytes	Data area of GPS Image File Directory		
	More IFDs (Makernote and Iteroperability, IFD1 for thumbnail image)	N bytes	N entries (number of fields, ISO speed, data area, index version, Compression,X/YResolution)		

APP1 Marker		FFE1	
	Thumbnail image	0xFF\0xD8	Start of image
		0xFFDB + *n* bytes	Define quantization table
		0xFF\0xC0 + *n* bytes	Baseline
		0xFF\0xC4 + *n* bytes	Define Huffman table
		n bytes	Thumbnail data
		0xFF\0xD9	End of image

Table 1: Basic structure of EXIF APP1 marker

In a JPEG/Exif file, every image file directory can be subdivided into *n* fields, and each field is of 12 bytes. The offset to the Global Positioning System field is given in IFD0.

The 12 bytes are always in the form of 2 bytes representing the tag ID (which are not unique across image file directories), then 2 bytes for type ID or data format (1: Byte, 2: ASCII, 3: Short, 4: Long, 5: Rational, 6: Signed Byte, 7: Undefined byte array, 8: Signed Short, 9: Signed Long, 10: Signed Rational, 11: Float, and 12: Double), followed by 4 bytes defining the byte count for byte arrays (size), followed again by the last 4 bytes, which give value or offset to the actual data.

What concerns us in this structure is understanding how to extract and analyze GPS data from an existing JPEG photo.

Consider the following portion of a hexadecimal dump of a photo containing GPS data:

```
Offset      0  1  2  3  4  5  6  7   8  9  A  B  C  D  E  F

00000000   FF D8 FF E1 8A 44 45 78  69 66 00 00 4D 4D 00 2A    ÿØÿáŠDExif MM *
00000010   00 00 00 08 00 0B 01 0F  00 02 00 00 00 06 00 00
00000020   08 9E 01 10 00 02 00 00  00 0A 00 00 08 A4 01 12    ž             ¤
00000030   00 03 00 00 00 01 00 01  00 00 01 1A 00 05 00 00
00000040   00 01 00 00 08 AE 01 1B  00 05 00 00 00 01 00 00              ®
00000050   08 B6 01 28 00 03 00 00  00 01 00 02 00 00 01 31    ¶ (             1
00000060   00 02 00 00 00 0E 00 00  08 BE 02 13 00 03 00 00                 ¾
00000070   00 01 00 01 00 00 87 69  00 04 00 00 00 01 00 00             ‡i
00000080   08 CC 88 25 00 04 00 00  00 01 00 00 62 3C EA 1C    Ì^%         b<ê
00000090   00 07 00 00 08 0C 00 00  00 92 00 00 6A 5A 1C EA          '   jZ ê
```

It contains the following:

- `0xFF\0xD8`: 2 bytes SOI for JPEG header.

- `0xFF\0xE1\0x8A\0x44`: 2 bytes APP1 header + 2 bytes data size.

- `0x45\0x78\0x69\0x66\0x00\x00`: 6 bytes APP1 Exif data type.

- `0x4D\0x4D\0x00\0x2A\0x00\0x00\0x00\0x08`: 8 bytes TIFF header with big-endian byte order, `0x002A` identifier, and `0x00008` IFD0 offset.

- `0x00\0x0B`: 2 bytes IFD0 `0x0b` entries (11 entries).

- `0x01\0x0F\0x00\0x02\0x00\0x00\0x00\0x06\0x00\0x00\0x08\0x9E`: 12 bytes IFD0-Field 0.

  IFD0-Field 0 is the 0th field of Image File directory 0 and is composed as follows:

  - **Tag ID**: `0x010F` -> TagName: Maker (image input equipment manufacturer)
  - **Format**: `0x0002` -> format is ASCII
  - **Size**: `0x00000006` -> 6 bytes
  - **Offset**: `0x0000089E` is an offset of the actual value

- `0x01\0x10\0x00\0x02\0x00\0x00\0x00\0x0A\0x00\0x00\0x08\0xA4`: 12 bytes IFD0-Field 1, Tag ID: `0x0110`, TagName: Model (image input equipment model) which is of a length of ten (`0x0000000A`) characters (`0x0002`) located at offset `0x000008A4`.

- `0x01\0x12\0x00\0x03\0x00\0x00\0x00\0x01\0x00\0x01\0x00\0x00`: 12 bytes IFD0-Field 2 holding Orientation.

- `0x01\0x1A\0x00\0x05\0x00\0x00\0x00\0x01\0x00\0x00\0x08\0xAE`: 12 bytes IFD0-Field 3 holding XResolution.

- `0x01\0x1B\0x00\0x05\0x00\0x00\0x00\0x01\0x00\0x00\0x08\0xB6`: 12 bytes IFD0-Field 4 holding YResolution.

- `0x01\0x28\0x00\0x03\0x00\0x00\0x00\0x01\0x00\0x02\0x00\0x00`: 12 bytes IFD0-Field 5 holding ResolutionUnit.

- `0x01\0x31\0x00\0x02\0x00\0x00\0x00\0x0E\0x00\0x00\0x08\0xBE`: 12 bytes IFD0-Field 6, TagID: `0x0131`, TagName: Software (software used to take photo) which is 14 bytes (`0x0000000E`) ASCII (`0x0002`) located at offset `0x000008BE`.

- `0x02\0x13\0x00\0x03\0x00\0x00\0x00\0x01\0x00\0x01\0x00\0x00`: 12 bytes IFD0-Field 7 holding YCbCrPositioning.

- 0x87\0x69\0x00\0x04\0x00\0x00\0x00\0x01\0x00\0x00\0x08\0xCC: 12 bytes IFD0-Field 8 holding ExifOffset.

- 0x88\0x25\0x00\0x04\0x00\0x00\0x00\0x01\0x00\0x00\62\0x3C: 12 bytes IFD0-Field 9, TagID: 0x8825, TagName: GPSInfo, Data Format: Long (0x0004, 4 bytes size and data located at offset 0x0000623C).

The last four bytes of any field (Image File Directory entry) indicate an offset to the location of the actual value data. However, *if and only if* the actual value can fit into four bytes, then this value is stored in the leftmost of the last four bytes.

Some interesting correlation can be addressed at this point between TagIDs, TagNames, and offsets:

TagID	TagName	Offset	Size in bytes
0x010F	Make	0x089E	0x06
0x0110	Model	0x08A4	0x0A
0x0131	Software	0x08BE	0x0E
0x8825	GPSInfo	0x623C	0x04

TagIDs are constants, and are defined in Exif standard. Based on what we've got until now, we can gather the input equipment, input equipment model, input software, and GPS location of the photo we are analyzing. Using a hexadecimal editor, let's go to the offset 0x089E:

```
Offset       0  1  2  3  4  5  6  7   8  9  A  B  C  D  E  F

00000890    00 00 00 00 00 00 00 00  00 00 00 00 00 00 4E 6F            No
000008A0    6B 69 61 00 4C 75 6D 69  61 20 39 32 30 00 00 00    kia Lumia 920
000008B0    00 48 00 00 00 01 00 00  00 48 00 00 00 01 57 69    H      H    Wi
000008C0    6E 64 6F 77 73 20 50 68  6F 6E 65 00 00 17 82 9A    ndows Phone  ,š
000008D0    00 05 00 00 00 01 00 00  11 F2 82 9D 00 05 00 00              ð,
```

The first offset holds the make value `Nokia`, the second offset holds the model value `Lumia 920`, and the third offset holds software value `Windows Phone`. The first important information we know at this stage is that the photo being analyzed was taken using a Nokia Lumia 920 device running Windows Phone.

Now we need to gather GPS data, so let's go directly to offset `0x623C` (which I remember is GPS info IFD):

```
Offset       0  1  2  3  4  5  6  7   8  9  A  B  C  D  E  F

00006230    56 F2 8B 5F 00 00 00 64  00 00 00 64 00 0A 00 00    Vò<_     d    d
00006240    00 01 00 00 00 04 02 02  00 00 00 01 00 02 00 00
00006250    00 02 4E 00 00 00 00 02  00 05 00 00 00 03 00 00      N
00006260    6A 42 00 03 00 02 00 00  00 02 57 00 00 00 00 04    jB          W
00006270    00 05 00 00 00 03 00 00  6A 2A 00 05 00 01 00 00            j*
00006280    00 01 00 00 00 00 00 06  00 05 00 00 00 01 00 00
00006290    6A 22 00 0A 00 02 00 00  00 02 33 00 00 00 00 0B    j"          3
000062A0    00 05 00 00 00 01 00 00  6A 1A EA 1C 00 07 00 00            j ê
```

The first two bytes at the offset `0x623C` are `0x00\0xA`–this means that our GPS IFD contains 10 fields (12 bytes of Image File Directory entries 10 times).

GPS – Field 0	0x0000	0x0001	0x00000004	0x02020000
	TagID of GPSVersionID	Format or TypeID of Byte	Byte count for Value (size): 4	Value: 2 2 0 0
GPS – Field 1	0x0001	0x0002	0x00000002	0x4E000000
	TagID of GPSLatitudeRef	Format or TypeID of String (ASCII)	Byte count for Value (size): 2	Value 0x4E decodes in ASCII to *N* indicating north latitude
GPS – Field 2	0x0002	0x0005	0x00000003	0x00006A42
	TagID of GPSLatitude	Format or TypeID of Rational	Byte count for Value (size): 3	Offset of latitude data 0x6A42

Before continuing, it's important to know that Rational is an 8 bytes long type, and in this case, the byte count needed to store latitude data is 3, which means that we need 3 x 8 bytes to store it—this is beyond 4 bytes, which is why `0x00006A42` indicates an offset, and not a value. The same thing is applicable for Longitude, Altitude, and GPSDOP (dilution of precision).

GPS – Field 3	`0x0003`	`0x0002`	`0x00000002`	`0x57000000`
	TagID of GPSLongitudeRef	Format or TypeID of String (ASCII)	Byte count for Value (size): 2	Value `0x57` decodes in ASCII to *W* indicating west longitude
GPS – Field 4	`0x0004`	`0x0005`	`0x00000003`	`0x00006A2A`
	TagID of GPSLongitude	Format or TypeID of Rational	Byte count for Value (size): 3	Offset of longitude data `0x6A2A`
GPS – Field 5	`0x0005`	`0x0001`	`0x00000001`	`0x00000000`
	TagID of GPSAltitudeRef	Format or TypeID of Byte	Byte count for Value (size): 1	Value: 0 indicates that it's above sea level
GPS – Field 6	`0x0006`	`0x0005`	`0x00000001`	`0x00006A22`
	TagID of GPSAltitude	Format or TypeID of Rational	Byte count for Value (size): 1	Offset of altitude data `0x6A22`
GPS – Field 7	`0x000A`	`0x0002`	`0x00000002`	`0x33000000`
	TagID of GPSMeasureMode	Format or TypeID of String (ASCII)	Byte count for Value (size): 2	Value `0x33` decodes in ASCII to 3 for 3-dimensional measurement
GPS – Field 8	`0x000B`	`0x0005`	`0x00000001`	`0x00006A1A`
	TagID of GPSDOP (data degree of precision)	Format or TypeID of Rational	Byte count for Value (size): 1	Offset of GPSDOP data `0x6A1A`

From the preceding table, we can recapitulate the following information about our photo:

TagID	TagName	Tag description	Offset or value	Size in bytes
`0x0001`	GPSLatitudeRef	Indicates whether the latitude is north or south	N	2
`0x0002`	GPSLatitude	Indicates the latitude	`0x6A42`	24

TagID	TagName	Tag description	Offset or value	Size in bytes
0x0003	GPSLongitudeRef	Indicates whether the longitude is east or west	W	2
0x0004	GPSLongitude	Indicates the longitude	0x6A2A	24
0x0005	GPSAltitudeRef	Indicates the altitude used as the reference altitude	Above sea level	1
0x0006	GPSAltitude	Indicates the altitude based on the reference in GPSAltitudeRef	0x6A22	8
0x000A	GPSMeasureMode	Indicates the GPS measurement mode (2 or 3 dimensional)	3	2

The hexadecimal values at offset `0x6A22` are as follows:

```
Offset     0  1  2  3  4  5  6  7   8  9  A  B  C  D  E  F
00006A10                           00 00 00 13 55 38 00 00              U8
00006A20   03 E8 00 00 D4 E4 00 00 03 E8 00 00 00 07 00 00   è  Ôä  è
00006A30   00 01 00 00 00 27 00 00 00 01 00 00 62 43 00 00       '    bC
00006A40   03 E8 00 00 00 21 00 00 00 01 00 00 00 20 00 00   è  !
00006A50   00 01 00 00 04 C7 00 00 03 E8 00 06 01 03 00 03       ç  è
```

We will decode GPSLatitude (`0x6A42`), GPSLongitude (`0x6A2A`), and GPSAltitude (`0x6A22`) respectively; the specification of GPS TIFF tags (`http://www.exiv2.org/tags.html`) defines those tags, as follows:

- **GPSLatitude**: This is expressed as three Rational values giving the degrees, minutes, and seconds. If the latitude is expressed as degrees, minutes, and seconds, a typical format would be *dd/1,mm/1,ss/1*. When degrees and minutes are used, and, for example, fractions of minutes are given up to two decimal places, the format would be *dd/1,mmmm/100,0/1*.

- **GPSLongitude**: This is expressed as three Rational values giving the degrees, minutes, and seconds. If the longitude is expressed as degrees, minutes, and seconds, a typical format would be *ddd/1,mm/1,ss/1*. When degrees and minutes are used, and, for example, fractions of minutes are given up to two decimal places, the format would be *ddd/1,mmmm/100,0/1*.

- **GPSAltitude**: This is expressed as one Rational value. The reference unit is meters.

- **GPSAltitudeRef**: If the reference is sea level, and the altitude is above sea level, 0 is given. If the altitude is below sea level, a value of 1 is given and the altitude is indicated as an absolute value in the GPSAltitude tag. The reference unit is meters. Note that this tag is of type Byte, unlike other reference tags.

Rationals are 8 bytes long, and each Rational is subdivided into two Longs representing the numerator of a fraction and the denominator. The "formula" is quite simple and is given as follows:

- **1st Rational (8 bytes)**: 4 bytes (numerator) / 4 bytes (denominator)
- **2nd Rational (8 bytes)**: 4 bytes (numerator) / 4 bytes (denominator)
- **3rd Rational (8 bytes)**: 4 bytes (numerator) / 4 bytes (denominator)

So, the GPSLatitude value: `00 00 00 21 00 00 00 01 00 00 00 20 00 00 00 01 00 00 04 C7 00 00 03 E8` decodes as follows:

- `0x00\0x00\0x00\0x21 / 0x00\0x00\0x00\0x01` => 33/1 = 33
- `0x00\0x00\0x00\0x20 / 0x00\0x00\0x00\0x01` => 32/1 = 32
- `0x00\0x00\0x04\0xC7 / 0x00\0x00\0x03\0xE8` => 1,223/1,000 = 1.223

Here, as we can see, Latitude is described in degrees and minutes: *33; 32; 1.223 N.*

In the same way, we can extract longitude from the GPSLongitude value `00 00 00 07 00 00 00 01 00 00 00 27 00 00 00 01 00 00 62 43 00 00 03 E8` from offset `0x6A2A`:

- `0x00\0x00\0x00\0x07 / 0x00\0x00\0x00\0x01` => 7/1 = 7
- `0x00\0x00\0x00\0x27 / 0x00\0x00\0x00\0x01` => 39/1 = 39
- `0x00\0x00\0x62\0x43 / 0x00\0x00\0x03\0xE8` => 25,155/1,000 = 25.155

Longitude is stored in degrees and minutes as well, and is equal to: *7; 39; 25.15 W.*

The Altitude value is 8 bytes in size, and is stored at the offset `0x6A22: 00 00 D4 E4 00 00 03 E8`. So we get:

- `0x00\0x00\0xD4\0xE4 / 0x00\0x00\0x03\0xE8` => 54,500/1,000 = 54.5

This means that the altitude is *54.5 meters above sea level.*

At this stage, we've gathered the GPS position successfully, which can help us locate where the photo that we analyzed had been taken:

- GPS altitude   : 54.5 m above sea level
- GPS latitude   : 33 deg 32' 1.223" N
- GPS longitude   : 7 deg 39' 25.15" W
- GPS position   : 33 deg 32' 1.22" N, 7 deg 39' 25.15" W

Now we can easily locate it in a map (via `http://www.gps-coordinates.net/`):

Figure 11: Location in map of the extracted GPS position

As a bonus for our exercise, we can now extract the thumbnail of the analyzed photo. In many forensic cases, thumbnails are used to authenticate original digital images. In a forensic context, the integrity of digital evidence is a daily struggle, so we will not go very deep into thumbnail analysis in this part, because its way beyond the scope of this chapter, and even this book. Instead, we will go through the very first step, which is extracting a valid thumbnail from an original photo.

On the basis of the JPEG/TIFF structure, we know that the thumbnail is always located at Image File directory 1 (IFD1), which is linked to IFD0 as follows:

```
Offset      0  1  2  3  4  5  6  7   8  9  A  B  C  D  E  F

00000000    FF D8 FF E1 8A 44 45 78  69 66 00 00 4D 4D 00 2A    ÿØÿáŠDExif  MM *
.........   .. .. .. [CUT CUT CUT CUT CUT CUT].. .. .. .. ..        ‡i
00000090    00 07 00 00 08 0C 00 00  00 92 00 00 6A 5A 1C EA              '   jZ ê
```

At the end of IFD0, the value `0x6A5A` points us to the offset of the next IFD, which is IFD1:

```
Offset      0  1  2  3  4  5  6  7   8  9  A  B  C  D  E  F

00006A50                            00 06 01 03 00 03
00006A60    00 00 00 01 00 06 00 00  01 1A 00 05 00 00 00 01
00006A70    00 00 6A A8 01 1B 00 05  00 00 00 01 00 00 6A B0    j¨        j°
00006A80    01 28 00 03 00 00 00 01  00 02 00 00 02 01 00 04    (
00006A90    00 00 00 01 00 00 6A B8  02 02 00 04 00 00 00 01        j,
00006AA0    00 00 1F 84 00 00 00 00  00 00 00 48 00 00 00 01      „      H
```

```
00006AB0    00 00 00 48 00 00 00 01  FF D8 FF DB 00 84 00 08      H     ÿØÿÛ „
00006AC0    06 06 07 06 05 08 07 07  07 09 09 08 0A 0C 14 0D
00006AD0    0C 0B 0B 0C 19 12 13 0F  14 1D 1A 1F 1E 1D 1A 1C
00006AE0    1C 20 24 2E 27 20 22 2C  23 1C 1C 28 37 29 2C 30      $.' ",#  (7),0
```

This IFD1 has `0x0006` entries. In order to avoid going through each entry, the IFD1-Field 4 here is ThumbnailOffset defined by its TagID `0x0201` located at `0x6A8C`:

- **TagID**: `0x0201` -> This entry holds the offset to the start byte (SOI) of the JPEG compressed thumbnail data
- **Format**: `0x0004` -> Format Long
- **Size**: `0x00000001` -> 4 bytes
- **Offset**: `0x00006AB8` -> `0x6AB8`

This is followed directly by IFD-Field 5, ThumbnailLength:

- **TagID**: `0x0202` -> This entry holds the number of bytes of the JPEG compressed thumbnail data
- **Format**: `0x0004` -> Format Long
- **Size**: `0x00000001` -> 4 bytes
- **Value**: `0x00001F84` -> 8,068 bytes

Based on this, our thumbnail is 8,068 bytes starting from offset `0x6AB8`; so, in our hexadecimal editor we can define a block of 8,068 bytes starting from the offset `0x6AB8`, which indeed contains the JPEG file header `0xFFD8` at its beginning, and the JPEG trailer `0xFFD9` at its end:

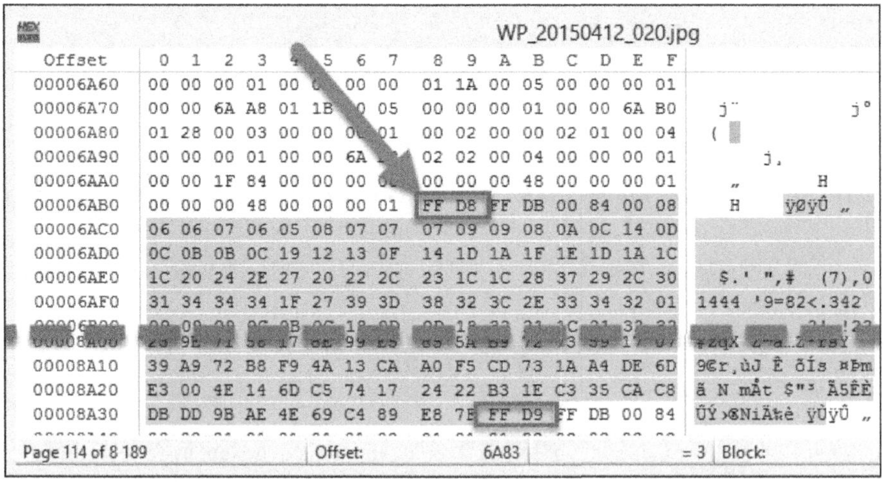

Figure 12: Thumbnail block defined

The dumped file is a 320 x 192 JPEG file representing the original thumbnail of the previously analyzed photo:

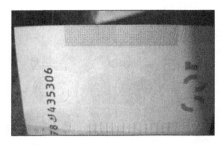

Figure 13: Thumbnail dumped from the original photo

String dump and analysis

Most digital investigations rely on textual evidence. This is obviously due to the fact that most stored digital data is linguistic, for example, logged conversation. A lot of important text-based evidence can be gathered while dumping strings from images (smartphone memory dumps); this can include e-mails, instant messaging, address books, browsing history, and more. Most of the currently available digital forensic tools rely on match and indexing algorithms to search for textual evidence at the physical level, so they search every byte to locate specific text strings.

Finding accurate hits is a critical need in every digital forensic case. In contrast to searching individual key terms or single words, things are much more complicated when an investigator wants to perform an advanced search such as for credit card numbers or phone number. Even if most digital forensic tools offer the capability to use regular expression for searching, the main difficulty resides in generating an accurate regular expression. A lot of effort has been put in this direction to help the law enforcing and digital forensic community generate efficient and accurate regular expressions. You can have a look at `http://www.dfcsc.uri.edu/docs/Perez_Thesis.pdf` and `http://www.cftt.nist.gov/ss-req-sc-draft-v1_0.pdf` for more information.

There are many tools and ways to extract and find strings within different supports, especially disk images. The `strings` command in Linux lists all printable characters from a given file; by default, it returns ASCII printable strings having at least four characters. The `strings` command is very effective in a preliminary analysis. This command is configurable—if you use it under Linux, always try to consider the option `--all` to examine the entire file, `--radix` to print the offset at which the string was found (`--radix=x` to print the offset in the hexadecimal format), and the option `--encoding` to select the character encoding of the looked-for string. The variants for the same functions in OS X are `-a`, `t`, and `x` respectively.

An example of using this command against an arbitrary bin file reveals that this binary is a photo tampered with using Photoshop CC 2015 for Windows, which contains hidden information within it at offset `0x4002`:

```
soufiane@soufiane-VirtualBox:~/Desktop$ strings --all --radix=x bin.bin
      6 Exif
     7e Adobe Photoshop CC 2015 (Windows)
     a0 2015:11:20 13:39:18
    144 Adobe_CM
    152 Adobe

   3f8c .gam
   3fe2 '54,u0
   4002 ?sSoufiane Tahiri : Passw0rd is hidden in a piccr
   408f E0juPS
   40ee U9\>oo
```

Figure 14: strings command against binary file

Adding the parameter `--encoding=b`, for example, will tell the command to find 16 bits of big-endian characters, and this can reveal deleted "strings" such as deleted e-mails. The `strings` command can be very useful for extracting names, phone numbers, e-mails, and a huge pack of information within a disk image; do not hesitate to try it with all the encoding options:

- `--encoding=s` for single 7-bit byte characters
- `--encoding=S` for single 8-bit byte characters
- `--encoding=b` for 16-bit big-endian characters
- `--encoding=B` for 32-bit big-endian characters
- `--encoding=l` for 16-bit little-endian characters
- `--encoding=L` for 32-bit little-endian characters

Running the `strings` command on a Windows Phone image reveals links to visited Facebook photos (the photo has been blurred intentionally):

Figure 15: Facebook photos' links found

The output can be saved to a text file for analysis by adding > `/path/to/file.txt`.

The Linux terminal environment offers another very versatile and powerful command: **Global Regular Expression Print (Grep)**. Grep dubbed to regular expressions to search for text patterns can be an extremely powerful tool if handled correctly.

For a demonstration, I'll be using the output of the previously executed `strings` command.

The basic usage of grep is searching for a word within a file, which means that grep will print out all the lines containing the desired word.

A basic grep command looks like this: `grep 'word' file`. We will use it to find lines that contain the word `facebook`:

```
grep 'facebook' Lumia005.txt

1d8b4176 ttps://www.facebook.com/diverteeWP

3afd0bcc ttps://www.facebook.com/pages/Webcam-
Remote/348280255226071?skip_nax_wizard=true

3afd0c70 ttp://www.facebook.com/pcremotewindows?sk=wall&filter=2

3f00fda2 ttp://m.facebook.com/policy.php>

...
```

The preceding search pattern is case sensitive. If we want it to find all instances ignoring the case, we can specify the `-i` argument: `grep -i "word" file`. We can also do an invert match; so, we can search for every line that does not contain a given word by specifying the `-v` argument: `grep -v "word" file`. Things get more interesting with the use of regular expressions and extended regular expressions.

Grep is extremely flexible, an exhaustive number of patterns can be used with it, as follows:

- **Find anchor matches**: Specify where in the line a match must occur:

  `grep "^word" file`

- **Match any character**: Any single character can occur at the given location:

  `grep ".o.d" file`

  `grep "..rd" file`

- **Brackets expression**: By placing just a few or a whole range of characters, we can find every line that contains what is between `[]`:

  `grep [A-Za-z ] file`

- **Escaping meta-characters**: Searching an opening bracket or a dot, for example, may be confusing. For grep to search characters with special meaning, we use backslash \ before the character.

- **Repeat pattern**: The use of wild card * means the previous pattern is to be repeated zero or more times:

  `grep "([A-Z]*)" file`

  The preceding command will find each line with opening and closing parentheses with only uppercase letters in between.

- **Plus character**: The plus character + finds all patterns that match at least one time.

Let's go directly to some interesting uses of grep and regular expressions. Assume that we want to find all address mails within our smartphone image or within a directory. The regular expression to use is: `"\b[a-zA-Z0-9.-]+@[a-zA-Z0-9.-]+\.[a-zA-Z0-9.-]+\b"`. Since this is an extended regular expression, the argument `-E` must be used with grep; the command will then be as follows:

```
grep -E -o "\b[a-zA-Z0-9.-]+@[a-zA-Z0-9.-]+\.[a-zA-Z0-9.-]+\b" -R  /
Directory
```

The `-o` argument is used to show only that part of the matching line that matches the given pattern:

Figure 16: E-mails found using grep

We can try to elaborate very accurate regular expressions with grep such as for finding phone numbers of different formats:

- **xxx-xxx-xxxx**: The command will be `grep -o '[0-9]\{3\}\-[0-9]\{3\}\-[0-9]\{4\}'  file`

- **(xxx)xxx-xxxx**: The command will be `grep -o '([0-9]\{3\})[0-9]\{3\}\-[0-9]\{4\}'  file`

- **xxx xxx xxxx**: The command will be `grep -o '[0-9]\{3\}\s[0-9]\{3\}\s[0-9]\{4\}'  file`

- **xxxxxxxxxx**: The command will be `grep -o '[0-9]\{10\}'  file`

The SANS Institute released a nice list of regular expression patterns (`https://www.sans.org/reading-room/whitepapers/forensics/regular-expression-search-primer-forensic-analysts-33929`) to be customized depending on your specific need:

File extensions	`grep -E '\.(txt|exe|xls|doc|docx|jpg|bmp)\b'`
URLs	`grep - E '\bhttps?://.+\.(com|net|org|uk|mil|gov|edu)'` (The ? following the s indicates that it is optional)
SSN	`grep -E '\b[0-9]{3}( |-)[0-9]{2}( |-)[0-9]{4}\b'`
MAC addresses	`grep -E '\b([0-9a-f]{2}:){5}[0-9a-f]{2}\b'`
IP addresses	`grep -E '\b[0-9]{1,3}(\.[0-9]{1,3}){3}\b'`
Credit Card	`grep -E '\b[0-9]{4}(( |-)[0-9]{4}){3}\b'`
American Express	`grep -E ''\b[0-9]{4}( |-)[0-9]{6}( |-)[0-9]{5}\b'`

There is also another command in the Linux environment for extracting printable characters from a file: `srch_strings`. Quite similar to the `strings` command, this command will, by default, print all the ASCII characters of at least four characters in length. The command, as taught in the SANS Forensic courses, is as follows: `srch_strings -a -t=d Input > Output.txt`, where –a tells the command to scan the entire file, -t to display the offset of the line with the occurrence shown in o (octal), x (hexadecimal), or d (decimal).

Encryption versus encoding versus hashing

Encryption, encoding, and hashing are quite confusing notions. Without digging very deep into the mathematical dimension, we will see the difference between all of these notions, keeping in mind that all of them transform data from one given format to another. The most important aspect to note is that the encryption and encoding functions are reversible but hashing is not.

Encryption

Encryption is a method or a set of methods for scrambling data. The process of encrypting aims to transform plaintext information by means of a given algorithm, referred to as cipher, to produce obscure/scrambled data, referred to as ciphertext. The process of encryption requires the use of a key to both encrypt plaintext and to decrypt ciphertext. The main differences between encryption and hashing are the fact that in contrast to hashing algorithms, encryption algorithms do not produce fixed length outputs, and encrypted data can be reversed back into the original format using the right key. This last difference brings us to one important thing to know about encryption: it has two primary types, symmetric key encryption and public key encryption.

In the case of symmetric key encryption (which is widely associated with encryption in general, when people think of encryption), the same key is used to produce both encrypted and decrypted data. In the case of public key encryption, instead of using one single key, it uses two different keys to encrypt/decrypt data; one public key, which, as its name invokes, is publicly shared, and is used to encrypt the desired data (message, string, or others), and one private key is used to decrypt this data — obviously, the private key is exclusively accessible to the intended recipients.

Symmetric key encryption

The most famous symmetric algorithm is **Advanced Encryption Standard (AES)**, also known as Rijndael, and is a specification of the encryption data established by the **National Institute of Standards and Technology (NIST)** in 2001 (`http://csrc.nist.gov/publications/fips/fips197/fips-197.pdf`). This algorithm can process data blocks (array of bytes) of 128 bits using keys with lengths of 128 and 192, and is recommended for most use cases with a key of 256 bits. Depending on the key length used, this encryption algorithm may be referred to as AES-128, AES-192 or AES-256.

AES is based on a series of linked mathematical operations known as the substitution-permutation network or **SP-network (SPN)**. The principle behind this network is to take a block of the plaintext and the key as input, and apply a fixed number (depending on the length of the used key) of cycles — or transformation rounds — (of substitution and permutation) in order to produce the ciphertext. The number of cycles is defined as follows:

- **128-bits key**: 10 cycles of repetition
- **192-bits key**: 12 cycles of repetition
- **256-bits key**: 14 cycles of repetition

Each round consists of four similar steps, which are as follows:

- **Key expansions**: Routine that generates a series of values derived from the cipher key
- **Initial Round**
  - **AddRoundKey**: Each byte of the intermediate cipher result (referred to as state) is combined with a block of values derived from the cipher key using the key expansion routine; the addition is done using bitwise XOR operation

- **Rounds**
  - **SubBytes**: Based on the non-linear Rijndael S-box (`https://en.wikipedia.org/wiki/Rijndael_S-box`), each byte is replaced with another
  - **ShiftRows**: Cyclically shifts the last three rows of the intermediate cipher result
  - **MixColumns**: Combines the four bytes in each column in the cipher in order to produce a new column
  - **AddRoundKey**
- **Final round**: At this step, no MixColumns is performed:
  - SubBytes
  - ShiftRows
  - AddRoundKey

Based on this high-level description of the AES encryption algorithm, a pseudo code of AES cipher may look like the following:

```
Cipher(byte in[16], byte out[16], key_array round_key[Nr+1])
begin
byte state[16]; state = in;
AddRoundKey(state, round_key[0]);

for i = 1 to Nr-1 stepsize 1 do
  SubBytes(state);
  ShiftRows(state);
  MixColumns(state);
  AddRoundKey(state,round_key[i]);
end for

SubBytes(state);
```

```
ShiftRows(state);
AddRoundKey(state, round_key[Nr]);
end
```

As an example of what AES produces, using the plaintext soufianetahiri@gmail.com and random 256-bits key 5575D3F563CB24BFDF55CFE252F857E4235CD23E645FAE5B235CD23E645FAE5B, the encrypted output looks like: 18 35 E2 EB F3 93 D7 34 DE 47 CF 52 2F 4F 4A 28 E4 F8 2D 01 C9 7B 73 8A 28 C9 87 C1 3B 05 FF 8D.

CryptoTool (https://www.cryptool.org/en/) is an awesome tool to play around with cryptography. I used it to decrypt the produced message as seen in the following screenshot:

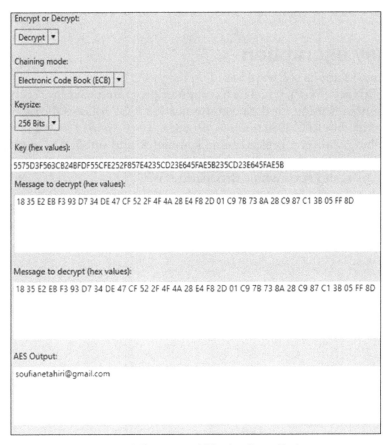

Figure 17: Decrypting AES using CryptoTool

AES-256 is somehow the gold standard, and has become ubiquitous since its adoption by the U.S. government in 2001 as the standard of encrypting data. The AES-256 encryption was also approved by the NSA, and believed to be unbreakable because of the length of the key (256 bits) and the number of cycles (14); even for a 128-bits key, recovering this length key requires 8×10^{37} steps. According to Leuven University, "on a trillion machines, that each could test a billion keys per second, it would take more than two billion years to recover an AES-128 key".

That said, at Black Hat 2015, Yu Yu, a research professor with Shanghai Jiao Tong University, used a side-channel analysis instead of brute-force attack to crack the encryption codes on 3G and 4G SIM cards, which use AES-128 encryption, and has successfully isolated 256 sections of the key (`https://www.blackhat.com/docs/us-15/materials/us-15-Yu-Cloning-3G-4G-SIM-Cards-With-A-PC-And-An-Oscilloscope-Lessons-Learned-In-Physical-Security-wp.pdf`).

Public key encryption

Some of the most famous software based on the public key encryption algorithm is **Pretty Good Privacy (PGP)**, which is a computer program providing cryptographic privacy and authentication for data communication. PGP follows the OpenPGP standard described in RFC 4880 (`https://tools.ietf.org/html/rfc4880`). PGP combines hashing, data compression, and symmetric and public key encryption to ensure confidentiality and integrity, and is often used for signing and exchanging texts, e-mails, files, and even whole disk partitions.

The schema that follows describes the general process of encrypting/decrypting in PGP:

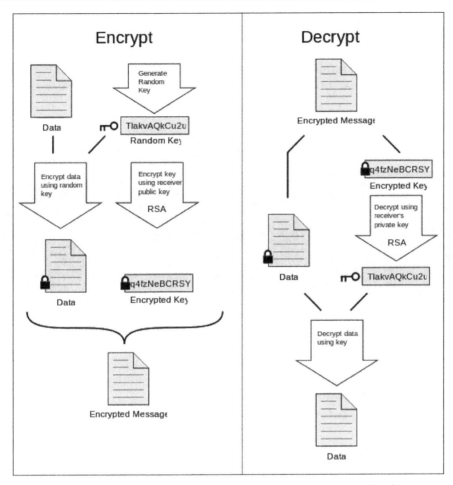

Figure 18: The encryption and decryption scheme of PGP (source: Wikipedia)

PGP uses an asymmetric scheme that uses a pair of keys for encryption, a public key that encrypts data, and a private key that decrypts it; the main goal of this approach is that anyone with your public key can then encrypt and send you information that only you can decrypt (using your private key), and it's computationally impossible to deduce the private key from the public key.

Each PGP message is constructed from a number of records called packets. Each packet is composed of a chunk of data, each chunk of data is associated with a tag specifying its meaning. Every packet consists of a packet header of variable length followed by the packet body.

If we refer to the RFC for the OpenPGP message format, in section 5.1 (`https://tools.ietf.org/html/rfc4880#section-5.1`), each encrypted message contains at least one public key encrypted session key packet. The body of this packet consists of a one-octet number giving the version number of the packet type, and an eight-octet number that gives the Key ID of the (sub) public key to which the session key is encrypted.

Tools like **PGPdump** (`http://www.pgpdump.net/about.html`) can extract this information from a given encrypted message/file, as seen in the following screenshot:

```
soufiane@soufiane-VirtualBox:~$ pgpdump /home/soufiane/Desktop/artifact.txt.gpg
Old: Public-Key Encrypted Session Key Packet(tag 1)(268 bytes)
        New version(3)
        Key ID - 0x3CF480556B845507
        Pub alg - RSA Encrypt or Sign(pub 1)
        RSA m^e mod n(2048 bits) - ...
                -> m = sym alg(1 byte) + checksum(2 bytes) + PKCS-1 block type 02
New: Symmetrically Encrypted and MDC Packet(tag 18)(95 bytes)
        Ver 1
        Encrypted data [sym alg is specified in pub-key encrypted session key]
                (plain text + MDC SHA1(20 bytes))
```

Figure 19: PGPdump

The Key ID can be used to deduce the intended recipient's identity, or, at least, can help us narrow down the identity of the intended recipient. Researchers at the University of Birmingham demonstrated how we can disclose an OpenPGP recipient's identity by exploiting the Key ID (`https://www.cs.bham.ac.uk/research/projects/infotools/leakwatch/examples/pgp.php`).

Elcomsoft (`https://www.elcomsoft.com/efdd.html`) also provides **Elcomsoft Forensic Disk Decryptor**, a tool that can perform a complete forensic analysis of encrypted disks and volumes protected with PGP.

A session key is a one-time-only secret key generated randomly from the movements of your mouse and the keystrokes that you type. Once the data is encrypted, the session key is then encrypted to the recipient's public key; this results in an encrypted session key.

Encoding

Ensuring the interchangeability of data between different types of systems relies, in part, on encoding. The main purpose of encoding data is to transform this data into another format so that it can be properly and safely consumed by different types of systems. This transformation is based on publicly available schemes so that it can be reversed with no pain. No keys are used in encoding/decoding processes, since the purpose is not to hide information; all we need to decode a given encoded information is to know the algorithm used. Sending files in e-mails, for example, is an encoding act.

Encoding is, to some level, a "character" related concept. This means that depending on the abstract layer and context, character encoding is used to describe a repertoire of units of information that roughly correspond to a grapheme of an encoding system (a system of rules to convert information from a given form of representation into another). This process is used in all kind of algorithms, protocols, data storage, and transmission of textual data. This abstraction is referred to as a character set or codeset.

There are four major terms that we must understand in order to go a bit deeper:

- **Character**: Sometimes abbreviated as char, this is a single visual object used to represent a symbol (text, number, and so on), and is equal to one byte (8 bits).

- **Character set**: A collection of characters.

- **Coded character set**: A collection of characters where each character is assigned a unique number.

- **Code point**: Also referred to as code position, this is any value that can be used in a coded character set, and is a 32-bit data type.

- **Code unit**: The minimal bit combination that can represent a unit of encoded text for processing or interchange. Code unit size is equivalent to the bit measurement for a given encoding scheme.

There are many widely and daily used character sets / encoding schemes, like ASCII, UNICODE/UTF-8, and URL encoding.

ASCII and UNICODE/UTF-8

The standard ASCII character set consists of 128 decimal numbers ranging from 0 through 127 mapped to letters, numbers, and the most common special characters; the code unit size in ASCII consists of 7 bits, but these days computers use an 8-bit byte to store each character in the memory, which extends the ASCII code units without modifying the original character-mapping, while adding additional characters. The original 7-bit ASCII was the most widely used encoding scheme until 2008 when UTF-8 became more common. A 7-bit ASCII table can be seen at `http://www.neurophys.wisc.edu/comp/docs/ascii/ascii-printable.html`.

Several mechanisms have been specified to come up with UTF-X (where X can be 8, 16, or 32 bits), and all depend on the available storage, compatibility, and system interoperability. UTF stands for **Unicode Transformation Format**. It's historically an effort of ISO/IEC 1046 (`https://www.ietf.org/rfc/rfc3629.txt`), and is defined by the UNICODE standard; it represents full ASCII compatibility, and obviously, can also contain any UNICODE character. UTF-8 means that it uses from one to four octets to represent a character.

RFC 2044 describes this as follows:

> *"The only octet of a "sequence" of a character has the higher-order bit set to 0, the remaining 7 bits being used to encode the character number. In a sequence of n octets, n>1, the initial octet has the n higher-order bits set to 1, followed by a bit set to 0. The remaining bit(s) of that octet contain bits from the number of the character to be encoded. The following octet(s) all have the higher-order bit set to 1 and the following bit set to 0, leaving 6 bits in each to contain bits from the character to be encoded."*

`https://tools.ietf.org/html/rfc2044`

The directly beneficial consequence is that no character will have null value when encoded. UTF-8 behaves just like ASCII when representing any character equal to or less than `0x7F` (127); this means that a plain ASCII string is a valid UTF-8 string.

To summarize the format of these octet types, please refer to the following table:

Character number range in hexadecimal	UTF-8 octet sequence in binary
0000 0000-0000 007F	0xxxxxxx
0000 0080-0000 07FF	110xxxxx 10xxxxxx
0000 0800-0000 FFFF	1110xxxx 10xxxxxx 10xxxxxx
0001 0000-0010 FFFF	11110xxx 10xxxxxx 10xxxxxx 10xxxxxx

Tableau 1: UTF-8 octet types format

To actually encode a character to UTF-8, three main steps are followed, as expressed in RFC3629:

1. Determine the number of octets required from the character number and the first column of the preceding table. It is important to note that the rows of the table are mutually exclusive, that is, there is only one valid way to encode a given character.

2. Prepare the high-order bits of the octets as per the second column of the table.

3. Fill in the bits marked x from the bits of the character number, expressed in binary. Start by putting the lowest-order bit of the character number in the lowest-order position of the last octet of the sequence, then put the next higher order bit of the character number in the next higher-order position of that octet, and so on. When the x bits of the last octet are filled in, move on to the next-to-last octet, then to the preceding one, and so on until all x bits are filled in.

I have been asked many time a simple question based on a lot of misunderstanding: "What is the difference between UNICODE and UTF-8?". I think at this stage, you can answer it by yourself: No comparison can be done for the simple reason that UTF-8 is an encoding and UNICODE is a character set. A character set is an abstract mapping between characters and numbers; for example, in ASCII and UNICODE, the character *S* corresponds to the number 53. On the other hand, encoding is the act of translating those numbers into binary format so they can be digitally stored. UTF-8, for instance, will encode the word *Forensic* like this: 01000110 01101111 01110010 01100101 01101110 01110011 01101001 01100011. Now let's see the inverse process—suppose that we want to read this binary back from disk. Let's say Notepad knows that a binary sequence represents Unicode string encoded with UTF-8, so Notepad will use the UTF-8 algorithm to convert each binary block to its hexadecimal value in order to produce the UNICODE code point from the Unicode character set, and correlate each number to its corresponding character:

Binary	Unicode code point	Character	UTF-8 (hex)
01000110	U+0046	F	0x46
01101111	U+006F	o	0x6F
01110010	U+0072	r	0x72
01100101	U+0065	e	0x65
01101110	U+006E	n	0x6E
01110011	U+0073	s	0x73
01101001	U+0069	i	0x69
01100011	U+0063	c	0x63

Tableau 2: Bin to Unicode / UTF-8

For the full UTF-8 encoding table and Unicode characters, you can refer to `http://www.utf8-chartable.de/`.

URL encoding

Under certain circumstances, the **Unified Resource Identifier** (**URI**) encodes information using the URL-encoding mechanism, also referred to as **percent-encoding**. This encoding mechanism is often used in the preparation of data of the *application/x-www-form-urlencoded* media type. It aims, principally, to replace any "unsafe ASCII" character with a `%` followed by two hexadecimal digits ("unsafe" here means when the character is outside the allowed set of characters). A percent encoding data octet is always encoded as the percent character followed by two hexadecimal digits representing the actual octet's numeric value. For example, the widely seen percent-encoding octet is `%20`; `0x20` in ASCII corresponds to the space character which is not allowed in URLs (or URIs to be more correct, since URI includes both **Uniform Resource Locator** (**URL**) and **Uniform Resource Name** (**URN**)).

There is a limitation to the characters allowed in a URI, and those characters can be split into two main categories: reserved and unreserved characters. Reserved characters are so called because they may be defined as delimiters of URI's dereferencing algorithm. So, if data for a URI component conflicts with a reserved character, this data must be URL-encoded (or percent-encoded) before the URI is formed. For example, forward slash (/) is a reserved character. As of January 2005, reserved characters are defined in RFC 3986 section 2.2 (`https://tools.ietf.org/html/rfc3986`) as follow:

!	?	$	@	&	=	+	*	'	#	/	(	)	;	,	:	[	]

Tableau 3: URI reserved characters

Every other character that is found within a URI, but does not have a reserved purpose, is considered an unreserved character; this includes uppercase and lowercase letters, decimal digits, hyphens, periods, underscores, and tildes.

If a reserved character is meant to be used as data in a given context, and the URI scheme says that a reserved character is necessary to be used as it is and not as a URI's delimiter, then this character must be URL-encoded.

URL-encoding a reserved character is done by converting this character to its corresponding byte sequence in ASCII or UTF-8, and then representing that value as a character triplet consisting of the percent character followed by a pair of hexadecimal digits. The percent character is used as an escape character.

The reserved character &, for example, has the special task of passing variables with data between pages using URLs. If we need to use this character itself as data, then it must be percent-encoded as %26. The following table shows reserved characters after URL-encoding:

!	?	$	@	&	=	+	*	'
%21	%3F	%24	%40	%26	%3D	%2B	%2A	%27
#	/	(	)	;	,	:	[	]
%23	%2F	%28	%29	%3B	%2C	%3A	%5B	%5D

Tableau 4: URI reserved characters URL-encoded

Following this, an encoded URL like this one `https%3A%2F%2Fwww.google.com%2Fwebhp%3Fsourceid%3Dchrome-instant%26ion%3D1%26espv%3D2%26es_th%3D1%26ie%3DUTF-8%23q%3Dsoufian+tahiri%26es_th%3D1` can be decoded as `https://www.google.com/webhp?sourceid=chrome-instant&ion=1&espv=2&es_th=1&ie=UTF-8#q=soufian tahiri&es_th=1`.

Hashing

The use of cryptography in the forensic processes is a normal and common task. Using hashing algorithms like MD5 and SHA help to maintain and verify evidence integrity, and by the same process, assist investigators with admissibility of evidence in court. Hashing can also be used as a tool to help quickly identify certain files when analyzing a filesystem.

Basically, hashing is an irreversible algorithm capable of producing (usually) a small fixed size output whatever the input used. **Message-Digest Algorithm (MD5)** and **Secure Hashing Algorithm (SHA)** are typical cryptographic hashing algorithms.

MD5 processes any input message into a fixed-length output of 128 bits, considered as a fingerprint of the input.

The input message (or data) is treated by blocks of 512 bits. If the data size is not divisible by 512, then the data is padded (extended) by adding 1 bit to the end of the message followed by as many zeros as necessary to bring the extended data to 448 modulo, 512. Without digging into mathematical details, we can simply say that the MD5 algorithm is composed of the following five main steps:

1. Append padding bits.
2. Append length.
3. Initialize MD buffer.

4. Process message in 16-word blocks.

5. Output.

The MD5 algorithm is described in RFC 1321 (`https://www.ietf.org/rfc/rfc1321.txt`).

SHA is, in fact, a family of cryptographic functions including SHA-0, SHA-1, SHA-2, and SHA-3. They were published by the National Institute of Standard and Technology. The most famous family is SHA-1, and was developed by the NSA. But since 2010, this function is no longer approved due to a weakness discloser (Henri Gilbert, Helena Handschuh. *Security Analysis of SHA-256 and Sisters*. Selected Areas in Cryptography 2003. pg 175–193). SHA-1 produces a 160 bit output (called message digest), and is still the algorithm that is widely used in forensic examinations (even if using SHA-2 is more secure). The SHA-1 algorithm has been available to the Internet community since 2001, and is well described in RFC 3174 (`https://tools.ietf.org/html/rfc3174`).

Whatever the hash algorithm we are talking about, it contains three interesting properties: generating a hash value is a relatively easy and not time-consuming task; theoretically, it's not possible to alter data without changing its hash value, and different data cannot produce the same hash value.

Based on these facts, hash functions are used to authenticate evidence, to verify data integrity, and can also be used to identify a file by looking up the hash in the hash databases.

Hash databases are often built by agencies of law enforcement to help in quickly identifying known files. There are many downloadable hash databases. The National Institute of Standard and Technology offers the **National Software Reference Library** (**NSRL**) that contains, among other things, **NSRL Reference Data Set** (**RDS**), a public dataset holding very large cryptographic hash values (MD5 and SHA-1) of known files. RDS is updated and published every three months. RDS is an interesting repository of hashes. The content of the RDS archive is `hashes.txt`, `NSRLFile.txt`, `NSRLMfg.txt`, `NSRLOS.txt`, and `NSRLProd.txt` (downloadable from `http://www.nsrl.nist.gov/Downloads.htm#isos`).

More repositories of interesting hashes can also be listed at Hashkeeper (even if it's not maintained anymore), SANS Hash Database, AccessData, EnCase, Shadowserver Bin Check Service, Project VIC, and more.

There are many ways to look for hashes (grep, hfind, and more); the main difference among them is time consumption.

The problem with MD5 and SHA-1 is that both are vulnerable to hash collision, which means that two arbitrary inputs can produce the same hash value, such as *hash(message1) = hash(message2)*. Back in March 2005, Xiaoyun W. and Hongbo Yu of Shandong University in China described an algorithm that can cause MD5 collision, and published an article about their exploit titled *How to break MD5 and other hash functions* (`http://merlot.usc.edu/csac-f06/papers/Wang05a.pdf`). But in my view, they are still at some point forensically sound, because statistically, the chance to produce the same hash from different inputs is one in 2^L (where L is the fixed size output result length), which is infinitesimally small for either MD5 or SHA-1.

To conclude this part, the important thing to keep in mind is that encoding, encrypting, and hashing are terms that do not say the same thing at all:

- **Encoding**: Is meant for data usability, is reversible using the same algorithm, and requires no key
- **Encrypting**: Is meant for confidentiality, is reversible, and depending on algorithms, relies on key(s) to encrypt and decrypt.
- **Hashing**: Theoretically, this is meant for data integrity, cannot be reversible, and depends on no keys.

Decompiling and disassembling

Decompiling and disassembling are both kinds of a reverse engineering process that do the opposite of what a compiler and an assembler do.

A **decompiler** translates a compiled binary's low-level code designed to be computer readable into human-readable high-level code. The accuracy of decompilers depends on many factors like the amount of metadata present in the code being decompiled and the complexity of the code (not in terms of algorithms, but in terms of sophistication of the high-level code used). The bytecode format used by **Java Virtual Machine (JVM)** and the intermediate language used by .NET framework **Common Language Runtime (CLR)** include, in most cases, a very extensive amount of information and high level features. This makes the process of creating a high-level code from a compiled input quite feasible, and in most cases, very reliable. Most of the decompilation processes pass through seven steps before producing a readable high level code: loading -> disassembling -> programming idiom -> program analysis -> data flow analysis -> type analysis -> structuring.

The output of a **disassembler** is, at some level, processor dependent. It maps processor instructions into mnemonics, which is in contrast to the decompiler's output, which is far more complicated to understand and to edit.

What is the point of this in a forensic context? Let's suppose this simple scenario: A user encrypts photo albums or SMS using a third-party application (for example, on Android, the *Droid Crypt* or *EDS* app). Then it would be more than interesting to look inside the application algorithms to have a clear idea of how things were done. Reverse engineering smartphone applications can be very interesting from the perspective of forensics—looking inside an application can reveal passwords, keys, SQL queries, and algorithms. Reverse engineering is always used in cases of malware infection forensic processes too. So reverse engineering a smartphone application can help you understand a given app's functioning, its data storage, and security mechanisms.

Reversing Android, iPhone, and Windows Phone applications require different skills, but to keep it simple, let's go ahead and see how things are done on the Android side.

Every Android application is coded using Java. Applications built to run under Android come with an APK extension, which is the extension of the application install file. Downloaded APKs are usually stored on the phone in the /data/app directory. An APK can be extracted from a phone image using FTK Imager, for example, and if you have root access on the phone, you can copy it from the given directory to /sdcard, or you can install a file manager like ES File Manager, and use the built-in app management function to copy the desired APK to the /sdcard directory. To deal with built-in applications and system applications like Gmail, Calendar, and so on, since they are in /system/app, the easiest and simple way to extract them is by starting with identifying the package name using the adb shell pm list packages command, which works on rooted and non-rooted devices:

```
adb shell pm list packages
package:com.android.emulator.smoketests
package:com.android.packageinstaller
package:com.svox.pico

...

package:com.facebook.lite
package:com.android.netspeed

...
```

After identifying the package name, we can identify the full path using the command adb shell pm path PACKAGENAME. If we suppose that we want to extract the APK file of the Facebook Lite application, the preceding command will be as follows:

```
adb shell pm path com.facebook.lite
package:/data/app/com.facebook.lite-1/base.apk
```

The full path is /data/app/com.facebook.lite-1/base.apk, so now we can extract this file using adb pull APKLOCATION DIRECTORYOUTPUT:

```
adb pull /data/app/com.facebook.lite-1/base.apk /home/soufiane/Desktop/
apk_pulled/
1473 KB/s (475823 bytes in 0.315s)
```

The interesting thing to know about APKs is that they are just ZIP files, so once in your process, you can modify the .apk extension to .zip, and extract the archive as follows:

Name		Description
jsr-305		folder
META-INF		folder
res		folder
AndroidManifest.xml		XML document
base.apk		Android package
classes.dex		unknown
resources.arsc		unknown

Figure 20: Extracted APK application

Classes.dex is the actual application binary, the res directory is the directory used to store application resources (for example, images), the META-INF directory holds the digital signature of the application, and like every Android application, AndroidManifest.xml includes important information about the application like permissions, and indents like "...". The file AndroidManifest.xml is not readable as is; in order to transform it into a human-readable file, we can use the aapt command, which is a debug tool included with adb. The command is of the format aapt l -a APK.apk > textfile.txt, as follows:

```
aapt l -a /home/soufiane/Desktop/apk_pulled/base.apk > /home/soufiane/
Desktop/apk_pulled/AndroidManifest.txt
soufiane@soufiane-VirtualBox:~$
```

At this point, the manifest file is readable, and you can eventually look for permissions, for example. Why are permissions important? Imagine you have a simple calculator application that has the permission to geolocalise the smartphone or to access camera.

As for our Facebook Lite example, the application can read the user's SMS (suspect?):

```
  A: android:name(0x01010003)="android.permission.READ_SMS" (Raw:
"android.permission.READ_SMS")
```

Now we can move to the main application binary, and a bunch of tools can be used to reverse a `.dex` file. The first tool we need is **dex2jar** (`https://github.com/pxb1988/dex2jar`). This tool will convert `classes.dex` to a Java JAR file; the command used is of the format `d2j-dex2jar APK.apk > Output.jar`, as follows:

```
d2j-dex2jar /home/soufiane/Desktop/apk_pulled/base.apk >/home/soufiane/
Desktop/apk_pulled/base-dex2jar.jar
```

Then we will use any Java decompiler to restore the Java source code of our class. In this example, I'll use **JD-GUI** (`http://jd.benow.ca/`) via the command `jd-gui Output.jar`:

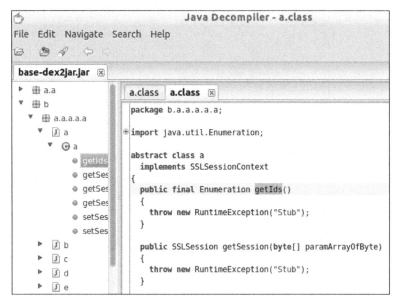

Figure 21: Java decomplier JD-GUI

The `a.a`, `b`, and `a.a.a.a` names reveal that this is an obfuscated JAR file, and this may be deobfuscated. But the technique is out of scope of this book, since the goal is to demonstrate the decompilation process. However, once you gain access to the source code, application analysis can be much easier and more useful.

The same "logic" can be applied to reverse most smartphone applications regardless of the operating system, but obviously, by using different tools and techniques.

If we take the example of a Windows Phone application, let's say WP8 Registry Tools, it has the XAP extension, and is coded using a .NET language (C# / VB.net). Just like Android applications, they are just ZIP files too. Once you have the `.xap` file in your computer, you can rename it by changing the extension to `.zip`, and extract the content:

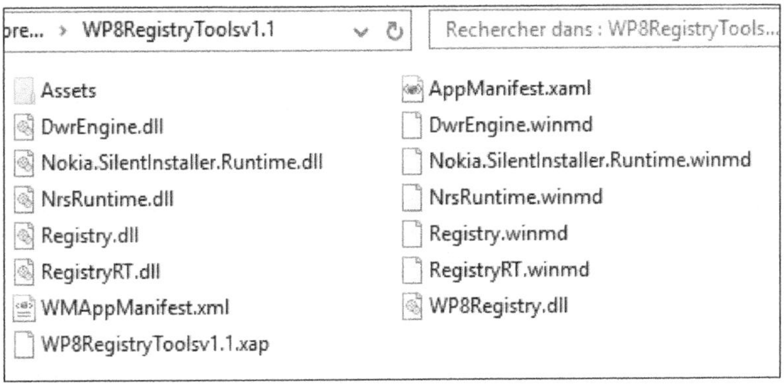

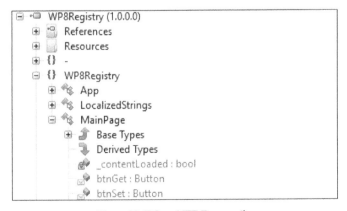

Figure 22: Extracted XAP application

As for Android, Windows Phone applications also have their WMAppManifest.xml files describing application permissions among other information. Permissions in Windows Phone are called "capabilities", as seen in our following example:

```
<Capabilities>
    <Capability Name="ID_CAP_NETWORKING" />
    <Capability Name="ID_CAP_IDENTITY_DEVICE" />
    <Capability Name="ID_CAP_PHONEDIALER" />
    <Capability Name="ID_CAP_LOCATION" />
    <Capability Name="ID_CAP_SENSORS" />
    <Capability Name="ID_CAP_WEBBROWSERCOMPONENT" />
</Capabilities>
```

The main application binary in our case is WP8Registry.dll, and we can use any .NET decompiler to see inside, I'll be using **ILSpy** (http://ilspy.net/), since it's a powerful and free .NET decompiler:

Figure 23: ILSpy .NET Decompiler

Here we've got an unobfuscated application, so we can navigate through it and see even original variables names, name spaces, and functions names:

```
private void btnGet_Click(object sender, RoutedEventArgs e)
{
    if (string.IsNullOrEmpty(this.txtRegKey.get_Text()) || string.
IsNullOrEmpty(this.txtRegVal.get_Text()))
    {
        MessageBox.Show("Please enter in values");
        return;
    }
....
    this.txtResult.set_Text(text.ToString());
}
```

.NET applications can be also obfuscated, and there are several tools to deobfuscate them; in my view, the most reliable one is **DE4DOT** (http://de4dot.com/).

On the other hand, we have the iOS applications—the bad news is that Apple changes the IDE at almost every release, making reversing iOS applications a real challenge. But the good news is that we belong to a world full of enthusiasts and researchers who have made a lot of progress in this direction. If you are interested in learning more about reversing iOS applications, you can refer to the book by Snakeninny named *iOS App Reverse Engineering*, available freely at https://github. com/iosre/iOSAppReverseEngineering.

Summary

Forensics is an extremely technical discipline, so this chapter was meant to help clarify the principles of file carving, to demystify GPS data, and to clearly explain how photos are made binary. We went through some deep technical aspects of computing in general, we saw some file formats and how metadata is stored within them, we went through characters and string data types, and explained how to extract strings from smartphone dumps. This chapter (hopefully) also clarified the difference between some common string related concepts like encryption, encoding, and hashing.

Seeing the importance of understanding how smartphone applications behave in a forensic context, we picked over some techniques of reverse code engineering smartphone applications.

Now that we are familiar enough with some low-level techniques, we can go ahead and discuss iOS forensics in the next chapter.

3
iDevices from a Forensic Point of View

The purpose of this chapter is to provide an overview of the forensic approach of an iOS device. We will introduce iOS architecture components and the filesystem. This chapter will indicate methodology, techniques, and tools used to acquire evidences from iOS devices, it will also point out the difference between different modes (DFU, recovery, and more), introduce the jailbreaking concept, and discuss the biometric aspect of iOS devices.

In this chapter, we will cover the following topics:

- The iOS architecture
- The iOS filesystem
- iOS platform and hardware security
- Identifying stored data
- iOS acquisition and forensic approaches
- iOS artifact recovery
- It's going biometric!
- Third-party application forensics

The iOS architecture

Originally called the iPhone OS, iOS is developed and distributed exclusively within Apple hardware (iPhones, iPads and iPod Touch). Similar to most operating systems, iOS is a layered OS. Applications deployed on any iOS device do not react directly with the underlying hardware, instead the operating system acts as a layer of system interfaces between those applications and the hardware; iOS is divided into four abstract layers as follows (from highest level at the top to the lowest-level at the bottom):

Cocoa Touch layer
Media layer
Core Services layer
Core OS layer

Table 1 - iOS layers

Let's look at the layers:

- **Cocoa Touch layer**: This contains the basic framework that provides multitasking, touch-based inputs, push notifications, and most of the high level system services. This layer contains some high-level features such as app extensions, which allow sharing media content to social entities, performing simple tasks with content, photo editing, and providing shared storage location (for applications that use document picking). It also contains TextKit, that offers a set of well-defined classes (NSAttributedString, NSLayoutManager, NSTextStorage and may other features; for more information you can refer to *Text Programming Guide for iOS* at https://developer.apple.com/library/ios/documentation/StringsTextFonts/Conceptual/TextAndWebiPhoneOS/Introduction/Introduction.html#//apple_ref/doc/uid/TP40009542) to enable application editing, creating, storing and displaying text, and integrating it with all UIKit text-based controls. Also, it contains multitasking, which is mainly designed to manage application resource consumption to maximize battery life; in addition to a bunch of other features, such as auto layout, UI state preservation, Apple Push Notification Service, and local notifications.

- **Media layer**: This implements all the necessary technologies to enhance the multimedia experience, including graphic technologies to handle advanced 2D and 3D rendering using hardware acceleration, such as OpenGL ES and GLKit; audio technologies, such as AV foundation and OpenAL; and video technologies, such as AVKit and AV Foundation to ensure video playback and recording capabilities.

- **Core Service layer**: This consists of services, such as Core Foundation and Foundation frameworks and holds the fundamental system services along with individual technologies offering features, such as geolocation, social media, networking, and iCloud. As for its high-level features, the Core Service layer offers features that support peer-to-peer connectivity, iCloud storage, data protection, file sharing support (making data available in iTunes), Grand Central Dispatch (BSD-level technology used to manage task execution), SQLite, and XML support.

- **Core OS layer**: Almost all the other previously cited technologies are built upon low-level features within this level; the Core OS layer contains frameworks dealing with security, digital signal and image-processing calculation (`Accelerate.framework`), Core Bluetooth framework (`CoreBluetooth.framework`), External Accessory framework (`ExternalAccessory.framework`) that provides support for accessories connected to the iDevice via its connector or via Bluetooth, Touch ID authentication support (`LocalAuthentication.framework`), and the Generic Security Service framework (`GSS.framework`) that gives a "basic" set of security services to iOS applications (the standardization of these services are well described in RFC 2743 at `https://www.ietf.org/rfc/rfc2743.txt` and RFC 4401 at `https://tools.ietf.org/html/rfc4401`). The Core OS layer also provides the system level that includes low-level UNIX interfaces, drivers and a match-based kernel environment that manages memory, threads, filesystem network, and inter-process communication.

It's important to note that above the kernel level, iOS uses Mac OS X's BSD Unix environment. To make it simple, iOS can be subdivided into three main layers: the XNU kernel, which is a hybrid kernel developed by Apple attempting to make the best use of a monolithic kernel and microkernel, **Portable Operating System Interface (POSIX)** layer, which is a set of standards for maintaining compatibility between operating systems, provided by a part of BSD's kernel that also provides among other things, system calls and filesystems, and lastly, the NeXTSTEP layer that implements the graphics stack of iOS.

The iOS filesystem

Just like all Apple operating systems, iOS is a derivative of the Mac OS X. Thus, iOS uses **Hierarchical File System Plus (HFS+)** as its primary filesystem. HFS+ replaces the first developed filesystem, HFS, and is considered an enhanced version of HFS. They are architecturally very similar. The main improvements seen in HFS+ are:

- Decrease in disk space usage on large volumes (efficient use of disk space)

- International-friendly file names (by the use of UNICODE instead of MacRoman)

- Allows future systems to use and extend files/folders' metadata

HFS+ divides the total space on a volume (a file that contains data and structure to access this data) into allocation blocks and uses 32-bit fields to identify them, this means that this allows up to 2^32 blocks on a given volume which simply means that a volume can hold more files.

All HFS+ volumes follow a well-defined structure and each volume contains a volume header, a catalog file, extents overflow file, attributes file, allocation file, and startup file. The general structure of an HFS+ volume is illustrated here:

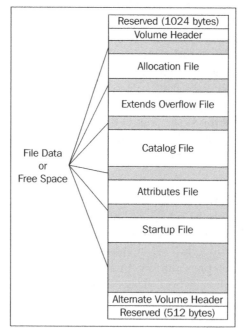

Structure of an HFS+ volume

Let's look at each part of the structure:

- **Volume Header**: The Volume Header is a reserved field of 512 bytes and contains information regarding the volume itself (size of block, total of blocks, and number of free blocks, creation, and modification date) and is described by the HFSPlusVolumeHeader type.

- **Allocation File**: This is a bitmap file used to store allocation information within a volume and determinates if a block is allocated or not. The allocation file can be up to 512 MB.

- **Extents Overflow File**: This maintains an appropriate order list of contiguous allocation blocks that belong to a file, if this file's fork contains more than eight extents; the extent records are described by the HFSPlusExtentKey type. The hierarchy of files and folders on a volume is kept as a B-Tree file in the Catalog File.

- **Catalog File**: This is used to locate a specific file or folder.

- **Attributes File**: It holds the fork data attribute, inline data attribute, and extension attribute (allowing a set of data associated with a filesystem to have more than eight extents).

- **Startup File**: This is a special file that keeps the information needed at system boot time and is used if the system does not support HFS+.

HFS+ under iOS has an activated journaling feature that keeps a transaction log of read/write activities on disk; this is meant to ensure stability of the operating system in case a system recovery is needed after a crash, but the filesystem keeping journal logs may contain the same data in catalog and attribute files; they may be forensically very valuable since they can be exploited to recover deleted files. An interesting read about filesystem journal analysis can be found at https://digital-forensics.sans.org/summit-archives/DFIR_Summit/File-System-Journaling-Forensics-Theory-Procedures-and-Analysis-Impacts-David-Cowen-with-Matthew-Seyer.pdf.

iOS platform and hardware security

This chapter cannot hold all the hardware and software security aspects of iDevices, thus we will see a general overview of how security is implemented on those devices.

All of Apple's iDevices have a combined built-in hardware/software advanced security and according to Apple's official *iOS Security Guide* can be categorized as follows:

- **System security**: Integrated software and hardware platform
- **Encryption and data protection**: Mechanisms implemented to protect data from unauthorized use
- **Application security**: Application sandboxing
- **Network security**: Secure data transmission
- **Apple Pay**: Implementation of secure payments
- **Internet services**: Apple's network of messaging, synchronizing and backing up.
- **Device controls**: Remotely wiping a device if lost or stolen
- **Privacy control**: Controlled access to geolocation and user data

The overview of the iOS security architecture is as follows:

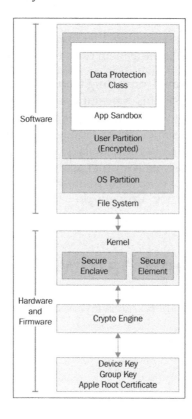

The hardware implementation in Apple's devices offer a dedicated AES-256 engine built into the **Direct Memory Access (DMA)** allowing the device to deal with data without involving the CPU, which maximizes file encryption/decryption efficiency. Each Apple device has its very **unique ID (UID)** and **group ID (GID)** which is AES-256 bits fused keys during manufacturing and is even JTAG resistant, those keys are used to encrypt and decrypt user's data, meaning that even if advanced techniques, such as chip-off are used encrypted data still is unreadable.

Data stored in the flash memory of any given iDevice is protected via Data Protection Technology (as Apple calls it); there are four main levels of data protection:

- **Complete Data Protection**: This is provided by the `NSFileProtectionComplete` class key and is protected with a key derived from the user passcode and the device UID; once the device is locked, the decrypted class key is removed from memory until next device unlock.

- **Data Protection Unless Open**: This is provided by the `NSFileProtectionCompleteUnlessOpen` class and is protected using asymmetric elliptic curve crypto.

- **Data Protected Until First User Authentication**: It is provided by the `NSFileProtectionCompleteUntilFirstUserAuthentication` class and is similar to a desktop full disk encryption, this class behaves like Complete Data Protection except the fact that the decrypted class key is not removed from memory.

- **No Protection**: This is provided by the `NSFileProtectionNone` class and is protected by the UID.

Each file created on data partition is assigned a new 256-bit key; this key is used by the AES engine to encrypt this file before writing it to the flash memory. Devices that use A8 processors encrypt files using XTS-AES (as described in *Recommendation for Block Cipher Modes of Operation: the XTS-AES Mode for Confidentiality on Storage Devices* presented by NIST in January 2010). Depending on the file (how and when it must be available), the generated per-file key is wrapped with a class key and stored in the same file's metadata under the `cprotect` attribute using AES key wrap algorithm, as described in RFC 3394 (`https://tools.ietf.org/html/rfc3394`). Files are decrypted somehow on demand, once a file is solicited, the filesystem key (the key that encrypts each file's metadata, including its class key) passes the revealed per-file key and the indication to the concerned class key to AES engine which decrypts the opened file.

The process is described in the following schema:

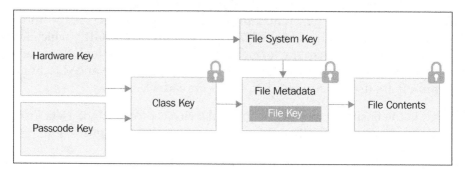

In addition to this, iOS offers **Keychain Data Protection**, which is implemented as a SQLite database present in the filesystem and provides a secure way to store sensitive information used by applications (such as login tokens and passwords). Keychain items are managed by the security daemon in order to determine which process can access which keychain and to facilitate this, a keychain-access group is set to facilitate sharing keychains between applications from the same developer.

Identifying stored data

All iDevices use a type of non-volatile memory chip using NOT AND gates called NAND memory, this memory in iDevices is divided into two partitions: system and data. As suggested by their respective names, the system partition holds the firmware including the operating system and built-in applications and in general it's a read-only partition. Depending on models, this partition can range anywhere from 1 to 2.5 GB. In general this partition does not hold any forensically interesting evidence; however, it's important to note that the `/private/etc/passwd` path holds the preconfigured user's "mobile" and "root" passwords, as shown in following screenshot:

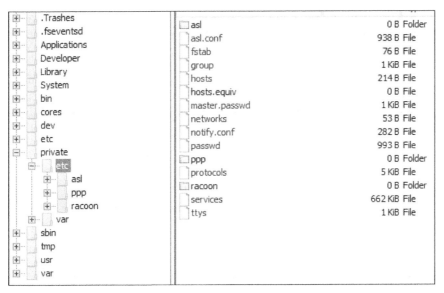

System partition of iOS 9.0

If you open the file with a text editor you should get the following:

```
 1  ##
 2  # User Database
 3  #
 4  # This file is the authoritative user database.
 5  ##
 6  nobody:*:-2:-2:Unprivileged User:/var/empty:/usr/bin/false
 7  root:/smx7MYTQIi2M:0:0:System Administrator:/var/root:/bin/sh
 8  mobile:/smx7MYTQIi2M:501:501:Mobile User:/var/mobile:/bin/sh
 9  daemon:*:1:1:System Services:/var/root:/usr/bin/false
10  _ftp:*:98:-2:FTP Daemon:/var/empty:/usr/bin/false
11  _networkd:*:24:24:Network Services:/var/networkd:/usr/bin/false
12  _wireless:*:25:25:Wireless Services:/var/wireless:/usr/bin/false
13  _neagent:*:34:34:NEAgent:/var/empty:/usr/bin/false
14  _securityd:*:64:64:securityd:/var/empty:/usr/bin/false
```

Default password of users root and mobile

The plaintext password is *alpine* and is the same in all iDevices. This password cannot be modified unless the device is jailbroken.

Data partition holds user's installed applications, iTunes media, settings, and all the user data, which leads to the fact that this partition constitutes the majority of NAND memory space, which can be up to 128 GB.

The majority of forensically interesting data is stored in /private/var, which is the mount point for device's user/data partition /dev/disk0s1s2 (or /dev/disk0s2 in older versions). Most applications run under the non-root user named "mobile" and all the data is present in /private/var/mobile.

The main children of /private/var/mobile are as follows:

- Containers (replaces Applications in versions prior to iOS 8)
- Applications (replaces Containers in versions prior to iOS 8)
- Documents
- Library
- Media

The Containers folder contains all applications downloaded from Apple Store and has the following children:

- Bundle
- Application
- Data
- Shared

As seen here, the Bundle folder holds an Application subfolder that holds the actual applications folders; this folder contains as many folders as there are downloaded and installed applications, each folder is named by the **Universally Unique ID (UUID)** of the application within it, the UUID uses a canonical format using hexadecimal text with inserted hyphens characters in this form: CCC7366E-AD57-476F-B7A4-30C060514BA1, each of these folders has the following general structure:

- Documents
- Library
- tmp
- Name.app
- iTunesArtwork
- iTunesMetadata.plist

The `Name.app` is the application bundle, `Name` is replaced by the actual application name, this file is digitally signed and verified at runtime and is not backed-up during sync. `Documents` is a folder containing the application's data and can be synchronized and backed-up, the data within this folder can also be accessed through iTunes File Sharing if this option is enabled in `iTunesMetadata.plist`. `Library` is also a folder containing application files; its content is backed-up except for its subfolder `Caches`. As its name suggests, `tmp` is a directory that contains volatile temporary files generated after the application launches. `iTunesArtwork` refers to the application icon used in iTunes and in general is 512 x 512 px. The `iTunesMetadata.plist` is basically an XML file containing the application's iTunes metadata and can be opened in Windows using **plist Editor Pro** (http://www. icopybot.com/plist-editor.htm); for example, this file may contain forensically interesting evidences, such as the Apple account name and the date of purchase. The following is a snippet of the LinkedIn application's `iTunesMetadata.plist` file:

```
<dict>
   <key>artistId</key>
   <integer>288429043</integer>
   <key>artistName</key>
   <string>LinkedIn Corporation</string>
   <key>asset-info</key>
......
   <key>bundleShortVersionString</key>
   <string>66</string>
   <key>bundleVersion</key>
   <string>5.1.6</string>
   <key>com.apple.iTunesStore.downloadInfo</key>
   <dict>
      <key>accountInfo</key>
      <dict>
         <key>AccountAvailableServiceTypes</key>
......
         <string>143469-2,2</string>
         <key>AccountURLBagType</key>
         <string>production</string>
         <key>AppleID</key>
         <string>edited@edited.com</string>
         <key>CreditDisplayString</key>
         <string></string>
         <key>DSPersonID</key>
         <integer>1067389897</integer>
      </dict>
```

```
<key>purchaseDate</key>
<string>2015-09-12T09:50:25Z</string>
</dict>
```

Timestamp is an important point to consider while manually analyzing artifacts, since the majority of (if not all) timestamps found on iDevices are either in UNIX timestamp format, also known as POSX time and Epoch time, or in MAC absolute format.

UNIX format represents the amount of seconds elapsed since the UNIX epoch, which is 00:00:00 UTC on 1 January 1970, so at UNIX epoch, UNIX time is equal to 0 and increases by 86400 seconds each day following the epoch. For example, 2016-01-04T00:00:00Z, meaning 16804 days after the epoch, will have a UNIX timestamp that will look like *16804 * 86400 =1,451,865,600*. There many free tools to do the conversion (http://www.unixtimestamp.com) or you can use your terminal in Linux, for example, by typing the following command date -u -d @1451865600 (or in OS X by typing OS X: $ date -ur 1451865600):

```
soufiane@soufiane-VirtualBox:~$ date -u -d @1451865600
Mon Jan  4 00:00:00 UTC 2016
```

The –u is used to indicate universal time and not local

The Mac Absolute Time format is almost the same except that the epoch time is considered as 00:00:00 UTN on 1 January 2001, making an exact difference of 978,307,200 seconds, so to convert a timestamp to this format, this difference must be added.

Depending on the iOS version (iOS 7, iOS 8+ or iOS 9+), the paths of different artifacts generated by the system or by the user's interaction with it are a bit different, but the general structure remains almost the same. In general, the main file formats that you will be analyzing in order to gather evidence are SQLite databases and **property list (plist)**.

Using the tree command against a mounted image either in a Windows, Mac, or Linux environment will bring up an easy-to-read list of how directories and files are sorted. The following list is a part of the result of the tree command in a Windows environment system partition of a mounted iOS 9.0 image:

```
+---Applications
|   +---AACredentialRecoveryDialog.app
|   |   \---_CodeSignature
|   +---AccountAuthenticationDialog.app
|   |   \---_CodeSignature
```

```
    |    +---AdSheet.app
    |    |    +---ar.lproj
...
    +---Managed Preferences
    |    \---mobile
    +---mobile
    |    +---Applications
    |    +---Library
    |    |    +---AddressBook
    |    |    +---Caches
    |    |    +---Cookies
    |    |    +---Inboxes
    |    |    +---Keyboard
    |    |    +---Logs
    |    |    |    \---CrashReporter
    |    |    |         \---DiagnosticLogs
    |    |    +---Preferences
    |    |    +---Safari
    |    |    +---WebClips
    |    |    \---WebKit
    |    \---Media
    |         +---DCIM
    |         +---PhotoData
    |         \---Photos
    +---MobileDevice
    |    \---ProvisioningProfiles
    +---msgs
    +---networkd
    +---preferences
    +---root
    |    \---Library
    |         \---Preferences
    +---run
    +---spool
    |    \---mdt
    +---tmp
    +---vm
    \---wireless
         \---Library
```

Generally, to gather the most valuable information about applications, such as Facebook, WhatsApp, Skype, and Dropbox, you should refer to either `private/var/mobile/Application/` for versions prior to iOS 8 or `/private/var/mobile/Containers/Bundle/Application/` in more recent versions.

iOS acquisition and forensic approaches

Before talking about acquisition, it's important to have at least an idea about some important iOS-related concepts: iOS boot process, operating modes, unique device identifier, and lockdown certificate.

iOS boot process and operating modes

Apple introduced what they call the **Secure Boot Chain** in which each step of the start-up process is cryptographically validated to ensure integrity and guarantee the chain of trust. The Apple root CA public key is shipped within the boot ROM code and is used to verify the **Low-Level Bootloader** (**LLB**). Once verified and loaded, LLB verifies and loads in turn the iBoot bootloader, which in turn verifies and loads the iOS kernel. This process is well described in the Apple's official *iOS Security guide* (`https://www.apple.com/business/docs/iOS_Security_Guide.pdf`). From these boot stages, three operating modes can be listed: LLB can be directly launched from **Device Firmware Upgrade** (**DFU**) mode; iBoot runs what is called the **recovery** mode, it has an interactive interface and can be used over USB, and then **normal** mode, which is the normal boot process showing the iOS interface. From a forensic point of view, both DFU and recovery modes are important and can be used to perform physical acquisition as we will see later in this chapter.

To put iOS 9 in recovery mode, follow these steps:

1. Turn off your iOS device by pressing and holding the Sleep/Wake button.
2. Take the USB cable (or lightning connector) and connect one end to your computer without connecting the other end to the device.
3. Hold down the Home button on your device, and while doing so, connect the device to the USB cable.

The iTunes player will open automatically.

To put iOS 9 in DFU mode, follow these steps:

1. Plug your device into your computer.

2. Turn off the device.

3. Hold the power button for 3 seconds.

4. Begin holding the Home button without releasing the power button for 10 seconds.

5. Release the power button and continue holding the Home button until you get a pop-up from iTunes.

Unique device identifier

Each iDevice is shipped with its own **unique device identifier** (**UDID**), which is 20 bytes and 40 characters long in hexadecimal values, which is calculated as follows:

$UDID = SHA1(serial + ECID + wifiMac + bluetoothMac)$

The serial is relative to the serial number as seen in the Settings App. ECID is an ID unique to every electronic or chip unit and can be obtained in Windows as follows:

1. Put your device in recovery mode or DFU mode.

2. Open Device Manager and right-click on **Apple Mobile Device** (Recovery or DFU mode) for properties.

3. Click on the **Details** tab.

4. Click on the drop-down box and select **Device Instance Path**.

You should find it in the textbox.

The easiest way to find the UDID is by connecting the device to the computer and running iTunes, then clicking on the iPhone icon, under **Settings**, clicking on **Summary**, and then clicking on the **Serial Number** to see the UDID:

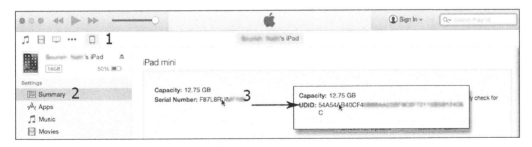

A simple method is to look for iTunes backups because files will be named using the UDID. Depending on the operating system iTunes backups are stored in:

- **Mac**: `~/Library/Application Support/MobileSync/Backup/{UDID}`

- **Windows Vista/7/8/10**: `\Users\(username)\AppData\Roaming\Apple Computer\MobileSync\Backup\{UDID}`

- **Windows XP**: `\Documents and Settings\(username)\Application Data\Apple Computer\MobileSync\Backup\{UDID}`

Lockdown certificate

Basically, a lockdown certificate is a pairing certificate created once an iDevice is connected to a computer with iTunes running. From a forensic perspective, obtaining this certificate can help obtain a partial access to a locked device. The important part is that you can copy this certificate to another computer and the process of paring won't be altered. Depending on the operating system of the computer used to sync the iDevice, lockdown certificates are `.plist` files named `UDID.plist` (where UDID replaces the unique identifier ID of the paired device) and stored in the following folders:

- **Mac OS X**: `/var/db/lockdown`

- **Windows 7/8/10**: `C:\ProgramData\Apple\Lockdown`

- **Windows Vista**: `C:\Users\username\AppData\roaming\AppleComputer\Lockdown`

- **Windows XP**: `C:\Documents and Settings\username\Application Data\Apple Computer\Lockdown`

This is shown in the following screenshot:

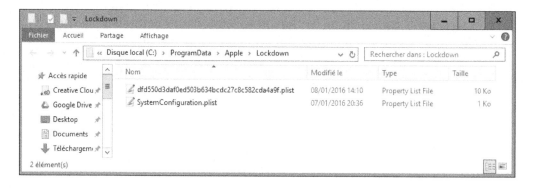

If you get a lockdown certificate, a lot of valuable information can be gathered via the **Apple File Conduit** (**AFC**) protocol (more information about this protocol is available at `https://www.theiphonewiki.com/wiki/AFC`), such as:

- Device information:
    - ◦ IMEI (for devices with telephone capability)
    - ◦ Bluetooth address
    - ◦ Language
    - ◦ Date and time
    - ◦ Timezone
    - ◦ Battery charge level
    - ◦ Total NAND memory size
    - ◦ Empty space size
- Backup configuration
- Installed application list
- Application distribution on Springboard
- File contained inside applications that are using iTunes File Sharing
- `iBooks` folder
- `Downloads` folder
- `iTunes_Control` folder:
    - ◦ `iTunes` subfolder
    - ◦ `Music` subfolder
- Videos loaded into the device from a PC/Mac

If you are dealing with a turned on device, you should always have the reflex of isolating it and searching for a lockdown certificate on a paired computer before turning the device off.

iOS acquisition

When dealing with seizure, it's important to activate the Airplane mode and if the device is unlocked, to set the auto-lock option to **Never** and to check whether the passcode was set or not (**Settings | Passcode**). Try to keep the phone charged if you are dealing with a passcode and you cannot acquire its content immediately; if no passcode was set, turn off the device.

There are four different acquisition methods when talking about iDevices:

- **Normal or direct**: This is the most perfect case when you can deal directly with a powered on device.

- **Logical acquisition**: This is when the acquisition is done using iTunes backup or a forensic tool that uses the AFC protocol and is in general not complete where e-mails, geolocation database, apps cache folder, and executables are missed.

- **Advanced logical acquisition**: This is a technique introduced by Jonathan Zdziarski (`http://www.zdziarski.com/blog/`) but is no longer possible with the introduction of iOS 8

- **Physical acquisition**: This generates a forensic bit-by-bit image of both system and data partitions. There are two categories of physical acquisition under iDevices:

    - The actual physical acquisition is feasible for iPhone, up to iPhone 4
    - Logical physical acquisition of the filesystem image requires a jailbroken device

Before choosing (or not, because the method to choose depends on some parameters) a method, the examiner should answer three important questions:

- What is the device model?
- What is the iOS version installed?
- Is the device passcode protected?

    - Is it a simple passcode?
    - Is it a complex passcode?

Identifying the device's model is quite simple because it's always located on the back of the device:

An exhaustive list of all iDevices models can be found at https://en.wikipedia.org/wiki/List_of_iOS_devices. Now to identify the operating system, you can use a tool called **ideviceinfo** (http://www.libimobiledevice.org), which is present in many Linux distributions dedicated to forensics, such as **Santoku** (https://santoku-linux.com) and can be used if the device is passcode locked. The command is as follows:

```
soufiane@santoku:~$ ideviceinfo -s
BasebandCertId: 3255536192
BasebandKeyHashInformation:
 AKeyStatus: 2
 SKeyHash: 7MQEUyvzG4gjjZc7KsNNAVTS8g4=
 SKeyStatus: 0
BasebandSerialNumber: BkauwQ==
BasebandVersion: 10.00.00
BoardId: 2
BuildVersion: 13C75
ChipID: 35152
```

```
DeviceClass: iPhone

DeviceColor: #3b3b3c

DeviceName: iPhone de Soufiane

DieID: 1593784934049508256

HardwareModel: N42AP

PartitionType:

ProductName: iPhone OS

ProductType: iPhone5,2

ProductVersion: 9.2

ProductionSOC: true

ProtocolVersion: 2

TelephonyCapability: true

UniqueChipID: 538818362632

UniqueDeviceID: dfd550d3daf0ed503b634bcdc27c8c582cda4a9f

WiFiAddress: 00:88:65:ae:d4:b6
```

If the device is passcode locked, several forensic tools can try to defeat the four-digit passcodes. **IP-Box**, which appears to work for up to iOS 8.1.2, is a black box device that basically sends predefined passcodes to a targeted iOS. Each attempt takes about 6 seconds, so it may take up to 17 hours to test the range from 0000 to 9999. The IP-Box kit consists of the actual box, iPhone cable, USB cable, an optical sensor, and the IP-Box software used to configure passcode patterns and to update the IP-Box firmware. The following is an image showing a successful attack where the passcode was 8664:

Detective Cindy Murphy documented this very well in *iP-BOX: Breaking Simple Pass Codes on iOS Devices,* available at `http://www.teeltech.com/wp-content/uploads/2014/11/IP-Box-documentation-rev2-1-16-2015.pdf`.

Normal/direct acquisition

If a device is not passcode protected or if the passcode or the lockdown certificates are known, a direct acquisition can be done using any iDevice browser. For example, iExplorer v 3.8.8.0 is iPhone 6s- and OS 9.2-ready and available for both Mac and Windows (`https://www.macroplant.com/iexplorer/release-notes`). The majority of tools like this act as a backup browser:

Logical acquisition

Creating a backup and working on it can be forensically interesting, since it avoids accidental writing operations caused by some non-forensic tools, as in the case of doing a direct acquisition. Making backups is possible if the device is not passcode protected, the passcode is known, or the examiner has a lockdown certificate (just like the conditions in direct acquisition).

The easiest way to back up an iDevice is via iTunes, there are two options to note: performing a fully unprotected backup of the computer, or performing a full password protected backup, and in both cases, the backup is done by clicking on **Back Up Now**:

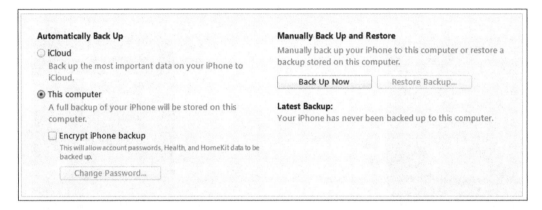

iTunes backups are stored in the following paths:

- **Windows XP**: Documents and Settings\(username)\Application Data\ AppleComputer\MobileSync\Backup\

- **Windows Vista/7/8/10**: Users\username\AppData\Roaming\Apple Computer\MobileSync\Backup\

- **Mac OS**: ~/Library/Application Support/MobileSync/Backup/

There are also many forensic tools that can make logical acquisition, we cannot cover them all in this chapter but the following example uses **MOBILedit! Forensic 8.2**. It's a commercial tool that offers a seven day trial period (http://www.mobiledit.com/downloads.htm). MOBILedit! offers three backup options: **MOBILedit backup** that will save contacts, organizer, and files; **device backup** is an iTunes backup with the ability to choose where to store the backup and **standard iTunes backup,** which will hold all the information, such as contacts, settings, and messages:

1. First step to do is to open MOBILedit! and connect your iDevice. Once detected, you can see it connected as follows:

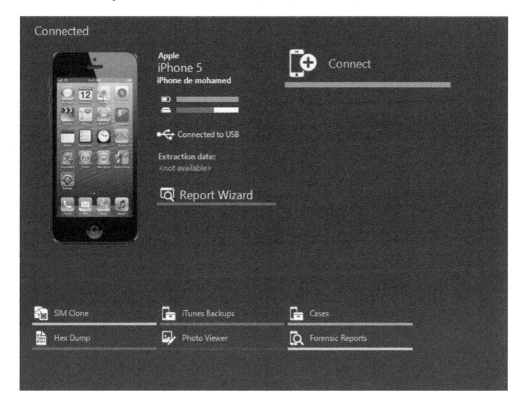

2. Click on **Report Wizard**, the tool here offers the possibility to use an existing detected backup (generally previously done using iTunes) or a simple extraction using the current connection:

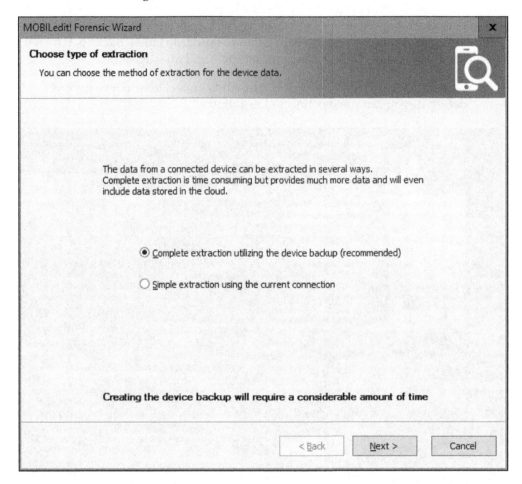

3. By choosing the second option and clicking **Next**, a new window invites you to fill in the current device information, such as the device label, name, owner, and so on and to choose device capabilities to extract:

4. The next step invites the examiner to choose a part of the filesystem to acquire:

5. In the next step, the tool starts extracting and parsing the previously selected parts of the filesystem. In this acquisition step, the tool may take a while to bring up the ready to use result:

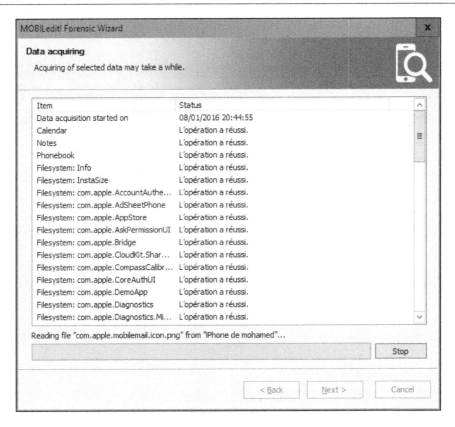

6. Once the acquisition is complete, a new window invites you to fill in the case details, by double-clicking on **< New Case >**:

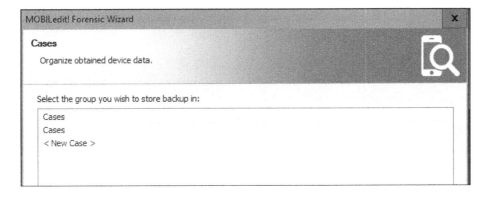

7. Fill in the case details, investigator details, and notes about the case then click on **Next** to create a new case for obtained data:

Physical acquisition

Every time physical acquisition is possible, the examiner does not hesitate to make it since it allows the extraction of almost everything from the device by providing an actual copy of the device's memory and access to all the files stored in there. There are many commercial tools that support physical acquisition of an iDevice, such as UFED Physical Analyzer, XRY, and Elcomsoft iOS Forensic Toolkit; the latter supports iOS up to 9.2 and also permits physical acquisition for 32-bit and 64-bit iDevices.

Always keep in mind that the passcode protection stat is important, since if the device is passcode protected and the passcode is complex, the analyst should brute-force or dictionary-attack the passcode; this option is offered by most commercial forensic tools, such as Elcomsoft iOS Forensic Toolkit that can brute-force a simple 4-digit passcode in 10-40 minutes. Complex passcodes require more time, since the recovery is being performed on the device and cannot be done on a faster equipment.

Physical acquisition also requires a jailbroken device most of time (if not all).

Jailbreaking iOS 9

Jailbreaking an iDevice is the process of gaining full access to all partitions; it's basically the process of mounting the system partition as read-write, modifying the AFC service to access the filesystem, and patching the kernel to bypass the code signing and Apple's restrictions. You can visit `https://www.theiphonewiki.com/wiki/Jailbreak` to learn more about it.

Even if it's principally a write activity and thus cannot be considered as forensically accepted, it offers the only way to perform physical acquisition with modern iDevices. A Chinese group called *PanGuTeam* has released the first jailbreak that supports iOS 9 versions 9.0.1 and 9.0.2 and also iPhone 6s and iPhone 6s+ (available for Windows and Mac free of charge at `http://en.pangu.io`). The process of jailbreaking an iPhone, iPad, and iPad touch on iOS 9 using Pangu Jailbreak is quite simple. After downloading the latest version of the jailbreak, simply follow these steps:

1. Using the USB cable, connect your iDevice to a PC or a Mac.
2. Be sure that iTunes is closed.
3. Disable the passcode and the *Find My iPhone* app and put the device in Airplane mode.
4. Launch Pangu Jailbreak.

5. Once your device is detected click on **Start**:

6. In the next window, click on the **Already backup** button:

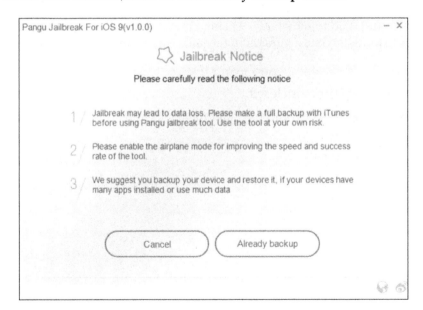

After this step, around 55% the device may reboot and around 65% will ask you to re-enable the Airplane mode.

7. At 75% you will be prompted to unlock the device and to run the Pangu app on the device:

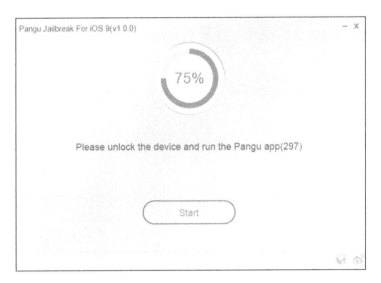

8. Next, on the device you will be prompted to click on the **Accept** button, then **Allow**, since for some reason this jailbreak needs access to the Photo app:

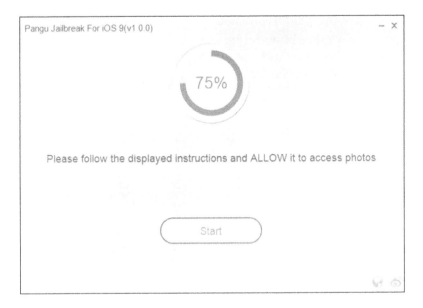

9. Once completed, the device will reboot and Pangu will tell you that your device is **Already jailbroken**:

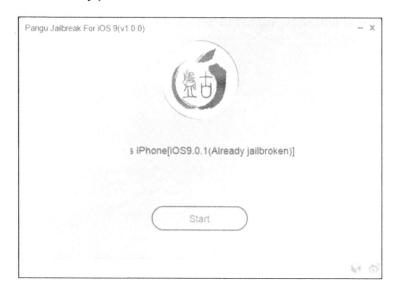

10. You can turn off the Airplane mode and run Cydia to prepare the filesystem.

Physical acquisition with Elcomsoft iOS Forensic Toolkit

As described on the vendor website (https://www.elcomsoft.com/eift.html), Elcomsoft iOS Forensic Toolkit performs the complete forensic acquisition of user data stored in the iPhone/iPad/iPod devices. Elcomsoft iOS Forensic Toolkit allows eligible customers to acquire bit-to-bit images of a device's filesystems, extract device secrets (passcodes, passwords, and encryption keys), and decrypt the filesystem image. Access to most of the information is provided instantly.

By executing Elcomsoft iOS Forensic Toolkit, you can see that the wizard is quite simple:

Elcomsoft iOS Forensic Toolkit main menu

Now, turn off your jailbroken device and connect it to your computer, then let Elcomsoft assist you in entering the DFU mode by typing 1:

Once this step is successfully completed, you will be prompted to let Toolkit Ramdisk load onto the device:

By typing y and then pressing *Enter* you will get the following screen:

```
          Welcome to Elcomsoft iOS Forensic Toolkit
           This is driver script version 2.0/Win

                (c) 2011-2015 Elcomsoft Co. Ltd.

Detecting device type...
Shutting down iTunes processes.
Checking the device type
Identified device as iPhone3,1
Initializing libpois0n
Shutting down iTunes processes.
Waiting for device in DFU mode to connect...
Found device in DFU mode
Checking if device is compatible with this Checking the device type
jailbreak
Identified device as iPhone3,1Preparing to upload limera1n exploit

Resetting device counters
Sending chunk headers
```

At this stage, the device will boot in the recovery mode and you can see the Elcomsoft logo on the phone. The device is ready to be acquired and the first thing to do is get the encryption keys:

```
          Welcome to Elcomsoft iOS Forensic Toolkit
           This is driver script version 2.0/Win

                (c) 2011-2015 Elcomsoft Co. Ltd.

Device keys file <keys.plist>: keys.plist

Write decrypted image to file <keychain.txt>: keychain.txt
```

`keys.plist` contains valuable information such as Apple ID/password and Wi-Fi network passwords, third-party and VPN credentials, and so on.

We can acquire all the user files by typing 8 on the main menu (choosing the **Aquire user's files from the device as a tarball** option):

```
Welcome to Elcomsoft iOS Forensic Toolkit
This is driver script version 2.0/Win

(c) 2011-2015 Elcomsoft Co. Ltd.

Please note that to obtain files from the device you need to load ramdisk
on the iOS device first. If you haven't done this yet, please return
to previous step and use corresponding menu item.

Continue? <Y/n>: y
Store files to archive <user.tar>: userfiles.tar


Mounting user partition...
Detecting iOS version...
Detected iOS
rawwrite dd for windows version 0.6beta3.
Written by John Newbigin <jn@it.swin.edu.au>
This program is covered by terms of the GPL Version 2.

3,075,584
```

This task may take a while and you will end up with a .tar file that has all the user data.

We can proceed with the actual physical acquisition by typing 6 (choosing the **Acquire physical image of the device filesystem** option), which will produce the system partition in plaintext and an encrypted data partition:

```
Welcome to Elcomsoft iOS Forensic Toolkit
This is driver script version 2.0/Win

(c) 2011-2015 Elcomsoft Co. Ltd.

Please note that to obtain device disk image you need to load ramdisk
on the iOS device first. If you haven't done this yet, please return
to previous step and use corresponding menu item.

Please select partition to image:
  1   System  <rdisk0s1s1> — this one is NOT ENCRYPTED
  2   User    <rdisk0s1s2> — this one is ENCRYPTED

  0   Back

>: 2
Save image to file <user.dmg>: userfiles.dmg

rawwrite dd for windows version 0.6beta3.
Written by John Newbigin <jn@it.swin.edu.au>
This program is covered by terms of the GPL Version 2.

28,958M
0+926506 records in
0+926506 records out
28958+1 records in
28958+1 records out
30365065216 bytes (30 GB) copied, 5019.23 s, 6.0 MB/s

Imaging done.

Press 'Enter' to continue
```

Here, we have the encrypted physical copy of the user data partition, which is almost 30 GB. Obviously, we cannot deal with it as it is but we can decrypt it using the previously extracted `keys.plist` file that holds all the encryption keys:

```
              Welcome to Elcomsoft iOS Forensic Toolkit
               This is driver script version 2.0/Win

                   (c) 2011-2015 Elcomsoft Co. Ltd.


Encrypted image file <user.dmg>: userfiles.dmg

Device keys file <keys.plist>: keys.plist

Write decrypted image to file <userfiles-decrypted.dmg>: ▪
```

Then, we can get the ready-to-mount decrypted images saved as `usefiles-decrypted.dmg`:

```
[INFO] Key "EscrowKeyBag" not found
[INFO] Complete key set is loaded, everything should be decryptable.
[INFO] Image encryption statistics:
[INFO]   6720 files total: 6626 encrypted + 94 not encrypted.
[INFO]   6626 files can be decrypted (out of 6626 encrypted files).
[INFO] Input image contains 3706673 blocks of 8192 bytes.
[100%] 28.28 of 28.28 Gb decrypted
SHA1(userfiles-decrypted.dmg) = 8a6049227629023fc809d9a62ee69d4eac5200d8

Press 'Enter' to continue
```

iOS artifacts recovery – evidence gathering and data recovery

Techniques of evidence gathering depends on the acquisition method used. The first interesting thing to know is how to deal with an iTunes backup, this usually allows the examiner to gain full access to data within this backup. iTunes backups contain almost every sensitive information an examiner can look for, such as:

- Contacts and call history
- Safari bookmarks, cookies, history, and offline data

- Calendar events
- iMessages, SMS and MMS
- Voicemail token and voice memos
- E-mail account passwords
- Location service preferences, map bookmarks, and recent searches
- App Store app data

iTunes backup folder contains uniquely named files with 40 hexadecimal character long names and without extensions:

Nom	Modifié le	Type	Taille
30cc5c0a1f5e5763a721cc302d4c5edce5e6...	09/01/2016 01:26	Fichier	3 Ko
30dec641efb1a1f07cf4fcf1a83907efb2d1b...	09/01/2016 01:22	Fichier	49 Ko
30e3f0efd9660bc6f05d0db328b25c7e944c...	09/01/2016 01:26	Fichier	193 Ko
30ea07192e37b825fbda968844364929c138...	09/01/2016 01:26	Fichier	118 Ko
30ee15927a823de257fd1f8af603b7beafe5...	09/01/2016 01:26	Fichier	3 025 Ko
30fe0bf2a52c93b07075d6fb8c85c15a568f...	09/01/2016 01:26	Fichier	17 Ko
031e7af4a46ce9d23fd49c1d5791754c6af3...	09/01/2016 01:28	Fichier	5 Ko
31bb7ba8914766d4ba40d6dfb6113c8b614...	09/01/2016 01:22	Fichier	1 041 Ko
31bc2525563764936ce99e637b188f962ec3...	09/01/2016 01:28	Fichier	2 Ko
31d0213710559efd6181d4f3ec65a409d4e2...	09/01/2016 01:22	Fichier	1 Ko
31e6bca0469c7d628091b945c45f996284f1...	09/01/2016 01:26	Fichier	27 Ko
32c8d0c7cce3693390e90fde3f7f4599d223...	09/01/2016 01:28	Fichier	4 Ko
32f3147958d2515390af648a7d9c6d6e41ac...	09/01/2016 01:22	Fichier	9 Ko
33a42b6417d713755842119f40d024faa6c5...	09/01/2016 01:27	Fichier	2 264 Ko
33e6b564d44d2909ef1beb7718389fb2e98...	09/01/2016 01:26	Fichier	1 Ko
034eac2aa80463d6b619f7e8169fd3b85dc2...	09/01/2016 01:26	Fichier	5 Ko
34b81f7ae8679864e18329d2ddecd5eae1d...	09/01/2016 01:28	Fichier	2 Ko
34e8b19d73bb2771c99d2ed497994ceb6c1...	09/01/2016 01:26	Fichier	40 Ko
35ad1741e313cbf56438eaf4bc20b53620e2...	09/01/2016 01:26	Fichier	30 Ko
35af7910c7262b99c97baf61a11d4454d5fb...	09/01/2016 01:22	Fichier	8 Ko
35bd84cceb82d804a3eefd3b9452fb49f5b...	09/01/2016 01:22	Fichier	1 Ko

Each filename is made by a SHA-1 hash of the original name, together with its path and domain separated by a dash. iOS contains several domains: `KeychainDomain`, `RootDomain`, `WirelessDomain`, `SystemPreferencesDomain`, `CameraRollDomain`, and so on. But there are two primary domains: `AppDomain` is used for applications downloaded from the App Store, and `HomeDomain` is the iOS domain that contains built-in applications data. For example, Facebook Messenger's property list backup file is `0ba8559bd5e366782b1e5d846c3bb94a71f435d8` and is calculated as follows:

SHA1('AppDomain-com.facebook.Messenger-Library/Preferences/com.facebook.Messenger. plist') = 0ba8559bd5e366782b1e5d846c3bb94a71f435d8

Some interesting hashes to know are as follows:

- **WhatsApp**: `1b6b187a1b60b9ae8b720c79e2c67f472bab09c0`
- **SMS and iMessage**: `3d0d7e5fb2ce288813306e4d4636395e047a3d28`
- **Call history**: `2b2b0084a1bc3a5ac8c27afdf14afb42c61a19ca`
- **Contacts and address book**: `31bb7ba8914766d4ba40d6dfb6113c8b614be442`
- **Calendar**: `2041457d5fe04d39d0ab481178355df6781e6858`
- **Notes**: `ca3bc056d4da0bbf88b5fb3be254f3b7147e639c`
- **Locations**: `4096c9ec676f2847dc283405900e284a7c815836`

In addition to these files, each iTunes backup contains four or more interesting files made by iTunes and holds valuable information about the device and the backup itself: `Info.plist`, `Manifest.mbdb`, `Manifest.plist`, and `Status.plist`. They are detailed as follows:

Key	Type	Value
Root	dict	
Applications	dict	
Build Version	string	13C75
Device Name	string	iPhone de mohamed
Display Name	string	iPhone de mohamed
GUID	string	3CE4210EA0AEDB84F23E0!
IMEI	string	013412008655534
Installed Applications	array	
	string	com.toyopagroup.picaboo
	string	com.cmplay.tiles2
	string	com.facebook.Facebook
	string	com.miniclip.8ballpoolmu
	string	com.google.chrome.ios
	string	com.facebook.Messenger
	string	InstaSize
	string	tr.com.tiramisu.driftxl
	string	net.whatsapp.WhatsApp
	string	com.burbn.instagram
	string	com.firsttouch.dts
Last Backup Date	date	2016-01-09T01:15:39Z
Product Name	string	iPhone 5
Product Type	string	iPhone5,2
Product Version	string	9.2
Serial Number	string	C37JWNN2DTWD
Target Identifier	string	dfd550d3daf0ed503b634bc
Target Type	string	Device
Unique Identifier	string	DFD550D3DAF0ED503B634
iTunes Files	dict	
iTunes Settings	dict	
iTunes Version	string	12.3.2.35

Info.plist

`Info.plist` is a property list file containing information about the device (device name, device type, IMEI, and so on) and also contains the iTunes version that is used to back up the device, date of backup, and so on.

```
     0  1  2  3  4  5  6  7    8  9  A  B  C  D  E  F   10 11 12 13 14 15 16 17   18 19 1A 1B 1C 1D 1E 1F
    6D 62 64 62 05 00 00 18   41 70 70 44 6F 6D 61 69   6E 2D 63 6F 6D 2E 61 70   70 6C 65 2E 4D 61 70 73    ▮bdb    AppDomain-com.apple.Maps
    00 00 FF FF FF FF FF FF   41 ED 00 00 00 00 00 00   01 F8 00 00 01 F5 00 00   01 F5 56 79 91 35 56 79    ÿÿÿÿÿÿAí         ø    õ    õVy´5Vy
    91 35 56 79 91 35 00 00   00 00 00 00 00 00 00 00   00 18 41 70 70 44 6F 6D   61 69 6E 2D 63 6F 6D 2E    ´5Vy´5            AppDomain-com
    61 70 70 6C 65 2E 4D 61   70 73 00 07 4C 69 62 72   61 72 79 FF FF FF FF FF   FF 41 ED 00 00 00 00 00    apple.Maps LibraryÿÿÿÿÿÿAí
    00 01 FA 00 00 01 F5 00   00 01 F5 56 7B 2D A6 56   7B 2D A6 56 79 91 35 00   00 00 00 00 00 00 00 00    ú    õ    õV{-¦V{-¦Vy´5
    00 00 18 41 70 70 44 6F   6D 61 69 6E 2D 63 6F 6D   2E 61 70 70 6C 65 2E 4D   61 73 00 13 4C 69 62        AppDomain-com.apple.Mas  Lib
    72 61 72 79 2E 50 72 65   66 65 72 65 6E 63 65 73   FF FF FF FF FF FF 41 ED   00 00 00 00 00 00 01 FC    rary.PreferencesÿÿÿÿÿÿAí
```

Manifest.mbdb

`Manifest.mbdb` is a binary database that holds information about all the backup content, such as file sizes and structures. Each entry of `Manifest.mbdb` is of a variable size and contains the following information about a given file:

- **Domain**: This is the domain the file belongs to
- **Path**: This is the file path
- **Target**: This is the absolute path for symbolic links
- **Encryption key**: For unencrypted files its `0xFF/0xFF`
- **Mode**: This identifies the file mode:
  - ° `0xA000`: Symbolic link
  - ° `0x4000`: Directory
  - ° `0x8000`: Regular file

- **Inode number**: This is the lookup entry in the inode table
- **User ID**: 501 is the default ID set by iOS
- **Group ID**: This is 501 as well
- **Last modification time**: This is the file's last modification date in UNIX format
- **Last accessed time**: This is the the last time the file was accessed in UNIX format
- **Creation time**: This is the file creation time in UNIX format
- **Size**: This is the size of the file in bytes:
  - ° 0 for symbolic links and directories

- **Protection class**: Data protection class from `0x1` to `0xB`
- **File hash**

MBDB as a file type has its own magic number that defines its header: `0x6D6264620500` (mbdb).

Key	Type	Value
⊟ Root	dict	
⊞ Applications	dict	
BackupKeyBag	data	...
Date	date	2016-01-09T01:15:33Z
IsEncrypted	boolean	false
⊟ Lockdown	dict	
BuildVersion	string	13C75
DeviceName	string	iPhone de mohamed
ProductType	string	iPhone5,2
ProductVersion	string	9.2
SerialNumber	string	C37JWNN2DTWD
UniqueDeviceID	string	dfd550d3daf0ed503b634b(
⊞ com.apple.Accessibility	dict	
com.apple.MobileDeviceCr	dict	
com.apple.TerminalFlashr	dict	
⊞ com.apple.mobile.data_syn	dict	
com.apple.mobile.iTunes.a	dict	
com.apple.mobile.wireless_	dict	
SystemDomainsVersion	string	24.0
Version	string	9.1
WasPasscodeSet	boolean	true

Manifest.plist

`Manifest.plist` is a property list file that holds information about the content of the backup, the application's bundle details, information about the device, iTunes version used to make the backup, and also contains flags to determine whether the backup is encrypted or not (`IsEncrypted`):

Key	Type	Value
⊟ Root	dict	
BackupState	string	new
Date	date	2016-01-09T01:15:38Z
IsFullBackup	boolean	false
SnapshotState	string	finished
UUID	string	B8F1118C-A251-4AA0-AC(
Version	string	2.4

Status.plist

`Status.plist` is a property list file that contains information about the backup process. It contains flags to determine whether the backup was a full backup or not, if it was successful or not, date and version, and so on.

These four files remain in plaintext, irrespective if the backup made is password-encrypted or not, meaning that the information is always available once you get an iTunes backup and there is no need to crack the password in case of an encrypted backup.

There are many tools that read and parse the `Manifest.mbdb` file and convert iTunes backup to a readable format. For Windows, you can use the iPhone Backup Browser (`https://code.google.com/p/iphonebackupbrowser/`) and iPhone Backup Extractor (`http://supercrazyawesome.com/`) in Mac, or iBackupBot, which is commercial but available for both Mac and Windows. The following is a screenshot from iPhone Backup Browser, which automatically detects backups found on the current computer and offers the possibility to open a backup from a custom directory. By clicking on a file, it sends you directly to where its located in the backup directory, and in the case of unencrypted backup, you can simply add the appropriate extension to open the file in a traditional viewer (in case of a JPG file, for example):

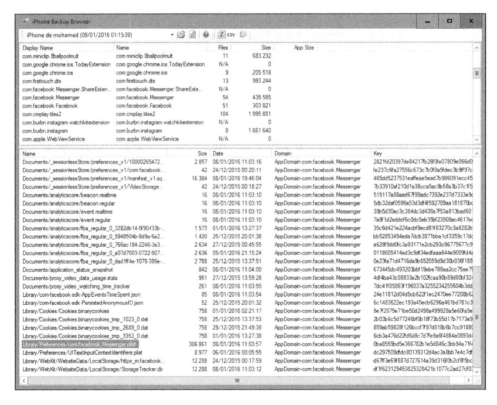

To extract data from an uncrypted iTunes backup, there are several free (iPhone Backup Analyzer, iPhone Analyzer, and more) and commercial tools (such as MOBILedit! Forensic, Oxygen Forensic Suite, Elcomsoft Phone Viewer, and so on). These tools allow you to gather all the data within a given backup.

Artifact recovery using iPhone Analyzer

iPhone Analyzer (`http://sourceforge.net/projects/iphoneanalyzer/`) is a Java-based tool that parses and brings all data in an easy-to-use user interface. This tool offers a native file browsing for plist and SQLite files, automatic bookmarks, address book, location map, voicemail, Facebook friends, map history, all sent and received messages, all incoming and outgoing calls, and all media files.

After running `iphoneanalyzer.fat.gui-2.1.0.jar`, the tool detects all the present iTunes backups on the current computer, you can either select one and click on the **Analyze IPhone Backup** button or click on **Browse** and manually select a backup folder.

Once the analyze button is clicked, the tool starts collecting media within the backup:

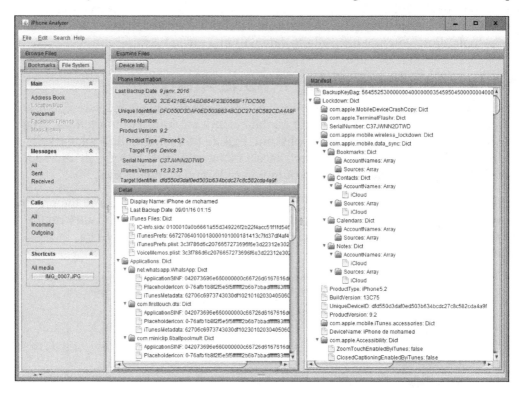

The tool brings up all kinds of information about the device and the backup and you can start browsing through the main menu to visualize the address book, as shown in the following screenshot:

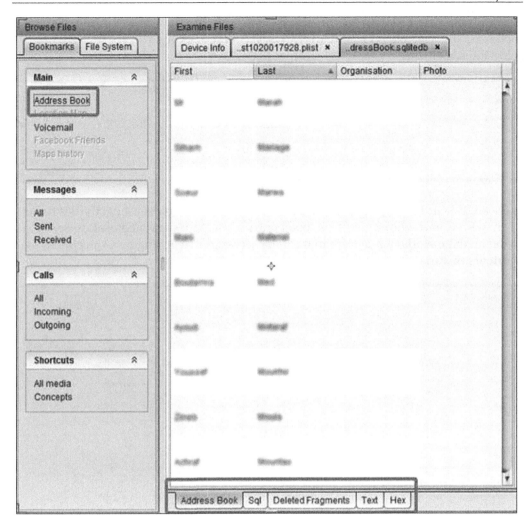

You can browse the address book SQLite database by clicking on the **Sql** tab and trying to recover deleted fragments too.

SMS and call history databases can also be viewed in the same way the address book was, and the deleted fragments can be recovered, as you can see in the following screenshot:

+21269		Sat Dec 26 22:18:03 WET 2015	RECEIVED	SMS
+21267		Sat Dec 26 17:35:06 WET 2015	SENT	SMS
+21269		Thu Dec 24 22:49:06 WET 2015	SENT	SMS
+21269		Mon Dec 28 23:44:29 WET 2015	SENT	SMS
+21269		Thu Dec 24 22:57:42 WET 2015	RECEIVED	SMS
+21269		Mon Dec 28 23:45:36 WET 2015	RECEIVED	SMS
+21263		Mon Dec 28 11:51:31 WET 2015	SENT	SMS
+21269		Sat Jan 02 16:29:09 WET 2016	RECEIVED	SMS
+21268		Fri Dec 25 16:33:53 WET 2015	SENT	SMS
+21269		Mon Dec 28 22:41:51 WET 2015	SENT	SMS
+21269		Mon Dec 28 23:38:19 WET 2015	SENT	SMS
+21268		Fri Dec 25 18:39:57 WET 2015	SENT	SMS

There are two interesting options that this tool offers: the first is user activities (what, when, where, and who) for address book entries, messages and geolocation based on the media metadata, a feature that can be accessed by clicking on **Concepts** in the **Shortcuts** menu:

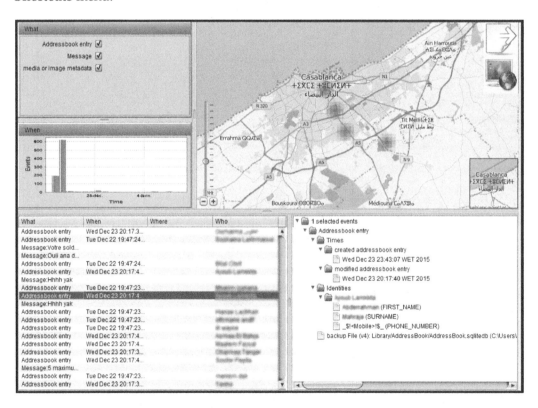

Here, we can see that the user created and modified an address book entry.

The second is the ability to search the entire backup for keywords using search options such as **Case sensitive, Case insensitive, Regular expression**, and **Fuzzy match** (via the top menu or *Ctrl + F*):

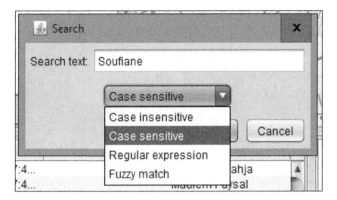

And the result is as follows:

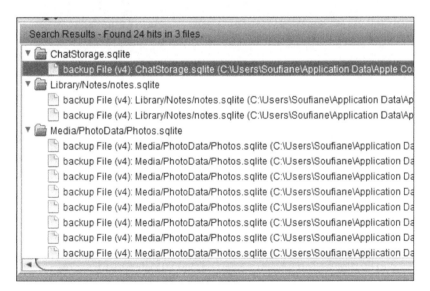

Artifact recovery using MOBILedit! Forensic

MOBILedit! Forensic can parse and present evidence from iTunes backups in a more fancy way:

1. To load an iTunes backup, from the **Navigation** menu, click on **iTunes Backups**:

2. Then click on **Reveal iTunes backups**:

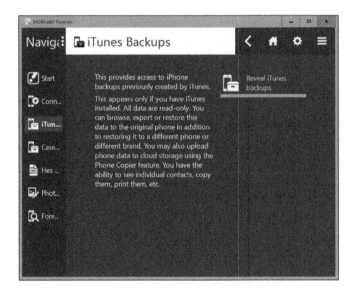

3. This will reveal all the existing iTunes backups on the current computer. Click on the desired backup:

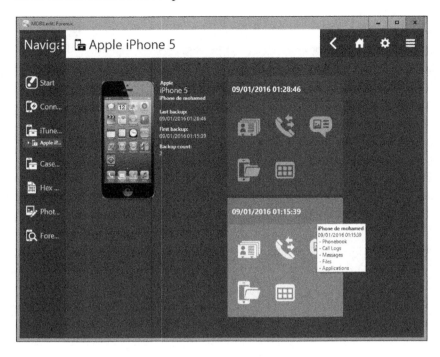

4. MOBILedit! Forensic will offer you the possibility to explore the phonebook, call logs, messages, application data, media, calendar, and notes (and the possibility to make a report):

5. In the following screenshot, you can see missed, outgoing, and incoming calls:

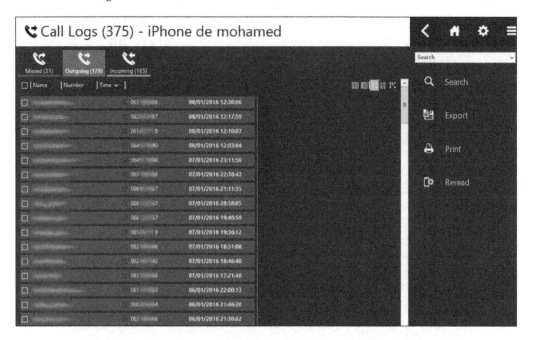

6. By clicking on **Application Data**, you get a tree of internal filesystem of all domains that has been backed up and you can copy each desired file for further analysis with external tools by clicking on the **Copy to** option in the right panel:

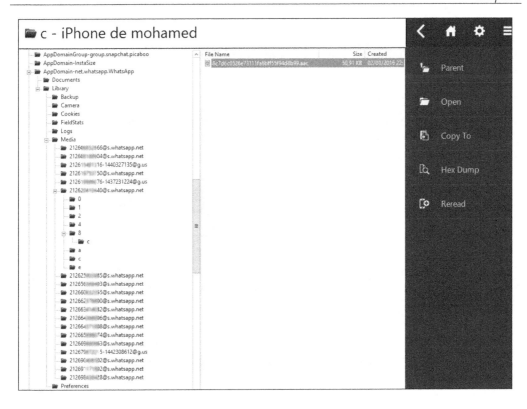

iTunes backups can be encrypted using a password, the backup is password protected from iTunes. If you are dealing with an encrypted backup, there are forensic tools that can try to crack this encryption by brute-forcing the password, such as Passware Kit 11.5, iPhone Backup Unlocker, or Phone Forensics Express.

The following section demonstrates how to crack the iTunes password using Phone Forensic Express (`http://www.mobiledit.com/forensic-express`). As described on the product website, with Forensic Express, you can extract all the data from a phone with only a few clicks. This data includes deleted data, call history, contacts, text messages, multimedia messages, files, events, notes, reminders, and application data from apps, such as from Skype, Dropbox, Evernote, Facebook, WhatsApp, Viber, and so on. Phone Forensic Express allows you to extract data from previous user-created backups. Especially, if you can't use a phone for evidence, a suspect's computer data can provide key insights into their phone behavior and this is the option that we will be using.

After opening the software, click on **Open File** and then click on **iTunes backup folder**. After selecting an encrypted backup, a window appears and asks you to enter the password used if known, if not you can choose either the **Dictionary attack** or the **PIN attack** option:

If the **Dictionary attack** option is chosen, you can choose single or multiple dictionaries as suggested by the tool or you can provide your own custom dictionary (text file), and you can choose a PIN length in case the **PIN attack** option is desired:

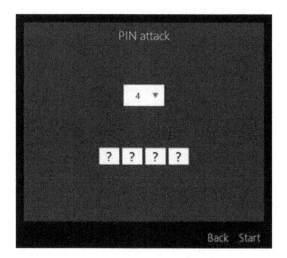

For this example, I'll be running a 4-digit PIN attack against my iTunes backup as shown in the following screenshot:

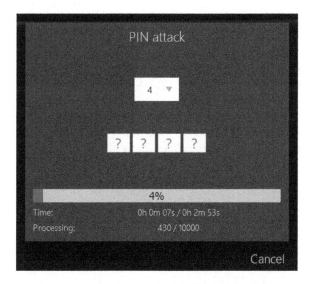

In less than a minute my pin *0558* was successfully cracked and the tool provided the password in order to use it if you want to analyze the backup with another tool:

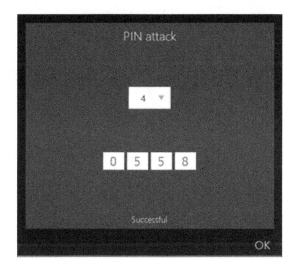

It's going biometric!

Apple introduced Touch ID fingerprint recognition with the iPhone 5S, it's believed to represent a significant improvement of iPhone users' data protection. In its basic description, Touch ID takes a 550 dpi resolution picture of your fingerprint by the help of a capacitive sensor, then iOS stores a mathematical representation of this image in the Secure Enclave, so technically, no image of your fingerprint is stored either in the device or in Apple's servers (including iCloud).

To match a fingerprint there are two main features of the fingerprint pattern: patterns (*Figure 1*) and minutia points (*Figure 2*), as you can see from the following images (images from https://en.wikipedia.org/wiki/Fingerprint_recognition):

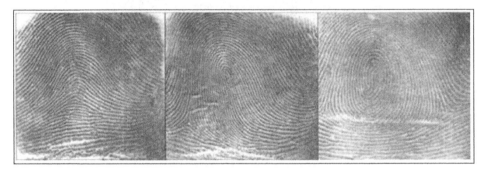

Figure 1

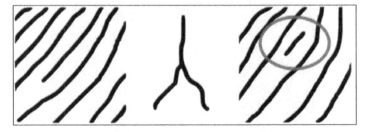

Figure 2: Minutia points from left to right: ridge ending, bifurcation, and short ridge (dot)

Basically, a fingerprint can be created from the difference in electrical conductivity between the epidermal and the dermal (not conductive) layers; this difference is "exploited" by the capacitive sensor to produce a digital image of the fingerprint pattern. *Starbug*, a member of the notorious **Chaos Computer Club (CCC)**, successfully bypassed Touch ID on iPhone 5S by faking a fingerprint using "the fingerprint of the phone user photographed on a glass surface." The used photo was 2400 dpi, the photo was inverted and printed out at 1200 dpi, later latex milk was poured onto the pattern and breathed on and the result was a success. The whole process is well documented at `https://www.ccc.de/en/updates/2013/ccc-breaks-apple-touchid`.

Apple improved Touch ID by the arrival of iPhone 6 but it was successfully bypassed using almost the same techniques if you can manage to lift a suitable fingerprint as demonstrated by researcher Marc Rogers at `https://blog.lookout.com/blog/2014/09/23/iphone-6-touchid-hack/`.

Third-party applications

All the third party applications are somehow organized the same way within iOS and they all belong to `AppDomain` and are stored in the Data partition. All commercially available forensic tools focus on interrogating application data. Most of the valuable information is stored in property list and SQLite formats. Media, such as videos, photos, and audio, is stored in general within a subdirectory in the same application folder.

Here, we will go through a forensic analysis of WhatsApp, the well-known cross platform mobile messenger that has replaced many cases traditional SMS services and offers the ability to exchange unlimited text messages, sending and receiving photos, videos, sharing geolocation, audio messages, making VoIP calls, and more. The following was an acquisition from an iPhone 5 running iOS 9.2.

All WhatsApp data can be found in `mobile/Application/net.whatsapp.WhatsApp/` and the most valuable files and directories are as follows:

- `ChatStorage.sqlite`
- `StatusMessages.plist`
- `Library/Logs/whatsapp-{dateTime}.log`

The `Documents/StatusMessages.plist` is a property list file that keeps a trace of the user's defined status:

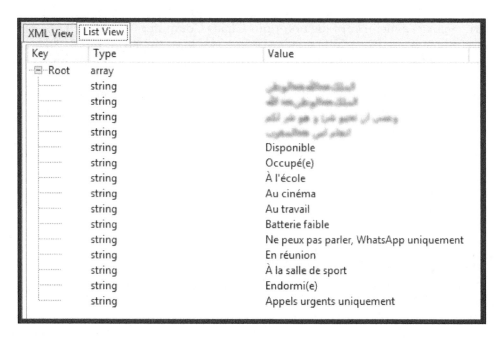

The `Library/Logs/` directory contains activity logs, each file contains the activity log of the defined period in the file's name:

Nom	Modifié le	Type
whatsapp-2016-01-05-22-11-29.279.134.log	09/01/2016 01:13	Fichier LOG
whatsapp-2016-01-05-22-14-08.588.135.log	09/01/2016 01:13	Fichier LOG
whatsapp-2016-01-05-22-59-50.589.136.log	09/01/2016 01:13	Fichier LOG
whatsapp-2016-01-05-23-31-02.198.137.log	09/01/2016 01:13	Fichier LOG
whatsapp-2016-01-06-00-01-15.963.138.log	09/01/2016 01:13	Fichier LOG
whatsapp-2016-01-06-00-50-16.166.139.log	09/01/2016 01:13	Fichier LOG
whatsapp-2016-01-06-13-21-24.385.140.log	09/01/2016 01:13	Fichier LOG
whatsapp-2016-01-06-14-13-21.000.141.log	09/01/2016 01:13	Fichier LOG
whatsapp-2016-01-06-14-31-24.079.142.log	09/01/2016 01:13	Fichier LOG

Logs contain interesting and very accurate information about the device and communications done, such as the carrier name, phone number, local time zone, time of received or sent buffers, IP addresses, notifications, and delivery time:

```
LL_A Device: iPhone 5
LL_A System: iPhone OS 9.2 (13C75)
LL_A WhatsApp version: 2.12.13
LL_A Carrier name: Méditel
LL_A Mobile country code: 604
LL_A Mobile network code: 000
LL_A Language: fr-YT
LL_A Locale: YT
LL_A Phone number: 212 619****76
LL_A JID: 212619****76@s.whatsapp.net
LL_A Time zone: Local Time Zone (Africa/Casablanca (UTC) offset 0)
[+0.0]
LL_A Uptime: 14.671 days
......
2016-01-07 12:24:43.234 [F] [xmpp] LL_N  stream/read/642b/buffer/642b/
processed/642b/elem-count/9
2016-01-07 12:24:43.248 [F] [xmpp] LL_N  < recv < [notification/status
id=3511138875 f=21269****28@s.whatsapp.net o=0 {0b}]
2016-01-07 12:24:43.248 [F] [xmpp] LL_N  < recv < [message/text
id=16F5331FB45A111D691 {0c} f=21266****06@s.whatsapp.net o=0 [enc
v='1' type='msg' {66b} ]
2016-01-07 12:24:43.248 [F] [xmpp] LL_N  < recv < [notification/
contacts id=1603672634 f=21261****515@s.whatsapp.net o=0 {0b}]
2016-01-07 12:24:43.248 [F] [xmpp] LL_N  connection/incoming-message/
first-offline-message/0.07s
2016-01-07 12:24:43.248 [F] [xmpp] LL_N  < recv < [notification/
contacts id=1875703281 f=212612****15@s.whatsapp.net o=0 {0b}]
2016-01-07 12:24:43.253 [F] [xmpp] LL_N  > send > [ack/receipt/
delivery t=212619****76-1437231224@g.us p=21263****466@s.whatsapp.net
id=D8F19DCB474D23A47E0]
2016-01-07 12:24:43.249 [F] [xmpp] LL_N  < recv < [message/
text id=C7A7952DB2EAD6ACEF6 {9c} f=21261****76-1437231224@g.us
p=21263****466@s.whatsapp.net o=0]
```

WhatsApp in iOS stores most of its valuable data in one single database, ChatStorage.sqlite, this database can be found under net.whatsapp.WhatsApp/ Documents/ChatStorage.sqlite and holds almost everything you may need to know from WhatsApp. This database can be browsed using DB Browser for SQLite (https://github.com/sqlitebrowser/sqlitebrowser), a visual and open source tool available for Windows and Mac to manipulate databases including SQLite.

This database is quite confusing, since its structure is a bit complicated, but to simplify things, here are the most important tables:

- ZWACHATSESSION: Contains contacts

- ZWASTATUS: Contains contacts

- ZWAMESSAGE: Contains data about the messages

- ZWAMEDIAITEM: Contains data about attachments

There are in total 12 tables in this database, as you can see in the following screenshot:

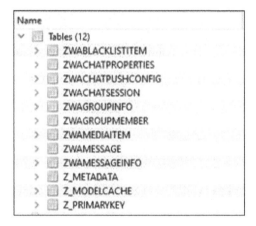

All messages can be found in the ZWAMESSAGE table under the ZTEXT column, if it's a sent message, the column ZFROMJID is kept NULL and the column ZTOJID contains the receiver ID, which is in the form of #phoneNumber@something.some and vice versa. All dates are stored in MAC Absolute format. The following is a screenshot showing this:

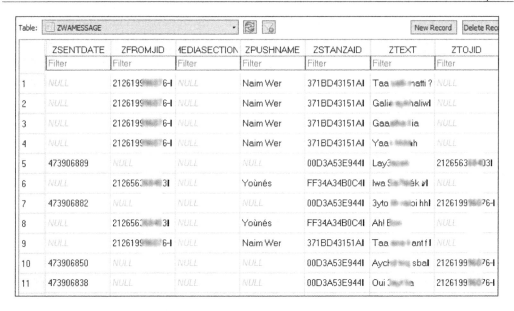

All attachments sent and received are stored in ZWAMEDIAITEM tables, the ZMEDIALOCALPATH column indicates the relative path to the exchanged media, each media file generates a thumbnail, and the location of the thumbnail is stored in the ZXMPPTH column:

DB Browser for SQL offers the option of querying the database via the **Execute SQL** tab. You can do whatever you want using SQL, for example, having an arranged chat history, as follows:

```
SELECT datetime(ZMESSAGEDATE + 978307200, 'unixepoch'),ZPUSHNAME,ZTEXT,ZT
OJID,ZFROMJID FROM ZWAMESSAGE ORDER BY 1;
```

The result will be as shown here:

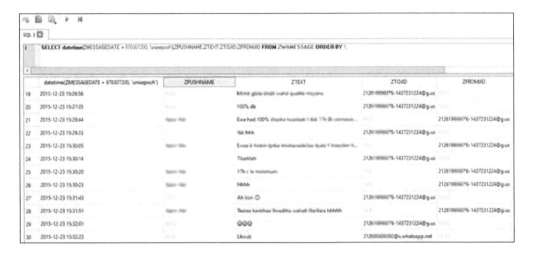

One important aspect of SQLite databases is that deleted records, in some cases, are recovered, which means that some of the deleted messages could be recovered. There are many free (Undark, SQLite-Parser, and more) and commercial (Oxygen Forensics SQLite Viewer) tools available to help recover deleted records. An interesting read about how this is technically possible is available at http://sandersonforensics.com/forum/content.php?222-Recovering-deleted-records-from-an-SQLite-database.

Basically, recovering deleted records exploits the SQLite file format, because the leaf table balance tree can contain areas of unallocated space (free blocks). Unallocated space is tracked by the leaf table balance trees and can contain deleted records. (You can learn more about SQLite file format at https://www.sqlite.org/fileformat.html.)

Here is an example of recovering some deleted records from `ChatStorage.sqlite` using SQLite-Parser. The output can be opened by any text editor. Usage is simple, as shown here:

```
sqlparse.py -p -f  dbname.db -o output.tsv
```

Here's the result:

```
495   Free Block   1861013 109 am  E5! ??121261    076-1437231224@g.us     371BD43151AB493C1E2 Yaak hhhhh
496   Free Block   1861473 7
497   Free Block   1861605 106 jC5^ ?>2126        03@s.whatsapp.net     FF34A34B0C42A6BFDF1 2Ah! Bon
```

However, this book does not focus only on iOS forensics. This is why this chapter did not cover iCloud and data acquisition from iCloud backups. If you are interested in digging this way too, I recommend you read *Learning iOS Forensics, Mattia Epifani and Pasquale Stirparo, Packt Publishing*.

Summary

In this chapter, we discussed some of the iOS internals including an overview of the iOS architecture and filesystem, we went through iOS platform and hardware security and also different boot modes. In this chapter, we introduced major methods of acquiring an iOS device normal, logical, and physical acquisitions and how to deal with some free and commercial forensic tools; this chapter also showed the data and how this data is stored within an iDevice. In this chapter, we also explained how iTunes backups are made, how lockdown certificates and property files are important, and how to gather data from unencrypted backups and then how to crack password protected backups. We also pointed to the fact that even if you cannot crack a password protected backup you are still able to know its actual content by inspecting property list files and `Manifest.mbdb`. We also had a look at the biometric aspect of new iDevices.

We illustrated how to approach the forensic analysis of the well-known messaging application WhatsApp, how we gathered data from its SQLite database, and how we can recover fragments of removed records; this approach is the same for almost any other application.

In the next chapter, we will be covering the Android platform and we will go through different techniques to acquire data with evidential value from the Android devices.

4
Android Forensics

Android-based smartphones have grown their consumer base in the past few years. At the same time, investigation needs have evolved as a consequence of the new smartphones that have entered the landscape. In order to answer some interesting questions about Android forensics, this chapter will bring to light some important points about Android OS internals, filesystem, data structure, and security models. It will discuss how it is possible to logically and physically acquire an Android device. We will also see what JTAGs are and what the chip-off technique is; this chapter will also explain how to bypass lock screens, security, and encryption. In this chapter, we will discuss a real case of forensic analysis of a third-party application.

This chapter will cover the following topics:

- Android OS – all you need to know
- Android security model
- Bypassing security
- Android logical data acquisition
- Android physical data acquisition
- JTAG and chip-off forensic examinations
- Third-party application and a real case study

Android OS – all you need to know

Android is an open source Linux-based operating system, which was first developed by Android Inc. in 2003. Then in 2005 it was acquired by Google and was unveiled in 2007. The Android operating system, like most operating systems, consists of a stack of software components roughly divided into four main layers and five main sections, as shown in the following diagram (source: `https://upload.wikimedia.org/wikipedia/commons/a/af/Android-System-Architecture.svg`). Each layer provides different services to the preceding layer:

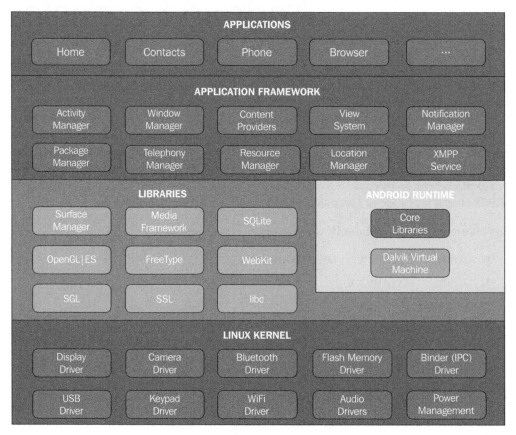

Figure 1: Android OS architecture

The lowest layer is the **Linux Kernel** layer, which was edited by Google to make some changes, such as the addition of the Flash filesystem (**YAFFS2**). The entire Android OS is built on top of this layer. This layer contains all the essential drivers to ensure the interaction between device hardware and the upper layers. The Linux Kernel is an abstract layer between the hardware and the software (all other layers); anything that needs hardware interaction is managed by this layer (from the screen's brightness to camera button clicks). Above the Linux Kernel layer comes the Software layer, which has two sections; the first section is **Libraries** section, which holds Android's native libraries and APIs written in C/C++ and are specific to a particular piece of hardware. They enable the device to handle different data types. For example, off-screen buffering (responsible for windows' transparency) is managed by the **Surface Manager** library. **Media Framework** is also an important library that provides different media codecs to allow the handling of different media formats. The second section is **Android Runtime**; before the launch of version 5.0, Android used Dalvik Virtual Machine, with trace-based **just-in-time** (**JIT**) compilation. However, with the release of Android 5.0 Lollipop, Android made **Android Runtime** (**ART**) the only runtime option. ART is an environment that makes use of **ahead-of-time** (**AOT**) compilation to compile the application intermediate language (Java bytecode) into a native, system-dependent machine code upon the installation of an application. This is meant to execute the resulting binary natively. ART and Dalvik use the same input bytecode to maintain downward compatibility.

Every Android application is coded using Java and compiled to a bytecode for the **Java Virtual Machine (JVM)**; this bytecode is then translated to a Dalvik bytecode in the form of `.dex` and `.odex` (optimized Dalvik executable) files, as a part of any APK file. ART and Dalvik make use of `.dex` files as the input while the `.odex` files are replaced with **Executable and Linkable Format (ELF)** files using the **dex2oat** utility responsible for the compilation process, so all applications compiled using ART on the device will be executed natively by the processor.

The major difference to note here is that instead of heuristically choosing a part of bytecode to compile during execution (Dalvik), ART compiles everything ahead of time. The following chart describes how this can improve performance significantly (source `https://en.wikipedia.org/wiki/Android_Runtime`):

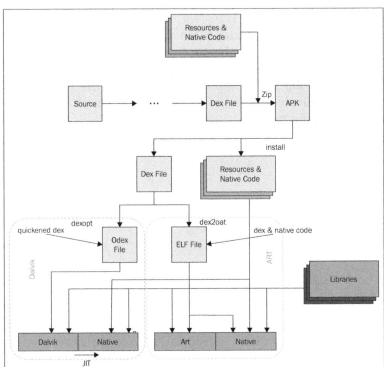

A comparison of Dalvik and ART architectures

Above the Library/Android Runtime layer is the **Application Framework** layer, mainly composed of Java-compatible libraries based on OpenJDK (in December 2015, Google announced that all Java implementation will be based on OpenJDK instead of Apache Harmony: `http://venturebeat.com/2015/12/29/google-confirms-next-android-version-wont-use-oracles-proprietary-java-apis/`). The basic functions of Android-based devices, such as voice calls and resource management, are managed via programs that interact directly with this layer. As you can see in *Figure 1*, this layer consists of nine important blocks or key services. **Activity Manager** controls and manages all the stack activities and lifecycle aspects of applications; **Content Providers** manage inter-applications data sharing; **Resource Manager** is responsible for managing all non-code embedded resources used in applications; **Notification Manager** is a service that allows applications to display alerts and notifications; **View System** provides an extensible set of views used to create application user interfaces; **Package Manager** is a service that allows applications to find out information about currently installed applications; **Telephony Manager** manages voice calls and gives applications information about the telephony capabilities of the device (such as status and subscriber information); and **Location Manager** gives access to geolocation information and the location service using GPS or cell towers. This layer is followed by the highest level and the topmost layer, the **Applications** layer, which represents the programs that are directly used by the device owner, and for most smartphone devices, we can distinguish two kinds of application: system apps that are shipped along with the device (default browser, contacts manager, SMS client, and so on). These apps are usually installed under `/system/priv-app/` starting from Android 4.4, and user installed apps that are downloaded and installed by the users are usually present in the `/data/` directory.

Android security model

Understanding every smartphone's OS security model is a big deal in the forensic context. All vendors and smartphones manufacturers care about securing their user's data, and in most cases, the security model implemented can cause a real headache to every forensic examiner, and Android is no exception. Android, as you know, is an open source OS built on the Linux kernel and provides an environment offering the ability to run multiple applications simultaneously. Each application is digitally signed and isolated in its very own sandbox; each application sandbox defines the application's privileges. Above the kernel, all activities have constrained access to the system.

Android OS implements many security components and has many considerations for its various layers; the following diagram summarizes the Android security architecture on ARM with TrustZone support:

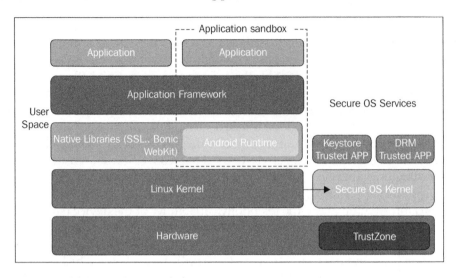

Most recent Android devices provide a secondary environment/OS: the Secure OS is dedicated to run security-sensitive operations, and this capability is usually implemented in a separate processor or it can also be shared on the same processor, such as the ARM TrustZone technology (to learn more about TrustZone, you can refer to http://www.arm.com/products/processors/technologies/trustzone/). The latest Samsung Galaxy S6 uses Samsung's in-house Exynos 7420 SoC, which is an ARM-based SoC providing a hardware cryptographic accelerator that uses a **Direct Memory Access (DMA)** engine to facilitate a full disk encryption. (An interesting paper about the Samsung Exynos 7420 can be found at http://www.anandtech.com/show/9330/exynos-7420-deep-dive.) There are at least seven manufacturers of SoC: Samsung, Qualcomm, MediaTek, Texas Instrument, Intel, nVidia, and ST-Ericsson. In general, OEMs use the Secure OS services to provide device-specific services and applications. All the cryptographic services based in the Secure OS are exposed to the Android application via the **KeyChain** API.

Android makes use of industry-standard algorithms to provide cryptography and data protection abilities in order to ensure three main functions: device encryption, application security, and network connectivity and encryption (SSL, VPN, and Wi-Fi).

Full disk encryption

Similar to iDevices and iOS, Android user data is also encrypted before writing it to the disk using an encrypted key, and all read operations automatically decrypt data before returning it. This encryption/decryption process is a kernel feature that works at the **dm-crypt** level. The encryption/decryption process relays on 128 AES with **cipher-block chaining (CBC)** and ESSIV:SHA256; the OEMs can use AES-128 bit or higher to encrypt the master key.

With the introduction of Android 5.0, some new encryption features have been offered as fast encryption, which only encrypts user's data partition if the ForceEncrypt flag is not set, which is also a newly introduced feature in order to gain time at first boot stage. Android 5.0 also introduced support of encryption without passwords and pattern support in addition to the hardware-backed storage of the encryption key.

Depending on the device's settings, Android 5+ offers four encryption types: default, PIN, password, and pattern. On the first boot, a randomly generated 128-bit master key is generated and hashed with a default password and stored salt and then signed through a trusted execution environment (such as TrustZone).

> The default password is default_password and is defined in the Android Open Source project cryptfs.c at https://android. googlesource.com/platform/system/vold/+/master/ cryptfs.c.

By setting up a PIN/password/pattern, the 128-bit key is re-encrypted and does not cause user data re-encryption. Encryption in Android is managed by init and vold.init calls **vold** (**volume daemon**) that sets a number of system properties to trigger various tasks and stages on the encryption/decryption/mounting processes and then communicates the current state to the services framework. In order to encrypt/decrypt the /data partition, a temporary filesystem (on-memory filesystem) is mounted, which allows the user interface to be shown, and then the physical partition is unmounted. To switch to the physical /data partition, all processes and system services with open files on the temporary filesystem are stopped and then restarted in the actual partition. These stop/start actions are triggered once the vold. decrypt property is set to trigger_restart_framework, trigger_restart_min_ framework, or trigger_shutdown_framework. vold and init communicate with each other by setting properties. A list of available properties for encryption is available at https://source.android.com/security/encryption/:

There are two main flows for Android devices: encrypting a previously unencrypted device and booting an encrypted one. Each flow has two options, respectively: encrypt a previously unencrypted device with ForceEncrypt and encrypt a previously unencrypted device at the user's demand (starting from Android L, users can initiate device encryption), then we have an option to boot an encrypted device with no password set (using default password) and boot an encrypted device that has a set password. Nikolay Elenkov describes, in detail, this last case where the device is encrypted using either PIN, password, or a pattern in his book *Android Security Internals: An In-Depth Guide to Android's Security Architecture*:

1. The password encrypted device is detected because of the flag `ro.crypto. state = "encrypted"` so vold sets `vold.decrypt` to `trigger_restart_ min_framework`.

2. Mount the **temporary filesystem (tmfs)** at this stage; based on the parameters passed from `init.rc`, init sets the following properties: `ro.crypto.fs_ type`, `ro.crypto.fs_real_blkdev`, `ro.crypto.fs_mnt_point`, `ro.crypto. fs_options`, and `ro.crypto.fs_flags` to save the initial mount options for the `/data` partition.

3. The framework starts up and sees that `vold.decrypt` is set to `trigger_ restart_min_framework`. This tells the framework that it is booting on a tmpfs `/data` disk and it needs a password.

4. Once `cryptfs cryptocomplete` is successful, the framework displays a UI asking for the disk password. The UI checks the password by sending the `cryptfs checkpw` command to vold. If the password is correct (which is determined by successfully mounting the decrypted `/data` at a temporary location, then unmounting it), vold saves the name of the decrypted block device in the property `ro.crypto.fs_crypto_blkdev` and returns status 0 to the UI. If the password is incorrect, it returns -1 to the UI.

> All encryptions featured in vold are invoked using `cryptfs` commands: `checkpw`, `restart`, `enablecrypto`, `changepw`, `cryptocomplete`, `verifypw`, `setfield`, `getfield`, `mountdefaultencrypted`, `getpwtype`, `getpw`, and `clearpw`.

5. The `vold.decrypt` property is set to `trigger_reset_main`. This stops all services and allows the temporary filesystem (tmpfs `/data`) to be unmounted.

6. The decrypted `/data` partition is prepared by vold and mounted.

7. All services boot using the decrypted `/data` filesystem.

KeyChain and KeyStore

Android implements a set of standard cryptographic algorithms. These algorithms are provided as APIs for several high level protocols (such as SSL and HTTPS) and applications to use the system credential storage for private keys and certificate chains.

Starting from Android 4.0, the KeyChain class allows applications to access private keys and their corresponding certificate chain through system credential storage. As for Wi-Fi and VPNs, once a private key is requested, the application receives a callback from an **X509KeyManager** (a key manager for X509 certificate-based key pairs). Then it calls choosePrivateKeyAlias, a public method that starts an activity for the user to select the alias for a private key/certificate pair then returns the selected alias (if not null) via the KeyChainAliasCallback callback. The private key and the X509Certificate are returned, respectively, after getPrivateKey(Context, String) and getCertificateChain(Context, String) are called.

After the appearance of Android 4.3 (API level 18), the KeyStore class was introduced and allowed applications to store credentials and cryptographic keys in containers to harden their extraction. The type of the system key store can be changed by setting the keystore.type property in the file named JAVA_HOME/lib/security/java.security.

Application security

As most mobile platforms, Android focuses on application security by providing several layers of protection in order to ensure application usability, stability, and integrity. There are several Android application security features; the main are application sandboxing and permissions, **Security Enhanced Linux** (**SELinux**), and application signing.

Application sandboxing and permissions

Each application in Android runs in its very own dedicated virtual sandbox; this is meant to isolate applications from each other. The application sandbox is in the kernel, which is an extended model of the native code; every application above the kernel layer runs within the application sandbox.

Application resources are identified and isolated based on the Linux user-based protection model, in which each application is assigned a **unique user ID (UID)** (which is automatically generated) and is executed by that user in a separate process. At the process level, security between the applications and the system is maintained via the Linux standard facilities, such as user and group IDs that are assigned to applications. Each application has its own `data` directory, which, at file level, ensures that this application has the permission to read and write to only its own `data` directory.

All systems with unique user IDs are defined in the `android_filesystem_config.h` header file, all application UIDs start from 10000 (`AID_APP`), and the corresponding usernames for devices that do not support multiple physical users are in the form uX_aYYY, where X corresponds to the Android user ID (for example, the root user is assigned 0) and YYY is the offset from `AID_APP`. The following command line snippet shows the Calendar application process executed as u0_a29:

```
$ ps
u0_a8 18788 182 925864 50236 ffffffff 400d073c S com.google.android.
dialer

u0_a29 23128 182 875972 35120 ffffffff 400d073c S com.google.android.
calendar

u0_a34 23264 182 868424 31980 ffffffff 400d073c S com.google.android.
deskclock
```

The ps utility lists process lists and supports the following parameters:

- `-t`: Shows threads
- `-x`: Shows time
- `-P`: Shows policy
- `-p`: Shows process priorities
- `-c`: Shows CPU #
- `<number>`: Filter by PID
- `<string>`: Filter by command name

Conceptually, an Android application sandbox can be represented as follows:

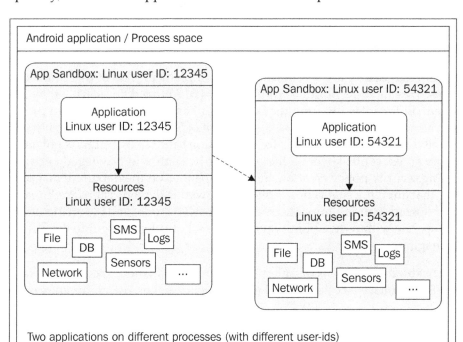

All applications are executed with no permission assigned; however, they can request permissions via their manifest files. Permissions are granted in two main ways, either by requesting the desired permissions through the appropriate manifest-permissions (AndroidManifest.xml) or by running the same process with other trusted applications.

The AndroidManifest.xml file is mandatory and every Android application contains one in its root directory. All permissions desired by a given application are declared within it. These permissions are meant to allow an application to access restricted APIs and resources; for example, if an application wants to capture audio output, the CAPTURE_AUDIO_OUTPUT permission must be declared in the manifest file. The following is an example of the AndroidManifest.xml file:

```
<manifest xmlns:android="http://schemas.android.com/apk/res/android"
package="com.example.soufiane">
<uses-permission android:name="android.permission. CAPTURE_AUDIO_
OUTPUT " />
</manifest>
```

You can find all manifest permissions at `https://developer.android.com/reference/android/Manifest.permission.html`.

Security Enhanced Linux – SELinux

SELinux is a **mandatory access control (MAC)** implementation of the Linux kernel as a Linux security module. Starting from version 4.3, Android has started integrating a modified SELinux version from the Security Enhancements for Android project (`http://seandroid.bitbucket.org`). The goal of SELinux in Android is to define well determined boundaries for application sandboxes. SELinux enhances mandatory access control over all the processes by confining privileged ones and automating security policy creation. SELinux operates on the default denial policy, meaning that anything that is not explicitly allowed is denied. There are three basic modes of operation in SELinux: disabled, permissive mode, and enforcing mode. They all operate within the SELinux policy (the set of rules that guide the SELinux security engine):

- **Disabled**: SELinux is disabled and no policy is loaded, except the default **Discretionary Access Control (DAC)** security, which remains enforced.
- **Permissive**: In this mode, the policy is loaded and SELinux only warns and logs permission denials.
- **Enforcing**: This mode enables and loads policy, which logs violations and also logs and enforces denials.

Starting from Android 5.0, full enforcement is enabled, covering all the Android domains (processes, group of processes, and so on); you can verify and change SELinux mode with the `getenforce` and `setenforce` commands.

Application signing

Application signing in Android is based on Java JAR signing. Basically, all application signing aims to guarantee authenticity (identifying and verifying the author's identity) and integrity (making sure the application is not altered in any way). The process of signing is implemented by a digital signature that makes the use of a private key and the X.509 certificates. In Android, the certificate is mainly used to verify that application updates are coming from the right authority, which applies the *same origin policy* and to establish an inter-application trust relationship.

Signing an Android application in release mode requires a **key store** (a binary file containing a set of private keys), a private key, adding the signing configuration to the build file for the app module, and invoking the `assembleRelease` build task from Android Studio.

The following screenshot shows the window to create a new key store in Android Studio:

A detailed step-by-step guide is available at `https://developer.android.com/tools/publishing/app-signing.html`.

Bypassing security

Without any doubt, lock screens represent the very first starting point in every mobile forensic examination. As for all smartphone OSes, Android offers a way to control access to a given device by requiring user authentication; the problem with recent implementations of lock screens in modern operating systems, in general and in Android (since it is the point of interest of this chapter), is that beyond controlling access to the system user interface and applications, lock screens have now been extended to more fancy (showing widgets, switching users in multi-users devices, and so on) and forensically challenging features, such as unlocking the system keystore, to derive the key-encryption key (used with the disk encryption key), and the credential storage encryption key.

The problem with bypassing lock screens (also called **keyguards**) is that techniques that can be used are very version/device dependent, thus there is neither a generalized method nor a technique that works every time.

The Android keyguard is basically an Android application, whose window lives on a high window layer with the possibility of intercepting navigation buttons in order to produce the "lock" effect. Each unlock method (PIN, password, pattern, and face unlock) is a view component implementation hosted by the KeyguardHostView, which is a view container class.

All of the methods/modes used to secure an Android device are activated by setting the current selected mode in the enumerable SecurityMode of the class KeyguardSecurityModel. The following snippet shows KeyguardSecurityModel. SecurityMode implemented, as seen in the Android open source project:

```
enum SecurityMode {
    Invalid, // NULL state
    None, // No security enabled
    Pattern, // Unlock by drawing a pattern.
    Password, // Unlock by entering an alphanumeric password
    PIN, // Strictly numeric password
    Biometric, // Unlock with a biometric key (e.g. finger print
or face unlock)
    Account, // Unlock by entering an account's login and
password.
    SimPin, // Unlock by entering a sim pin.
    SimPuk // Unlock by entering a sim puk
}
```

Before starting our bypass and lock cracking techniques, dealing with system files or "system protected files" assumes that the device you are handling meets some requirements:

- Using **Android Debug Bridge (ADB)**:
    - The device must be rooted
    - USB debugging is enabled on the device
- Booting into a custom recovery mode
- JTAG or chip-off to acquire a physical bit-by-bit copy

Bootloader/recovery mode

Besides the normal booting process of Android, there are some maintenance modes: **fastboot** (also called bootloader) and **recovery** mode. Either of the two can be accessed via the start-up key combination (depending on the device model) or via ADB commands.

Bootloader, or fastboot, is a BIOS-like system that packages the instructions to boot an operating system kernel and is designed to run its own debugging environment. Bootloader is extremely processor specific since it's the very first layer that has to be executed; every Android device has a bootloader, but depending on the hardware device, most of the OEMs have their own version especially designed for their hardware. That's why most of the bootloaders are "locked". This is meant to force users to stick with the Android version shipped within the device.

Bootloader in Android has a basic interactive mode and can be accessed in different ways depending on the device; the following is a list of the most common devices and how to get them to boot into fastboot mode:

Device	Instruction	Image
Samsung devices	• Power off your Samsung phone. • Press and hold the Power, Volume Down, and Home buttons for several seconds.	

Device	Instruction	Image
HTC devices	• Power off your HTC phone. • Press and hold the Power and Volume Down buttons for several seconds.	
Sony devices	• Power down your Sony Xperia phone. • Download and install DooMLoRD's FlashTool Xperia Driver Pack. • Check and install fastboot drivers. • Connect your USB cable to the computer, but not the phone. • Press and hold Volume Up. Connect the other end of the already attached USB cable to your phone.	

Device	Instruction	Image
Motorola devices	• Power off your Motorola phone. • Press and hold Volume Down. Then press and hold the Power key for about 2 seconds. Release the Power key whilst still holding down the Volume Down key for a second or two more. On some Motorola devices, you'll need to connect the phone to your PC whilst holding the Volume Down and Power keys.	
Nexus devices	• Power off your Nexus device. • Press and hold the Power, Volume Up, and Volume Down keys simultaneously. Don't release until you're inside the menu.	

Device	Instruction	Image
LG devices	<ul><li>Power off your LG device.</li><li>Connect your USB cable to your computer, but not your phone.</li><li>Press and hold the Power and Volume Up keys simultaneously. Hold for about 5 to 8 seconds.</li><li>Connect the other end of the USB cable to your phone.</li></ul>	

You can also boot in both modes via the command line using ADB if USB debugging is enabled on the device; this does not require a rooted device:

1. Install ADB (`https://developer.android.com/sdk/index.html`) and USB drivers for the device model.

2. Connect the device to the computer using a USB cable.

3. To boot into bootloader mode for most Android devices, type this command in the command window: `adb reboot-bootloader`:

```
C:\Users\Soufiane\AppData\Local\Android\sdk\platform-tools>adb reboot-bootloader
```

4. To boot into recovery mode for all Android devices, in the command window type this: `adb reboot recovery`.

Rooting an Android device

Having a rooted device can also cause the examiner a lot of pain. A group of young developers (called KingRoot Studio) interested in the underlying system of mobile device publically released an easy-to-use root tool, **KingRoot**. This tool can work on almost all devices from Android 2.x to 5.1.1.

KingRoot offers two methods for gaining root access on a given device, one using a computer and the second directly on the device:

1. Download and install the KingRoot app directly on the device and run it (the latest release at time of writing this book is `http://king.myapp.com/myapp/kdown/img/NewKingrootV4.85_C139_B255_en_release_2016_03_29_105203.apk`). Before proceeding, make sure the device is connected to Internet (even if this is not recommended in a forensic investigation, it's necessary to have an Internet connection when you root the device)

   You should allow application installation from unknown sources by following these steps:

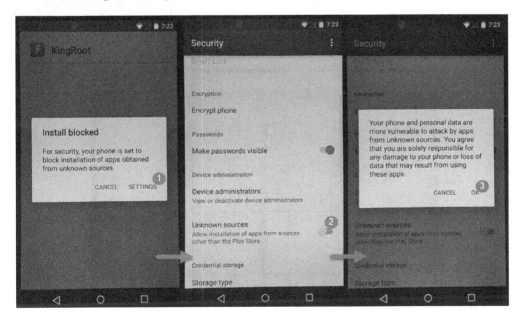

2. Now you can proceed with KingRoot installation. The process is very simple, as you can see in the following screenshot:

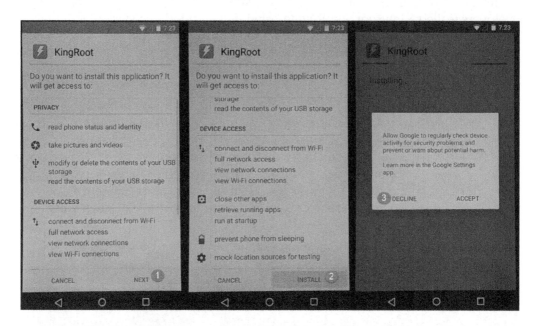

3. Once the installation complete, press **Open** to continue:

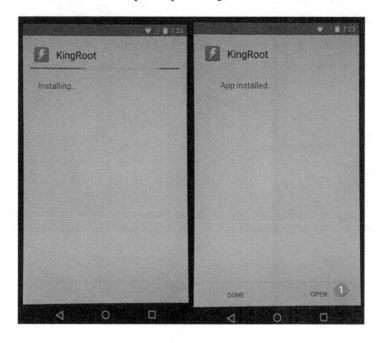

4. At this stage, the application will verify the root status; if it's not rooted, the application will prompt you to click on **Start Root**. All you need to do after clicking is to wait until the process finishes:

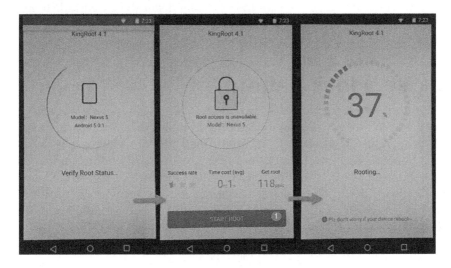

5. If you are prompted to allow Google to regularly check the device activity for security problems, press **Decline**. Once done you will get a message telling you root was successfully installed:

If you want to root the device by booting the system using a custom recovery image, you can use **Team Win Recovery Project (TWRP)**; it's an open-source recovery image for Android-based devices that is supported by almost all Android devices (`https://twrp.me`). You can find a detailed step-by-step guide at `http://galaxys6root.highonandroid.com/galaxy-s6-root-news/how-to-root-galaxy-s6-or-s6-edge-with-twrp-recovery/`.

Cracking a lock pattern

The lock pattern mode `KeyguardSecurityModel.SecurityMode.Pattern` implementation requires drawing a predefined pattern on a 3 x 3 grid. The pattern grid points are registered in order, starting from 0 at the top-left corner to 8 at the bottom-right point. To be valid, a pattern must join at least 4 points and a maximum of 9, and each used point cannot be reused within the current pattern, which statistically means that the number of variations in a pattern lock is considerably low compared to a nine-digit PIN. Having all combinations between 0123 and 876543210 is not a big deal.

The following is an "indexed" pattern lock screen:

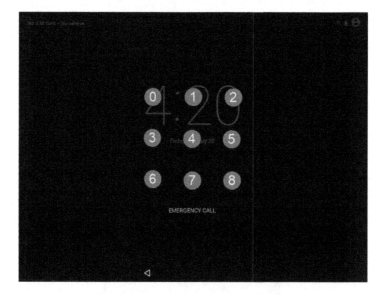

Furthermore, the pattern lock is stored as an unsalted SHA-1 value, as we can see from the `LockPatternUtils` class from the Android project:

```
private static byte[] patternToHash(List<LockPatternView.Cell>
pattern) {
```

```
    if (pattern == null) {
        return null;
    }
    final int patternSize = pattern.size();
    byte[] res = new byte[patternSize];
    for (int i = 0; i < patternSize; i++) {
        LockPatternView.Cell cell = pattern.get(i);
        res[i] = (byte) (cell.getRow() * 3 + cell.getColumn());
    }
    try {
        MessageDigest md = MessageDigest.getInstance("SHA-1");
        byte[] hash = md.digest(res);
        return hash;
    } catch (NoSuchAlgorithmException nsa) {
        return res;
    }
}
```

In all Android versions, the hash value of the pattern lock is stored in the `/data/system/gesture.key` file (and `/data/system/users/<user ID>/gesture.key` on devices that support multi-user access):

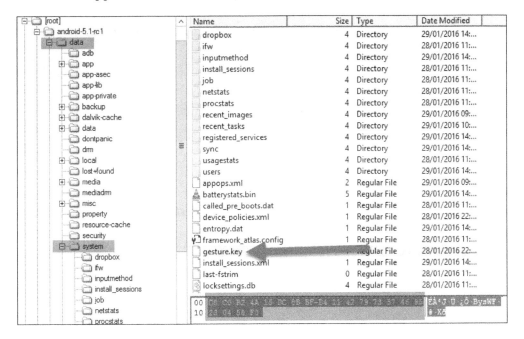

In the preceding screenshot, the `gesture.key` content C8C0B24A15DC8BBFD411427973574695230458F0 is the hashed value of the swipe pattern. The generated hash is always the same because there is no randomly generated salt addition. There are several freely available scripts to generate all the possible hashes and their respective patterns (`https://github.com/kevinis/ AndroidPatternCracker`) and there are freely available precompiled tables (`http://www.android-forensics.com/tools/AndroidGestureSHA1.rar`):

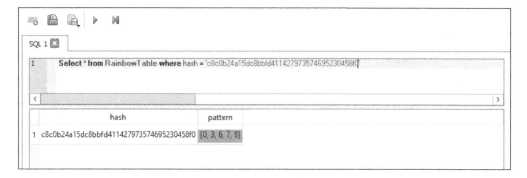

The actual pattern in our case was *03678*, meaning it draws an *L* starting from the upper-left corner:

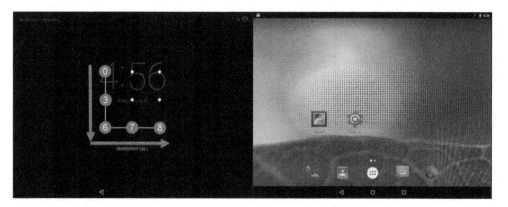

You can also just "pull" the `gesture.key` file using ADB via the `adb pull /data/ system/gesture.key` command:

```
C:\Users\Soufiane\AppData\Local\Android\sdk\platform-tools>adb pull /data/system/gesture.key
3 KB/s (20 bytes in 0.006s)
C:\Users\Soufiane\AppData\Local\Android\sdk\platform-tools>
```

If you get the *Permission denied* message, try to restart ADB as root by typing `adb root`:

```
C:\Users\Soufiane\AppData\Local\Android\sdk\platform-tools>adb root
restarting adbd as root
```

Cracking a PIN/password

The major difference between PIN/password and pattern lock (in addition to the different way they are stored) is that the PIN/password are salted and as we saw, pattern locks are not. Essentially, PINs and passwords are equivalent; they compare the hash of the user's inputs to a stored salted hash. The salt used is a random 64-bit value stored in `/data/system/password.key` (and `/data/system/users/<user ID>/ password.key` on devices that support multi-user access).

The following is an example of a hash in the `/data/system/password.key` file:
`F507780CA6762594B2C39F61279D544EA06AF3C95AA4CA29D6221FC7D E4AEC5349C257F3`.

As we can learn from the `LockPatternUtils` class (`https://github.com/android /platform_frameworks_base/blob/master/core/java/com/android/internal /widget/LockPatternUtils.java`), the hash is in fact a concatenation of the SHA1 hash and the MD5 hash:

```
public byte[] passwordToHash(String password, int userId) {
        if (password == null) {
            return null;
        }

        try {
            byte[] saltedPassword = (password + getSalt(userId)).
getBytes();
            byte[] sha1 = MessageDigest.getInstance("SHA-1").
digest(saltedPassword);
            byte[] md5 = MessageDigest.getInstance("MD5").
digest(saltedPassword);

            byte[] combined = new byte[sha1.length + md5.length];
            System.arraycopy(sha1, 0, combined, 0, sha1.length);
            System.arraycopy(md5, 0, combined, sha1.length, md5.
length);
```

```
                      final char[] hexEncoded = HexEncoding.encode(combined);
                      return new String(hexEncoded).getBytes(StandardCharsets.
         UTF_8);
              } catch (NoSuchAlgorithmException e) {
                  throw new AssertionError("Missing digest algorithm: ", e);
              }
          }
```

This means that the PIN/password can be seen as *password.key = SHA1($pass . $salt) . MD5($pass . $salt).*

Starting from Android 4.4, the salt used for calculating the preceding hash is stored in a dedicated database named `locksettings.db`, the latest version has a single table and can be found under `/data/system/locksettings.db`.

The database contains one interesting table with the same name as `locksettings`, and the following screenshot shows the columns:

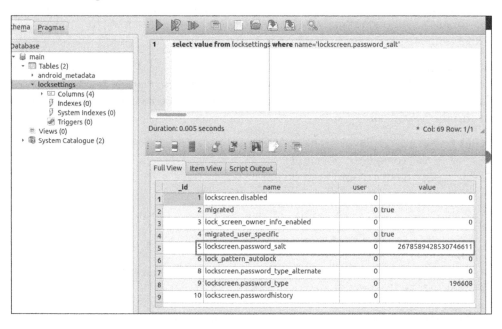

The following SQL query returns the salt:

```
select value from locksettings where name='lockscreen.password_salt'
```

It is 64-bit (long integer): `2678589428530746611`. As you can see at this point we know that our PIN is as follows:

- **SHA1**: `F507780CA6762594B2C39F61279D544EA06AF3C9`

- **MD5**: `5AA4CA29D6221FC7DE4AEC5349C257F3`

- **Salt**: \ (the hexadecimal form of the salt)

We can gather even more hints about the PIN/password from the `/data/system/device_policies.xml file`:

```
<policies><active-password quality="196608" length="4" uppercase="0"
lowercase="0" letters="0" numeric="4" symbols="0" nonletter="4"/></
policies>
```

We can now try to crack the weakest hash (MD5) using freely available tools, such as **Hashcat**, which you can grab from `https://hashcat.net/hashcat/`.

We will run Hashcat with the following parameters: `-m 10` (hash attack type is `md5($pass.$salt)`), `-a 3` (attack mode is brute-force) `?d?d?d?d` (built in charset as `?d` is a decimal). Using this, our execution query will be something similar to `hashcat-cli64.exe -m 10 hash.txt -a 3 ?d?d?d?d` (with `hash.txt` containing our `hash:salt` values):

```
C:\Users\Soufiane\Downloads\hashcat-2.00>hashcat-cli64.exe -m 10 hash.txt -a 3 ?d?d?d?d
Initializing hashcat v2.00 with 8 threads and 32mb segment-size...

Added hashes from file hash.txt: 1 (1 salts)
Activating quick-digest mode for single-hash with salt

5aa4ca29d6221fc7de4aec5349c257f3:252c42e4bab114f3:0912

All hashes have been recovered

Input.Mode: Mask (?d?d?d?d) [4]
Index.....: 0/1 (segment), 10000 (words), 0 (bytes)
Recovered.: 1/1 hashes, 1/1 salts
Speed/sec.: - plains, 9.65k words
Progress..: 9694/10000 (96.94%)
Running...: 00:00:00:01
Estimated.: --:--:--:--


Started: Tue Feb 02 19:34:40 2016
Stopped: Tue Feb 02 19:34:41 2016
```

The PIN here was successfully cracked in no time and is equal to 0912.

It may be interesting to note that an Android 5.x lock screen bypass, by exploiting a vulnerability in Android 5.x (before build LMY48M), allows one to crash the lock screen and gain full access to a locked device even if encryption is enabled. The vulnerability affects password-protected devices (PIN and pattern locks are not vulnerable).

The vulnerability is referenced as **Elevation of Privilege Vulnerability in Lockscreen** (CVE-2015-3860) and you can trigger it using the following steps:

1. From the locked screen, open the Emergency Call window.

2. Type a few characters, for example 10 asterisks. Double-tap the characters to highlight them and then tap the copy button. Then tap once in the field and tap paste, doubling the characters in the field. Repeat this process to highlight all, and then copy and paste until the field is so long that the double-tapping can no longer highlight the field.

3. Go back to the lockscreen, then swipe left to open the camera. Swipe to pull the notification drawer down from the top of the screen, and then tap on the settings (gear) icon in the top-right corner. This will cause a password prompt to appear.

4. Long-tap in the password field and paste the characters into it. Continue to long-tap the cursor and paste the characters as many times as possible, until you notice that the UI crashes and the soft-buttons at the bottom of the screen disappear, expanding the camera to fullscreen. Getting the paste button can be finicky as the string grows. As a tip, always make sure that the cursor is at the very end of the string (you can double-tap to highlight all, then tap towards the end to quickly move the cursor there) and long-tap as close to the center of the cursor as possible. It may take longer than usual for the paste button to appear as you long-tap.

These steps are fully documented with screenshots at `http://sites.utexas.edu/iso/2015/09/15/android-5-lockscreen-bypass/`, and more details about CVE-2015-3860 can be found at `https://web.nvd.nist.gov/view/vuln/detail?vulnId=CVE-2015-3860`.

Android 3.0 introduced **Full Disk Encryption** (FDE) for the first time, the implementation remained the same until Android 4.3. All Android versions use **crypto footer**, which is an implementation similar to the encryption partition header used by **Linux United Key Setup** (LUKS) but in a very light way (with all anti-forensic, split/merge, and more capabilities removed). Android supports only one decryption passphrase and the only way to check if the entered passphrase is correct or not is by trying to mount the encrypted partition; if you succeed, the passphrase is right, otherwise the passphrase is wrong.

If you visit `cryptfs.h` from the Android Open Source Project, you can see that the crypto footer in Android 4.3 looks similar to the following:

```
struct crypt_mnt_ftr {
    __le32 magic;      /* See above */
    __le16 major_version;
    __le16 minor_version;
    __le32 ftr_size;   /* in bytes, not including key following */
    __le32 flags;      /* See above */
    __le32 keysize;    /* in bytes */
    __le32 spare1;     /* ignored */
    __le64 fs_size;    /* Size of the encrypted fs, in 512 byte sectors */
    __le32 failed_decrypt_count; /* count of # of failed attempts to
decrypt and mount, set to 0 on successful mount */
    unsigned char crypto_type_name[MAX_CRYPTO_TYPE_NAME_LEN]; /* The
type of encryption needed to decrypt this partition, null terminated
*/
};
```

Considered as version 1.0 of FDE, the master key is encrypted using an AES-128 key-encryption key derived from the user PIN/password and the salt using 2000 iterations of **Password-Based Key Derivation Function 2 (PBKDF2)**. This makes brute-forcing it require obtaining a copy of the crypto footer, which resides in a dedicated partition whose name is specified in `encryptable` flag in the `fstab` file and the encrypted `userdata` partition.

A very interesting discussion about cracking the FD3 v1.0 can be found at `https://hashcat.net/forum/thread-2270.html`.

A 4-digit PIN can be brute-forced with a very high success rate using the `bruteforce_stdcrypto.py` script (`https://github.com/santoku/Santoku-Linux/blob/master/tools/android/android_bruteforce_stdcrypto/bruteforce_stdcrypto.py`). A detailed step-by-step guide is available on `https://santoku-linux.com/howto/mobile-forensics/how-to-brute-force-android-encryption/`.

The most effective difference in Android 4.4 is replacing PBKDF2 with **scrypt** (`https://www.tarsnap.com/scrypt.html`), after generating the **disk-encryption key (DEK)**. Android 4.4 applies scrypt with $N=15$, $r=3$, and $p=1$ to the user PIN/password and salt to produce a 32-bit key-encryption key, so as a part of the upgrade, the crypto footer in Android 4.4 looks similar to the following:

```
struct crypt_mnt_ftr {
    __le32 magic;
```

```
    __le16 major_version;
    __le16 minor_version;
    __le32 ftr_size;
    __le32 flags;
    __le32 keysize;
    __le32 spare1;
    __le64 fs_size;
    __le32 failed_decrypt_count;
    unsigned char crypto_type_name[MAX_CRYPTO_TYPE_NAME_LEN];
    __le32 spare2;
    unsigned char master_key[MAX_KEY_LEN];
    unsigned char salt[SALT_LEN];
    __le64 persist_data_offset[2];
    __le32 persist_data_size;
    __le8  kdf_type;
    /* scrypt parameters. See www.tarsnap.com/scrypt/scrypt.pdf */
    __le8  N_factor; /* (1 << N) */
    __le8  r_factor; /* (1 << r) */
    __le8  p_factor; /* (1 << p) */
};
```

This structure is considered as version 1.2 of FDE, which is still vulnerable to a brute-force attack if the PIN used was simple, using the same script distributed within Santoku Linux.

Android 5.0 and above brings with it a 1.3 version of FDE with a new crypto footer:

```
struct crypt_mnt_ftr {
    __le32 magic;           /* See above */
    __le16 major_version;
    __le16 minor_version;
    __le32 ftr_size;        /* in bytes, not including key following */
    __le32 flags;           /* See above */
    __le32 keysize;         /* in bytes */
    __le32 crypt_type;      /* how master_key is encrypted. Must be a
                             * CRYPT_TYPE_XXX value */
    __le64 fs_size;
    __le32 failed_decrypt_count;
    unsigned char crypto_type_name[MAX_CRYPTO_TYPE_NAME_LEN];
    __le32 spare2;
    unsigned char master_key[MAX_KEY_LEN];
    __le64 persist_data_offset[2];
    __le32 persist_data_size;
```

```
    __le8  kdf_type; /* The key derivation function used. */
    /* scrypt parameters. See www.tarsnap.com/scrypt/scrypt.pdf */
    __le8  N_factor; /* (1 << N) */
    __le8  r_factor; /* (1 << r) */
    __le8  p_factor; /* (1 << p) */
    __le64 encrypted_upto;
    __le8  hash_first_block[SHA256_DIGEST_LENGTH];
    __le8  keymaster_blob[KEYMASTER_BLOB_SIZE];
    __le32 keymaster_blob_size;
    unsigned char scrypted_intermediate_key[SCRYPT_LEN];
};
```

The major improvement in this implementation is the fact that there is no need for a PIN/password and the key-encryption key has hardware protection, as suggested by `keymaster_blob[KEYMASTER_BLOB_SIZE]`, which refers to the size of the asymmetric hardware-bound private key (KBK).

As described by the official documentation (`https://source.android.com/security/encryption/`):

The encrypted key is stored in the crypto metadata. Hardware backing is implemented using **Trusted Execution Environment** (TEE) signing capability. Previously, we had encrypted the master key with a key generated by applying scrypt to the user's password and the stored salt. In order to make the key resilient to off-box attacks, we extend this algorithm by signing the resultant key with a stored TEE key. The resultant signature is then turned into an appropriate length key by one more application of scrypt. This key is then used to encrypt and decrypt the master key. To store this key, follow these steps:

- Generate a random 16-byte disk encryption key and a 16-byte salt.
- Apply scrypt to the user password and the salt to produce a 32-byte intermediate key 1 (**IK1**).
- Pad IK1 with zero bytes to the size of the hardware-bound private key (HBK). Specifically, we pad as follows: *00 || IK1 || 00..00*; that is, one zero byte, 32 IK1 bytes, and 223 zero bytes.
- Sign a padded IK1 with HBK to produce 256-byte IK2.
- Apply scrypt to IK2 and salt (same salt as step 2) to produce 32-byte IK3.
- Use the first 16 bytes of IK3 as KEK and the last 16 bytes as IV.
- Encrypt DEK with AES_CBC, with key KEK, and initialization vector IV.

This means that at the time of writing this book, brute-forcing Android 5+ encrypted disks is no longer efficient and no technique has been disclosed at the time of writing.

Android logical data acquisition

Logically acquiring the Android device allows gathering user data on the basis of communication with the base operating system. In most cases, and if prerequisites are verified (mostly a rooted device with USB debugging mode enabled), a logical acquisition can expose most of the valuable information on the device, including SMS, call history, application data, system logs, and media.

Gaining root access is a very important step in most Android forensic scenarios, and the decision to root a device or not must be taken with approval from a court of law. Most of the commercially available forensic tools offer automated, temporary root for Android devices (such as XRY, Oxygen Forensic Suite, Paraben's Device Seizure, or NowSecure Forensics Suite), but the result is still very device/Android version dependent.

If you are willing to do it manually, most of the logical acquisition process in Android devices can be conducted using ADB functionalities.

Logical data acquisition using ADB

In addition to development/debugging purposes, ADB offers a bunch of capabilities that are welcome in a forensic context, since ADB lets an examiner copy files and folders from and to the device, executing shell commands on the device, getting system and app logs, installing and removing applications, and debugging applications running on the device.

Assuming that the ADB environment is correctly configured in the examiner computer (a step-by-step guide can be found at `http://www.howtogeek.com/125769/how-to-install-and-use-abd-the-android-debug-bridge-utility/`), you can also use the Universal ADB Driver if you are on a Windows machine, since it supports ADB and fastboot interfaces for most Android devices (you can grab it from `https://github.com/koush/UniversalAdbDriver`). You must make sure that USB debugging is enabled on the target device and the correct drivers are installed.

To enable USB debugging mode in different Android versions, do the following:

- For Android 2.0-2.3.x, go to **Settings | Applications | Development | USB Debugging**.
- For Android 3.0- 4.1.x, go to **Settings | Developer Options | USB Debugging**.
- For Android 4.2.x and higher, enable the Developer Options menu. Go to **Menu | Settings | About phone** or **About tablet**. Then, locate the **Build Number** option and tap on it seven times to enable Developer Options. Tap a few times more until you see **You are now a developer!**. Then go to **Settings | Developer Options | USB Debugging**.
- For Android 5.x Lollipop, the procedure is the same as Android 4.2.x.

Starting from Android 4.2.2, a new feature was introduced to enhance USB debugging security. Secure USB Debugging allows only explicitly authorized hosts to connect to the ADB daemon. The confirmation dialog looks similar to the following screenshot:

The choice can be made persistent by checking the **Always allow from this computer** option, which will let the device store the computer's RSA keys (2048-bit RSA keys locally generated by the ADB server), in order to avoid popping this dialog up each time the device is connected to the same host.

The interesting thing to do in a forensic examination is seize any computer that was previously trusted, since the generated keys are stored as `adbkey` and `adbkey.pub` in the following locations:

- **Windows**: `%USERPOFILE%\.android` or `C:\Windows\System32\config\systemprofile\.android`
- **Mac OS**: `/Users/<username>/.android`

By storing these files on the examiner computer, it will be considered to be trusted by the device.

An interesting vulnerability that allows you to bypass Secure USB Debugging has been disclosed and affects Android 4.4.2. No CVE reference was assigned to the vulnerability, and you can get technical details about this vulnerability at `https://labs.mwrinfosecurity.com/advisories/2014/07/03/android-4-4-2-secure-usb-debugging-bypass/`.

If the previously mentioned conditions are verified, we can start pulling evidence from the device, and the very first command to use is `adb pull`. The syntax is as follows:

```
adb pull [-p] [-a] < remote file path on device. > [<local file path>]
```

Here, `-p` and `-a` are optional parameters to respectively show the transfer's progress and to copy a pulled file's timestamp and mode.

The first thing to do is open a terminal/command window and navigate to the Android ADB folder (available once you install Android SDK), after enabling Secure USB Debug mode on the device and connecting it to the computer using a USB cable. Make sure that it's connected correctly:

```
$ adb devices
List of devices attached
* daemon not running. starting it now on port 5037 *
* daemon started successfully *
90000a7854ca  device
```

Our device is connected and correctly recognized. ADB offers a UNIX shell to issue commands without entering the ADB remote shell on the device; the basic command is `adb shell`:

```
$ adb shell
root@generic:/ #
```

The sharp # symbol means that you have root access on the device. Now we can start exploring partitions:

```
#  ls -l data/data/
drwxr-x--x u0_a0      u0_a0          2016-02-03 01:10 com.android.
backupconfirm
drwxr-x--x u0_a15     u0_a15         2016-02-04 13:16 com.android.
browser
drwxr-x--x u0_a16     u0_a16         2016-02-03 01:11 com.android.
calculator2
drwxr-x--x u0_a17     u0_a17         2016-02-03 01:18 com.android.
calendar
drwxr-x--x u0_a31     u0_a31         2016-02-03 01:12 com.android.camera
......
drwxr-x--x u0_a4      u0_a4          2016-02-03 01:18 com.android.dialer
drwxr-x--x u0_a24     u0_a24         2016-02-03 01:11 com.android.
documentsui
drwxr-x--x u0_a14     u0_a14         2016-02-03 01:11 com.android.
dreams.basic
drwxr-x--x u0_a25     u0_a25         2016-02-03 01:19 com.android.email
......
drwxr-x--x u0_a5      u0_a5          2016-02-03 01:12 com.android.
gallery
drwxr-x--x u0_a48     u0_a48         2016-02-03 01:12 com.android.
gesture.builder
drwxr-x--x u0_a29     u0_a29         2016-02-03 01:12 com.android.
htmlviewer
drwxr-x--x system     system         2016-02-03 01:11 com.android.
inputdevices
drwxr-x--x u0_a30     u0_a30         2016-02-03 01:16 com.android.
inputmethod.latin
drwxr-x--x system     system         2016-02-03 01:18 com.android.
keychain
drwxr-x--x u0_a5      u0_a5          2016-02-03 01:19 com.android.
providers.media
drwxr-x--x system     system         2016-02-03 01:13 com.android.
providers.settings
drwxr-x--x radio      radio          2016-02-03 01:18 com.android.
providers.telephony
```

```
drwxr-x--x u0_a2      u0_a2           2016-02-03 01:16 com.android.
providers.userdictionary

drwxr-x--x u0_a10     u0_a10          2016-02-03 01:11 com.android.
proxyhandler

drwxr-x--x u0_a41     u0_a41          2016-02-04 13:43 com.android.
quicksearchbox

...etc
```

All `/data/data/<app package>` folders on the devices have the same subdirectory architecture:

Folder	Description
shared_prefs	XML of shared preferences
lib	Custom library files required by app
files	Developer saved files
cache	Files cached by the app
databases	SQLite databases and journal files

In Android, similar to most smartphone operating systems, the most valuable evidences resides on SQLite databases. Let's assume that we want to grab the database of Android Browser `/data/data/com.android.browser/`. The file name is `browser2.db` and its full path is `/data/data/com.android.browser/databases/browser2.db`, as you can see in the following screenshot:

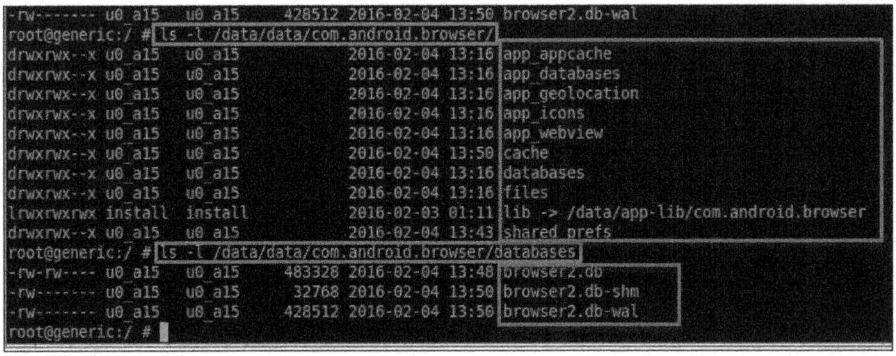

Exit the shell mode by typing `exit` and pull the database file (and the temporarily created `.db-shm` and `.db-wal` files) using `adb pull`, as shown here:

```
$ adb pull /data/data/com.android.browser/databases/browser2.db /home/
soufiane/Desktop/AndroidBrowserDBs/browser2.db
```

```
1466 KB/s (483328 bytes in 0.321s)
```

```
$ adb pull /data/data/com.android.browser/databases/browser2.db-shm /
home/soufiane/Desktop/AndroidBrowserDBs/browser2.db-shm
```

```
395 KB/s (32768 bytes in 0.080s)
```

```
$ adb pull /data/data/com.android.browser/databases/browser2.db-wal /
home/soufiane/Desktop/AndroidBrowserDBs/browser2.db-wal
```

```
1242 KB/s (428512 bytes in 0.336s)
```

Now we can browse the database extracted using any SQLite utility. The `browser2.db` database contains all the information related to user activity via the browser, as you can see from the table and column names:

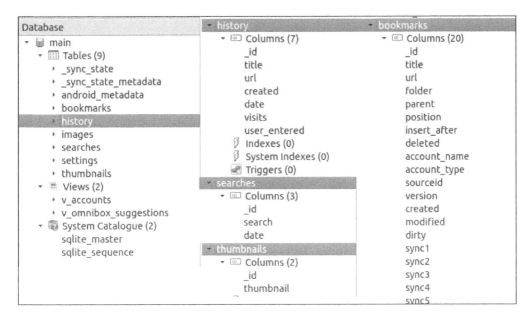

Querying the `history` table, for example, can return the titles of the visited pages, URLs, and how many times the page was visited and when:

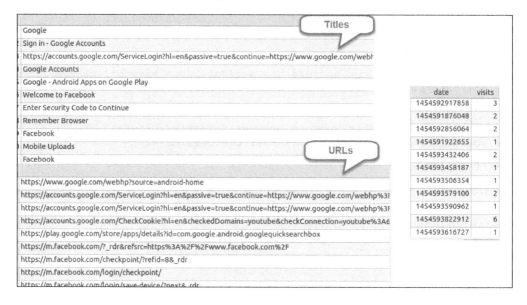

All dates are in UNIX time format, as described in previous chapters. The example of `1454599232` (from the preceding screenshot) is equivalent to the following:

- *2016-02-04T15:20:32+00:00 in ISO 8601*
- *Thu, 04 Feb 2016 15:20:32 +0000 in RFC 822, 1036, 1123, 2822*
- *Thursday, 04-Feb-16 15:20:32 UTC in RFC 2822*
- *2016-02-04T15:20:32+00:00 in RFC 3339*

Paths of traditional Android browsers are as follows:

- `/data/data/org.mozilla.fennec`
- `/data/data/com.android.browser`
- `/data/data/com.opera.mini.android`
- `/data/data/opera.browser`
- `/data/data/com.skyfire.browser`

The `adb pull` command can extract an entire application directory; for example, to pull the `telephony` folder that contains SMS database, the command will be as follows:

`adb pull /data/data/com.android.providers.telephony/ /Destination/Path/`

The result will be as shown here:

```
root@generic:/ # exit
soufiane@soufiane-VirtualBox:~$ adb pull /data/data/com.android.providers.telephony /home/soufiane/Desktop/Telephony
pull: building file list...
pull: /data/data/com.android.providers.telephony/databases/mmssms.db-journal -> /home/soufiane/Desktop/Telephony/databases/mmssms.d
b-journal
pull: /data/data/com.android.providers.telephony/databases/mmssms.db -> /home/soufiane/Desktop/Telephony/databases/mmssms.db
pull: /data/data/com.android.providers.telephony/databases/telephony.db-journal -> /home/soufiane/Desktop/Telephony/databases/telep
hony.db-journal
pull: /data/data/com.android.providers.telephony/databases/telephony.db -> /home/soufiane/Desktop/Telephony/databases/telephony.db
pull: /data/data/com.android.providers.telephony/databases/HbpcdLookup.db-journal -> /home/soufiane/Desktop/Telephony/databases/Hbp
cdLookup.db-journal
pull: /data/data/com.android.providers.telephony/databases/HbpcdLookup.db -> /home/soufiane/Desktop/Telephony/databases/HbpcdLookup
.db
pull: /data/data/com.android.providers.telephony/shared_prefs/preferred-apn1.xml -> /home/soufiane/Desktop/Telephony/shared_prefs/p
referred-apn1.xml
pull: /data/data/com.android.providers.telephony/lib -> /home/soufiane/Desktop/Telephony/lib
failed to copy '/data/data/com.android.providers.telephony/lib' to '/home/soufiane/Desktop/Telephony/lib': No such file or director
y
8 files pulled. 0 files skipped.
262 KB/s (222899 bytes in 0.829s)
soufiane@soufiane-VirtualBox:~$
```

This also means that if you want to pull the majority of a user's application data, you can execute `adb pull /data/data /Path/To/Your/Case/` and you will get a ready-to-examine logical copy of a user's data:

`$ adb pull -p /data/data/ ~/Desktop/Data`

`pull: building file list...`

`pull: /data/data/com.android.backupconfirm/lib -> /home/soufiane/Desktop/ Data/com.android.backupconfirm/lib`

`pull: /data/data/com.android.providers.calendar/databases/calendar.db -> /home/soufiane/Desktop/Data/com.android.providers.calendar/databases/ calendar.db`

`pull: /data/data/com.android.providers.calendar/lib -> /home/soufiane/ Desktop/Data/com.android.providers.calendar/lib`

`failed to copy '/data/data/com.android.providers.calendar/lib' to '/home/ soufiane/Desktop/Data/com.android.providers.calendar/lib': No such file or directory`

`pull: /data/data/com.android.contacts/lib -> /home/soufiane/Desktop/Data/ com.android.contacts/lib`

`......`

`pull: /data/data/com.android.launcher/cache/widgetpreviews.db -> /home/ soufiane/Desktop/Data/com.android.launcher/cache/widgetpreviews.db`

```
pull: /data/data/com.android.launcher/databases/launcher.db-journal -> /
home/soufiane/Desktop/Data/com.android.launcher/databases/launcher.db-
journal

pull: /data/data/com.android.launcher/databases/launcher.db -> /home/
soufiane/Desktop/Data/com.android.launcher/databases/launcher.db

pull: /data/data/com.android.launcher/shared_prefs/com.android.launcher2.
prefs.xml -> /home/soufiane/Desktop/Data/com.android.launcher/shared_
prefs/com.android.launcher2.prefs.xml

pull: /data/data/com.android.launcher/files/launcher.preferences -> /
home/soufiane/Desktop/Data/com.android.launcher/files/launcher.
preferences

pull: /data/data/com.android.launcher/lib -> /home/soufiane/Desktop/Data/
com.android.launcher/lib

......

478 files pulled. 0 files skipped.

265 KB/s (12818177 bytes in 47.143s)
```

ADB offers the possibility to extract a full backup of the device using the following command:

```
adb backup [-f <file>] [-apk|-noapk] [-shared|-noshared] [-all]
[-system|nosystem] [<packages>]
```

The command parameters are as follows:

- -all: This will back up applications and user data without including APKs to the current directory as a backup.ab file.

- -f: Lets you choose the path and backup file name.

- -apk or -noapk: Lets you choose whether or not APKs should be included in your backup.

- -shared or -noshared: Lets you choose whether or not to back up data from shared storage and the SD card.

- -system or -nosystem: Indicates whether or not the -all flag includes system applications.

- <packages>: Explicitly lists packages that you especially want to backup.

To proceed with a backup, you must already know or bypass any lock screen, if set, because when you back up a device, you will be prompted to interact with the device (Android will ask you if you want to encrypt the backup using a password then confirm (or not) the backup process).

The basic `adb backup -f Path/backup.ab -shared -all` command will extract all the possible user data and produce `backup.ab` on the given `/Path/`:

```
C:\Users\Soufiane\AppData\Local\Android\sdk\platform-tools>adb backup -f e:\case1\backup.ab -shared -all
Now unlock your device and confirm the backup operation.
```

The extracted backup is in fact a compressed TAR file using a combination of the LZ77 algorithm and Huffman coding (deflated), but it can be parsed using **Android Backup Extractor**, a Java open source tool that you can download from `http://sourceforge.net/projects/adbextractor/` and can be executed with the command `abe.jar unpack backup.ab backup.tar`, as shown here:

```
E:\case1\android-backup-extractor-20151102-bin>abe.jar unpack backup.ab backup.tar
```

If the command was successful, you should find the `backup.tar` file created and you can explore/extract it using any compression/decompression utility (WinRAR, 7Zip, and so on):

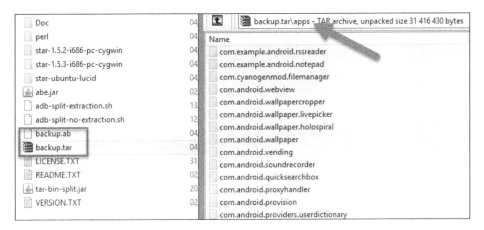

Logical data acquisition using AFLogical OSE

AFLogical OSE is an open source Android forensics app, and the framework available at `https://github.com/viaforensics/android-forensics` allows an examiner to extract CallLog calls, contacts, MMS messages, MMSParts, and SMS messages from Android devices. AFLogical OSE is already bundled with Santoku Linux.

The first thing to do is enable USB debugging on the device and connect it to the computer. In a terminal window type `aflogical-ose`. You will be asked to enter the password of the machine's superuser. Type it and press *Enter*:

```
$ aflogical-ose
Make sure android device is connected to USB
[sudo] password for soufiane:


321 KB/s (28794 bytes in 0.087s)
    pkg: /data/local/tmp/AFLogical-OSE_1.5.2.apk
Success
Starting: Intent { cmp=com.viaforensics.android.aflogical_ose/com.
viaforensics.android.ForensicsActivity }


Press enter to pull /sdcard/forensics into ~/aflogical-data/
```

If the SD card is ready, then before pressing *Enter*, select the data you want to extract from AFLogical UI on the device and click on **Capture**:

The terminal will show the following:

```
pull: building file list...
pull: /sdcard/forensics/20160204.1815/MMSParts.csv -> /home/soufiane/
aflogical-data/20160204.1815/MMSParts.csv
pull: /sdcard/forensics/20160204.1815/Contacts Phones.csv -> /home/
soufiane/aflogical-data/20160204.1815/Contacts Phones.csv
pull: /sdcard/forensics/20160204.1815/SMS.csv -> /home/soufiane/
aflogical-data/20160204.1815/SMS.csv
pull: /sdcard/forensics/20160204.1815/MMS.csv -> /home/soufiane/
aflogical-data/20160204.1815/MMS.csv
pull: /sdcard/forensics/20160204.1815/CallLog Calls.csv -> /home/
soufiane/aflogical-data/20160204.1815/CallLog Calls.csv
pull: /sdcard/forensics/20160204.1815/info.xml -> /home/soufiane/
aflogical-data/20160204.1815/info.xml
......
12 files pulled. 0 files skipped.
46 KB/s (59796 bytes in 1.244s)
```

All data acquired is stored in separated CSV files. The following is a preview from `CallLog Calls.csv` and `SMS.csv`:

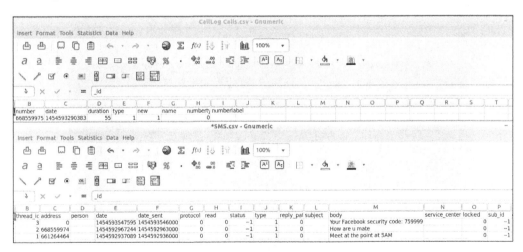

Android physical data acquisition

Acquiring the physical image of any device means extracting an exact bit-by-bit copy of the original device's flash memory. In contrast to logical acquisition, physically acquired images hold unallocated space, files, and the volume stack, in addition to the extraction of data remnants present in the memory.

In the Android context, we need to root the device to obtain a superuser privilege to fully access the ADB shell. A physical acquisition can be performed via a custom bootloader, by changing the custom recovery image or using flashing tools. We even have hardware-based acquisition techniques including JTAG and chip-off. Physically acquiring a device means that you have indirectly acquired everything within the device.

Linux-based operating systems include a built-in command-line tool called dd, used (by definition) to copy from source to destination, block-by-block, regardless of their filesystem type or operating system. This utility is included in Android!

Connect your rooted devices and in a terminal window type adb shell. As seen earlier in this chapter, this will let us run the remote shell interactively. If your device is rooted and correctly connected, you can now run the mount command to attach the filesystem found on the device to one file tree, as you can see in the following screenshot:

As highlighted in the preceding screenshot, the data partition is at `/dev/block/mtdblock1`. Now that we know which partition we want to physically acquire, we will need to extract it bit-by-bit. At this point, we have a choice to either dump the partition into an SD card or via a network directly on the examiner's computer.

If the device's SD card can be replaced by the examiner's one, make sure that the SD card has sufficient space to hold the phone image. In the shell window, type `ls -all` to determine the partition to which the SD card is linked:

```
drwxr-x--- root     root                1970-01-01 00:00 sbin
lrwxrwxrwx root     root                2016-02-05 11:20 sdcard -> /storage/sdcard
-rw-r--r-- root     root            471 1970-01-01 00:00 seapp_contexts
```

As shown in the preceding screenshot, in my case the SD card is symbolically linked to `/storage/sdcard`.

And now, using the `dd` command, we can dump `mtdblock1` to `/sdcard`. The command is as follows (the `of` parameter indicates the output file; other parameters are explained later on in the chapter):

```
dd if=/dev/block/mtdblock1 of=/storage/sdcard/physicalImage.dd bs=512
conv=notrunc,noerror,sync
```

Once dumping is done, you will see this result:

```
v/block/mtdblock1 of=/storage/sdcard/physicalImage.dd
^C879855+0 records in
879854+0 records out
450485248 bytes transferred in 681.856 secs (660675 bytes/sec)
```

Now we can pull the physical image from the SD card to the examiner's computer using the `adb pull` command, `adb pull /storage/sdcard/ /path/`, or simply by exploring the SD card via explorer:

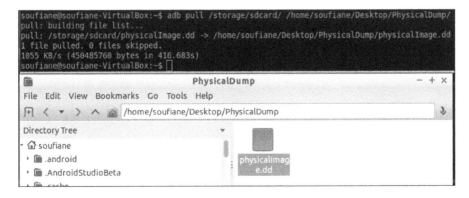

If we want to acquire the image over the network, we will not write the image dump to an SD card; instead, we will be enabling port forwarding on the device via ADB. You can choose any port number if you are using Windows and any port between 1023 and 65535 on Linux/Mac. The command is adb forward tcp:1986 tcp:1986, as shown here:

```
root@generic:/ # exit
soufiane@soufiane-VirtualBox:~$ adb forward tcp:1986 tcp:1986
soufiane@soufiane-VirtualBox:~$ 
```

In the shell window, we will run the dd command:

```
dd if=/dev/block/mtdblock1 conv=notrunc,noerror,sync | nc -l -p 1986
```

The dd parameters are as follows:

- if: Input file
- conv: Conversion options: notrunc to not truncate the output file, noerror to ignore errors and continue dumping, and sync is used in conjunction with noerror and allows a padding block with null \(x00) to maintain actual offsets within the image.

The nc parameters are as follows:

- -l: Puts Netcat in listen mode (default is client mode)
- -p: Defines the local port (in this case, 1986 is the port that is being listened to)

Open a new terminal window and be sure that Netcat (a UNIX built-in utility abbreviated to nc), which is a network utility to read from and write to network connections using TCP or UDP, is correctly installed on the computer and on the device.

If Netcat is not installed on the device, you can download an Android version and push it to the device. You can find many nc implementations for Android online, such as **SimpleNetCat** (`https://github.com/dddpaul/android-SimpleNetCat`) or **NetCat** (`https://github.com/MobileForensicsResearch/netcat`)

It's preferable to install it directly on the RAM, keeping the process forensically sound. This can be done by pushing nc on the `/dev` partition via the `adb push nc /dev/netcat/nc` command; then be sure to give it permission to execute (`chmod 111`):

```
$ adb push netcat-master/new_nc /dev/netcat/nc 241 KB/s
(20172 bytes in 0.081s)
$ adb shell
root@generic:/ # chmod 111 /dev/netcat/nc
root@generic:/ #
```

If you are on Windows, you can download and install **Nmap** (`https://nmap.org/download.html`), which will let you use NetCat via the command `ncat`.

Type in the following commands to establish a connection on the port `1986`:

- **For *nix**: `nc 127.0.0.1 1986 > /path/to/save/PhysicalImage.dd`
- **For Windows**: `ncat 127.0.0.1 1986 > X:/PATH/PhysicalImage.dd`

The `PhysicalImage.dd` file should be created in the given directory. Once the transfer is finished, which depends on the partition size, both terminals will return to the command prompt and the shell window will confirm the data transfer:

```
16771797+0 records in
16771797+0 records out
8587160064 bytes transferred in 1222.404 secs (7024813 bytes/sec)
root@x86:/ #
```

The acquired image can be mounted and explored. In Windows, we can use tools such as **AccessData FTK Imager** (`http://accessdata.com/product-download/digital-forensics/ftk-imager-version-3.4.2`), which will give us access to a logically mounted image, allowing us to view file types with Windows associations in their native or associated applications, and copy files from the mounted image to another location.

To mount the dumped image, open FTK Imager after downloading and installing it. Click on **File | Image Mounting**, then click on the **Browse** button, and locate the `Image.dd` file you previously acquired. Then click on the **Mount** button; once the operation succeeds, click on **Close**:

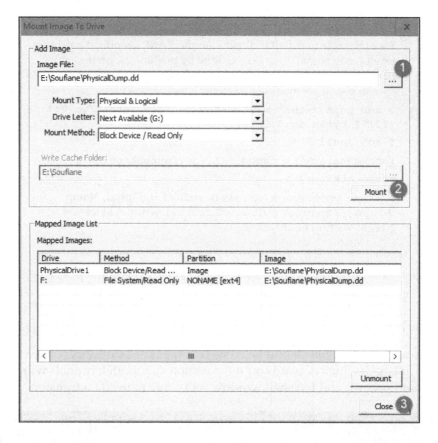

You can now find a drive mounted on the explorer, or via FTK Imager you can click on **File | Add all attached devices** and start browsing the mounted disk:

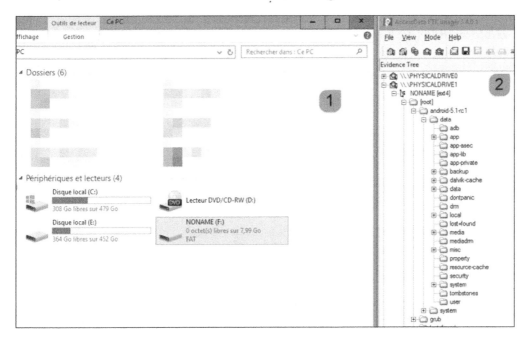

This said, a new acquisition technique was introduced by researchers Seung Jei Yang, Jung Ho Choi, Ki Bom Kim, and Tae Joo Chang; the new method is based on firmware update protocols by analyzing the commands used by the in-firmware update process. The full paper has been released and can be viewed at `http://www.sciencedirect.com/science/article/pii/S1742287615000535`.

Analyzing the acquired image using Autopsy

Autopsy is a tool by Basis Technologies; it's a free digital forensics platform and graphical interface to The Sleuth Kit (a library and collection of command line tools that allow you to investigate disk images) and other digital forensics tools. It is used by law enforcement, military, and corporate examiners to investigate what happened on a computer. Autopsy is available on Linux, Mac OS, and Windows. You can download it from `http://www.sleuthkit.org/autopsy/`.

Autopsy is an end-to-end moldable platform that, among other things, offers the **Android Analyzer** module, which we will use to explore our image.

After downloading and installing Autopsy, create a new case by filling in the case information (the base directory is where your analyzed data will be stored), as follows:

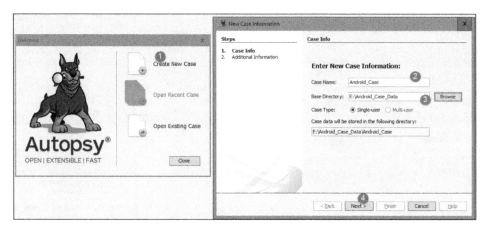

Click on **Next** and fill in the case number and examiner's name. After clicking on **Finish**, a new wizard will be displayed that will invite you to enter the data source (or your physical image) information. Make sure that the **Select source type to add** option is set to image file, browse for your image file, and click on **Next**:

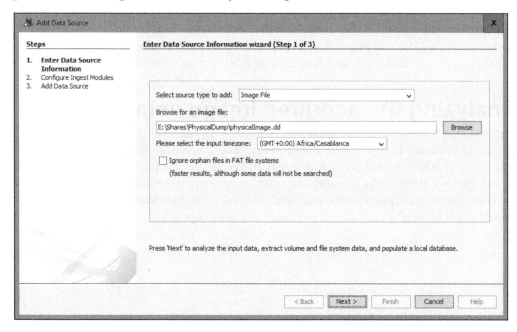

Autopsy, as specified earlier, comes with a set of modules that provide different capabilities, such as timeline analysis, hash filtering, keyword search, web artifact, and so on. It's important to know that usually, it's preferable to keep them all even if analysis will take time depending on the selected modules, but if you are dealing with an Android image, make sure that you select the **Android Analyzer** module and then click on **Next**:

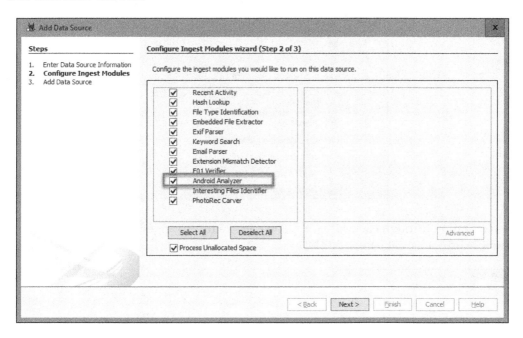

After clicking on **Next**, the main interface of Autopsy shows up and starts analyzing the loaded image dump in order to parse and to categorize eventual evidences; the analysis progress is visible and is divided into each module's status:

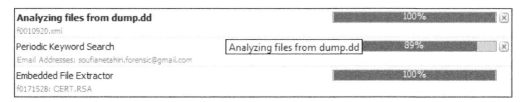

Along with your computer performance, the time taken to analyze this process depends on how big the image is and how many modules you checked before. You can see in the following screenshot that the Android Analyzer module stored the extracted content in a very fancy way:

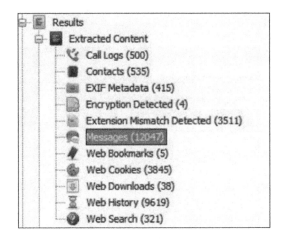

By navigating through each category, you can see the arranged evidences, for example, contacts, calls logs, or SMS:

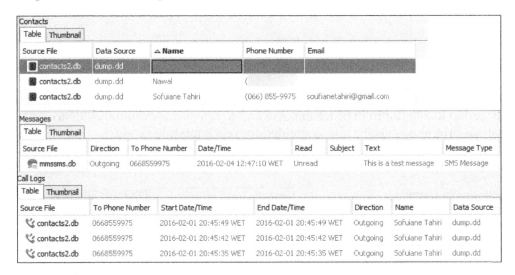

You can also navigate through the image and preview and extract files and folders within all partitions. Autopsy offers a very interesting feature, timeline analysis, which is a point not to be neglected in any forensic examination. Timeline analysis correlates time and date and all device activities (SMS, calls, e-mails, web activities, read/write, and so on). The feature can be triggered by clicking on the **Tools** menu and then the **Timeline** option and offers two different visualization types: the **Counts** view, which sums the activities that occurred in a given time frame via a stacked bar chart, and the **Details** view, which shows individual events or groups of related events:

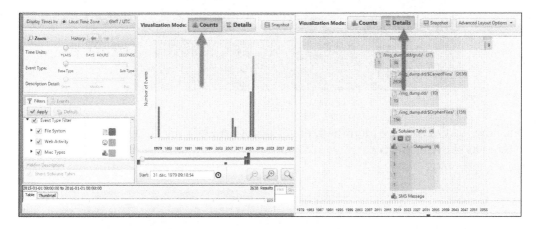

The colors in both the views represent different event types: filesystem (file modified, file accessed, file created, and file changed), web activity (downloads, cookies, bookmarks, and so on), and misc types (messages, GPS route, location history, calls, and so on). The event types can be filtered depending on your needs.

Autopsy is a user-friendly yet very efficient tool that offers a bunch of features, and in most cases it can save you from paying a forensic tool license.

JTAG and chip-off forensic examinations

Joint Test Action Group (**JTAG**) is an association created by the electronics industry for developing a method of verifying designs and testing printed circuit boards after manufacture. Even if the name is still commonly used, this industry effort has become an **Institute of Electrical and Electronics Engineers** (**IEEE**) standard entitled *Standard Test Access Port and Boundary-Scan Architecture*. Applied in a forensic context, JTAG consists usually of connecting to the standard **Test Access Port** (**TAP**) on a device and then instructing the processor to transfer raw data to a connected computer, meaning that JTAG usually requires disassembling the device.

The following are the JTAG TAPs on a disassembled Samsung Galaxy S4 (source `http://forensicswiki.org/wiki/JTAG_Samsung_Galaxy_S4_(SGH-I337)`):

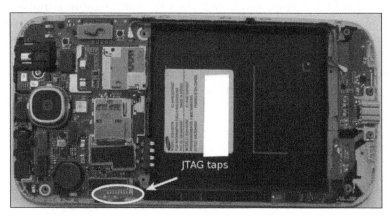

Figure 2

Once the JTAG TAPs are identified, the examiner solders the JTAG connectors to them as shown (source: `http://forensicswiki.org/wiki/JTAG_Samsung_Galaxy_S4_(SGH-I337)`):

Figure 3

Now, via the respective used JTAG box software, the acquisition can be conducted as shown (source: `http://forensicswiki.org/wiki/JTAG_Samsung_Galaxy_S4_(SGH-I337)`):

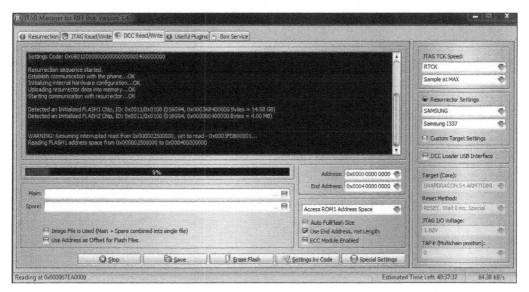

Figure 5

In this case, a RIFF Box (`http://www.riffbox.org/`) was used, which is probably the most used box in forensic examinations, as it comes with a variety of pin-outs and device support. You can find an exhaustive list of JTAG (and chip-off) boxes and tool manufacturers at `http://forensicswiki.org/wiki/JTAG_and_Chip-Off_Tools_and_Equipment`.

Acquiring a physical image using JTAG is usually an extremely technical approach and if it can be correctly conducted, the examiner can eventually gather the evidence from a turned off or even a damaged device. However, the approach is not always successful due to manufacturing constraints; this is why examiners can attempt the chip-off technique, which consists of basically removing a chip (tested and programmed using JTAG standards) from a circuit board and reading it using commercial tools.

Chip-off is by far the most expensive and intrusive method to acquire a physical image. The process itself requires heating the device's circuit board in order to melt the solder holding the chip:

The preceding image shows a device's chip about to be removed (source: `https://pressdispensary.co.uk/image_library/q991448.html`). Once the chip is successfully removed, the examiner must prepare adequate memory-reading hardware, a chip adapter, and the software that goes with it. Depending on the chip's nature (**Thin Small Outline Package (TSOP)** type, or **Bag Grid Array (BGA)** type), the cost of handling it varies.

This being said, the major difference between JTAG and chip-off remains the destructive side of chip-off, but both techniques, if successfully operated, can result in a full flash memory dump.

Third-party applications and a real case study

In today's mobile forensic world, a very big part of valuable evidence can be found by examining social media and messaging applications. The following will be a walkthrough forensic analysis of Facebook Messenger.

Facebook Messenger is the official Facebook app that lets users have text conversations with all of their connections (friends) on Facebook. Facebook Messenger offers the possibility to send and receive text messages in conversations, send and receive voice notes, make VOIP calls, share location and photos, and so on. It becomes mandatory for examiners to be prepared to investigate crimes related to online dating and social networks.

For the following investigation, a Samsung Galaxy J1 Ace running Android L 5.1.1 was the user. Facebook Messenger version 56.0.0.27.64 was installed and logically acquired from the rooted device using the `adb pull` command:

```
soufiane@soufiane-VirtualBox:~$ adb pull /data/data/com.facebook.orca /media/HostSh
ares/
pull: building file list...
pull: /data/data/com.facebook.orca/cache/image/v2.ols100.1/11/-JslGRfeva7VX79cG-QM4
7q3bk8.cnt -> /media/HostShares/cache/image/v2.ols100.1/11/-JslGRfeva7VX79cG-QM47q3
bk8.cnt
pull: /data/data/com.facebook.orca/cache/image/v2.ols100.1/11/vzlVdHTIgHSVb_XFmsuSD
fbc8eI.cnt -> /media/HostShares/cache/image/v2.ols100.1/11/vzlVdHTIgHSVb_XFmsuSDfbc
8eI.cnt
pull: /data/data/com.facebook.orca/cache/fb_voicemail_asset_725078935 -> /media/Hos
tShares/cache/fb_voicemail_asset_725078935
pull: /data/data/com.facebook.orca/files/image/v2.ols100.1/33/lFiMFn3SLjurnUb_3iNFi
_yRUY.cnt -> /media/HostShares/files/image/v2.ols100.1/33/lFiMFn3SLjurnUb_3iNFi_y
pull: /data/data/com.facebook.orca/lib -> /media/HostShares/FacebookMessenger/lib
failed to copy '/data/data/com.facebook.orca/lib' to '/media/HostShares/FacebookMes
senger/lib': Is a directory
153 files pulled. 0 files skipped.
866 KB/s (37802839 bytes in 42.586s)
```

All Facebook Messenger data can be found under `/data/data/com.facebook.orca`. The directory contains a bunch of folders and subfolders organized as follows:

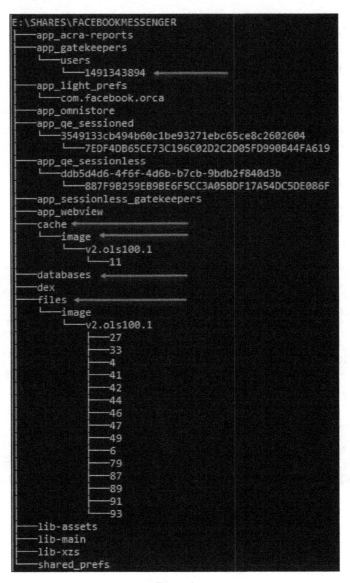

Figure 4

The screenshot highlights directories and subdirectories that potentially have valuable information. The `app_gatekeepers\users\` folder contains a directory named by the active user's Facebook ID:

```
├──app_gatekeepers
│   │   file_lock
│   │   gk_names
│   │   gk_state
│   │   gk_state.old
│   │
│   └──users
│       └──1491343894
│                   file_lock
```

You can find the corresponding profile by navigating directly using a browser to `facebook.com/1491343894`.

The `cache\image\v2.ols100.1\` and `files\image\v2.ols100.1\` folders contain numbered subdirectories, each holding a number of `.cnt` files; each file has a 27-character-long name, as follows:

By attempting to classify the filesystem of `.cnt` files using the `file` command, we can find that in fact they are just JPEG files that are renamed (*not* all `.cnt` files are JPEGs):

```
soufiane@soufiane-VirtualBox:~$ file /media/HostShares/FacebookMessenger/cache/imag
e/v2.ols100.1/11/vzlVdHTIgHSVb_XFmsuSDfbc8eI.cnt
/media/HostShares/FacebookMessenger/cache/image/v2.ols100.1/11/vzlVdHTIgHSVb_XFmsuS
Dfbc8eI.cnt: JPEG image data, JFIF standard 1.02
soufiane@soufiane-VirtualBox:~$
```

This eventually can be opened by a default viewer by changing the `.cnt` extension or by dragging and dropping individual files in a photo editor:

The `.cnt` extention is certainly an abbreviation of contact, since all files within `files\image\v2.ols100.1\` reveal the profile pictures of contacts in Messenger conversations.

Photos in `cache\image\v2.ols100.1\` can contain, in addition to profiles pictures, photos exchanged within a conversation.

You should verify each `.cnt` file's header either manually or by running the `file` command on it to determine the actual file type, as it may be, in some cases, videos, photos, or audios for audio messages.

From highlights in *Figure 4*, we can also see a `databases` folder that contains many SQLite databases named without the `.db` extension. Among the most interesting ones we can find are `contacts_db2`, `threads_db2`, `prefs_db`, and `analytics_db2`.

The `contacts_db2`, as its name reveals, holds information about the contacts in the user's Facebook Messenger account and contacts scraped from a user's phone book. It has eight tables:

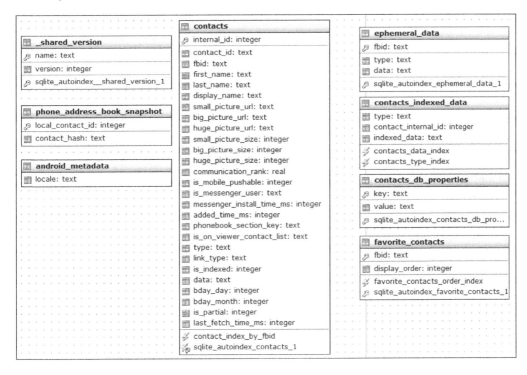

 SQLite's `sqlite_squence` table is automatically created whenever a table contains an autoincrement column. This table keeps a track of the largest `ROWID` (the physical location of a row) that a table has ever had.

Most of the valuable information is found in the `contacts` table, which is made up of 21 columns:

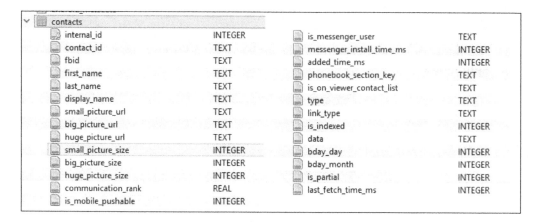

This table, as you can see from the preceding screenshot, contains the first name, the last name, Facebook ID, and the public link of a contact's profile picture for each contact:

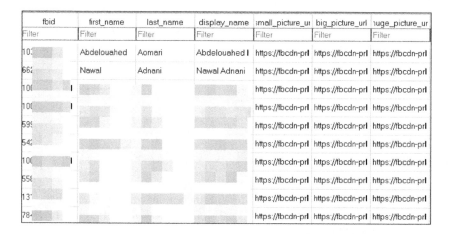

The `data` column within the same table contains a huge repository of information about each contact in the JSON/metadata format, such as the contact's day and month of birth, city name, last fetch time, and so on:

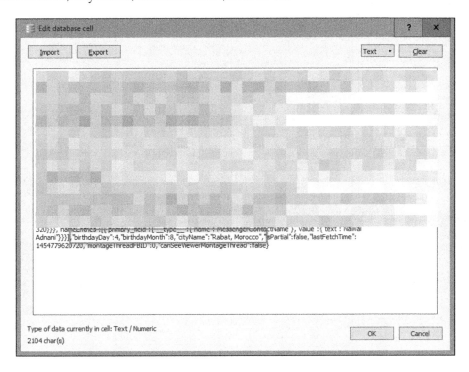

The database contains the `favourite_contacts` table, which has two columns: Facebook ID and display order:

The table holds the IDs of Facebook users that have been favored by the user. You can correlate each user back to the contacts table using its `fbid`.

The `threads_db2` database is composed of 11 tables and contains information related to sent/received messages:

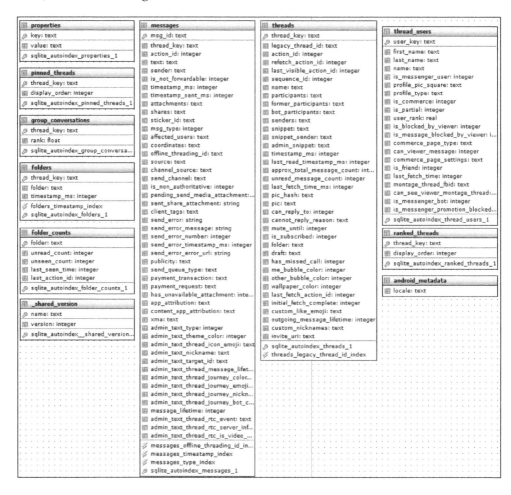

The `folders` table contains folders that the user created and when the user created them. The table `group_conversations` contains the column `thread_key`, which points to the `messages` table and contains the values for each group chat.

The main table that remains is the `messages` table; the major columns are described in the following table:

Column	Description
`msg_id`	Uniquely generated ID for each message.
`thread_key`	Uniquely generated ID for each chat session.
`text`	Contains the content of each sent/received message.
`sender`	Contains JSON data about the message sender, including sender's e-mail address, full name, and Facebook user's ID. An example is as follows: `{"email":EDITEDFORPRIVACY, "user_key":"FACEBOOK: EDITEDFORPRIVACY ","name":"Nawal Adnani"}`
`timestamp_ms`	Contains the time a message was received or sent in UNIX format.
`attachments`	Contains JSON data about sent or received attachments (file name, mime-type, file size, attachment URL, and so on).
`pending_send_media_ attachment`	Indicates the path to recover sent attachments.
`client_tags`	Contains the client used to send message (web or mobile).

You can identify the voice calls by looking for *You called Facebook User.*, *Facebook User called you.*, and *You missed a call from Facebook User.* in the `text` column of the `messages` table.

The `prefs_db` database is made of three tables, but the most interesting is the `preferences` table:

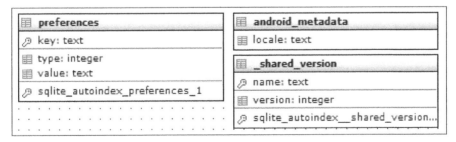

The preference table is a key-value table that contains useful metadata about sessions, user's account, and the used Messenger application. The `/auth/user_data/fb_session_cookies_string` key, for instance, holds cookie information (useful for session hijacking):

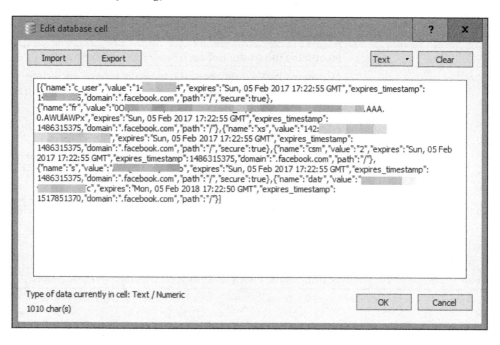

The `/auth/user_data/fb_me_user` key contains information about the authenticated user including their full name, date of birth, link to public profile picture, e-mail address, gender, phone number, and even the authentication token:

{"uid":"1491343894","first_name":"Soufiane","last_name":"Tahiri","name":"Soufiane Tahiri","birth_date_year":   "birth_date_month"   "birth_date_day"   ,"gender"   ,"emails":
[   ],"phones":[{"full_number":"+212668559975","display_number":"0668-559975","is_verified":true,"android_type":0}],"pic_square":"https://fbcdn-profile-a.akamaihd.net/hprofile-ak-xta1/v/t1.0-1/
p160x160/11949452_10204987185587960_1479973895921253134_n.jpg?_nc_ad=z-
m&oh=3a53d9240cc77f8fa4b217ea612ba532&oe=57383FF9&_gda__=1463144513_2ff976d3240a2326edbb0976c51f9e61","profile_pic_square":[{"url":"https://fbcdn-profile-a.akamaihd.net/hprofile-ak-xta1/v/t1.0-1/
p160x160/11949452_10204987185587960_1479973895921253134_n.jpg?_nc_ad=z-m&oh=3a53d9240cc77f8fa4b217ea612ba532&oe=57383FF9&_gda__=1463144513_2ff976d3240a2326edbb0976c51f9e61","size":160},
{"url":"https://fbcdn-profile-a.akamaihd.net/hprofile-ak-xta1/v/t1.0-1/p320x320/11949452_10204987185587960_1479973895921253134_n.jpg?_nc_ad=z-
m&oh=068c1476f65a76b54f62bdeebf5f900e&oe=572767EE&_gda__=1462958422_da32e8dac6307ba68df767015a5e0f6d","size":320},{"url":"https://fbcdn-profile-a.akamaihd.net/hprofile-ak-xta1/v/
t1.0-1/11949452_10204987185587960_1479973895921253134_n.jpg?_nc_ad=z-m&oh=e88a029c38d04e4a2c8442f57940a56d&oe=576941488&_gda__=1462227997_1451488017a18bd402a292d2ce171e4a","size":
960}],"is_pushable":true,"type":"user","auth_token":"   ","profile_picture_is_silhouette":false,"montage_thread_fbid":
0,"can_see_viewer_montage_thread":false,"is_deactivated_allowed_on_messenger":false}

Finally, the `analytics_db2` database contains four tables, as shown:

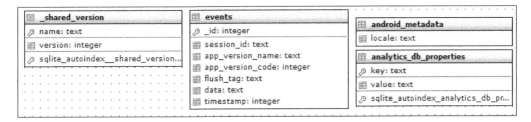

The `analytics_db_properties` table contains the active session ID, the active user's ID, and last activity time, which is very important from a forensic point of view:

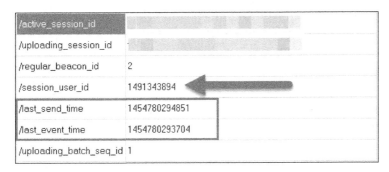

The `events` table contains exhaustive details about every single activity within a session in the form of JSON data and stored in the `data` column. Data can be extracted when a notification is dropped and when a message is read locally, when a message is sent or received, and when it is delivered, including the message ID (which can be correlated with the `msg_id` of `messages` table). The `events` table contains some kind of in-depth analytics related to all the activities using Facebook Messenger. An example of how the data is stored is as follows:

{"time":"1454779996.318","log_type":"client_event","name":"messaging_pub_ack","extra":{"status":"success_puback","retry_count":"0","sent_timestamp_ms":"1454779970023","first_message_first_send_delta":"25002","client_tag_trigger":"neue_main_recent
{"time":"1454779996.800","log_type":"client_event","name":"delivery_receipt_received","extra":{"watermark_timestamp":"1454779917721","message_id":"mid:1454779937712ew158e1acb393305:2","sequence_id":"46394","user_fbid":"1
{"time":"1454780001.091","log_type":"client_event","name":"messaging_send_via_mqtt","extra":{"status":"success","first_send_delta":"29656","initial_mqtt_push_state":"CONNECTED","current_time":"1454780000949","mqtt_push_state":"CONNECTED","retry}

Summary

In this chapter, we had a look at the Android architecture and its security models, how they are inherited and implemented; we saw how disk encryption has evolved through Android versions, and how Android deals with sandboxes, SELinux, and application signing; then we discussed various techniques for bypassing lock screens and how to crack PINs and passwords. This chapter tried to clarify the importance of rooting Android devices in order to help investigators gather the most evidence from it.

Having a sound knowledge of Android internals, security implementation, and lock screen bypasses lets us understand some techniques related to logical and physical acquisitions using different techniques. This chapter explained how we can acquire (logically and physically) an Android image and how we can analyze it using a free and open source tool (Autopsy), and introduced the JTAG and chip-off techniques, the differences between them, and how they are used in a forensic context.

This chapter demonstrated how the widely used instant-messaging application Facebook Messenger is stored and how it stores its data on an Android device, and then we went through its different databases to determine how evidence is stored.

The next chapter will discuss techniques and tools used in order to forensically acquire and analyze a Windows Phone 8.x device.

5
Windows Phone 8 Forensics

The purpose of this chapter is to introduce **Windows Phone 8 (WP8)**. In the first part of this chapter, we will see the main differences between WP7 and WP8. Further on, we will go through Windows 8 internals and describe the WP8 security models and their implementation. This chapter will also describe the WP filesystem, following which we will go through the steps to logically acquire a Windows Phone 8 device and describe WP PINs and hardware encryption. We will also describe evidence location in the Windows Phone registry and analyze the Windows Phone PIN.

This chapter will cover the following topics:

- Windows Phone 8 internals
- Partitions and the filesystem
- Windows Phone 8 security models
- Windows Phone 8 data protection
- Windows Phone 8 logical acquisition
- Windows Phone cloud acquisition
- JTAG and physical acquisition
- Artifact location and user PIN study

Windows Phone 7 versus Windows Phone 8

Windows Phone is Microsoft's smartphone operating system developed as a successor of Windows Mobile. In contrast to Windows Mobile, Windows Phone mainly targets customer markets rather than the enterprise market. This explains the significant progress it has made in the global smartphone market, moving it to third position based on market share.

Windows Phone 7 was the first public release announced in 2010. In 2011, Microsoft announced WP 7.5, which included the mobile version of Internet Explorer 9, Twitter integration of People Hub, multitasking of third-party applications, and Windows SkyDrive access. In October 2012, Microsoft announced Windows Phone 8, a newly built operating system based on the Windows NT kernel (instead of Windows CE) sharing many components with Windows 8. In April 2014, Windows Phone 8.1 added new features like the notification center, separate volume control, and inclusion of Apple's Siri-like voice assistant, **Cortana**.

Basically, the major difference between WP 7.x and WP 8.x is the fact that WP 8.x is the first mobile OS that uses the Windows NT kernel, the same kernel found in desktop versions of Windows 8; this switch is very important from both security and forensic points of view.

The implementation of the Windows NT kernel in WP 8.x implied core improvement of the filesystem and security components and enables support for multicores CPUs, support for microSD cards, native BitLocker encryption, and Secure Boot. Windows Phone 8.x uses **Windows Runtime (WinRT)**, proposing a totally new programming model. Unmanaged APIs based on a lightweight version of **Component Object Model (COM)** allow the WinRT component to be interfaced with from both managed and unmanaged languages. On the other hand, Windows Phone 7.x supports only managed code and can run only applications coded using C# or VB.Net; there is no native access to the system or phone hardware, and therefore, it's impossible to update WP 7.x to WP 8 due to limitations in hardware capabilities on previously released WP hardware.

The kernel adopted is the same as Windows 8 and includes two distinct components when it comes to smartphones: the NT Kernel, the **NT filesystem (NTFS)**, and the network layer as part of the Windows Core System and Mobile Core that includes relevant components for a mobile platform such as Internet Explorer's rendering engine (Trident) and CoreCLR.

Windows Phone 8 internals

Based on the Windows NT kernel, Windows Phone 8.x uses the Core System to boot, manage hardware, authenticate, and communicate on networks. The Core System is a minimal Windows system that contains low-level security features and is supplemented by a set of Windows Phone-specific binaries from Mobile Core to handle phone-specific tasks; this makes it the only distinct architectural entity (from desktop-based Windows) in Windows Phone. The following is an abstract representation of the Windows 8 and Windows Phone 8.x layers:

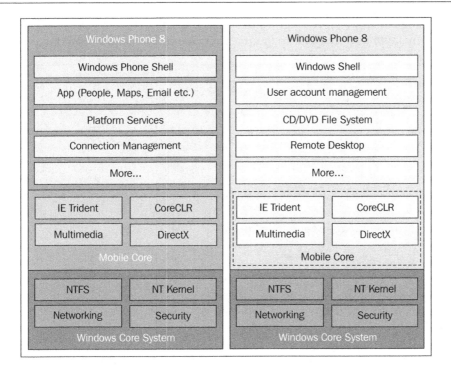

 Windows contains the same components as Mobile Core, but they are part of a larger set of functionality.

Windows and Windows Phone are completely aligned at the Windows Core System and run exactly the same code at this level. The shared core actually consists of the Windows Core System and Mobile Core where the APIs are the same, but the code at the backend has been changed to serve mobile needs.

As most mobile operating systems, Windows Phone has a pretty layered architecture. The kernel and OS layers are mainly provided and supported by Microsoft, but some layers are provided by Microsoft's partners, depending on hardware properties. These layers are provided in the form of a **Board Support Package (BSP)**, which usually consists of a set of drivers and support libraries that ensure low-level hardware interaction and boot process created by the CPU supplier. Additionally, it comes through **Original Equipment Manufacturers (OEMs)** and **independent hardware vendors (IHVs)** that write the required drivers to support the phone hardware and specific components.

The following is a high-level diagram describing the Windows Phone architecture organized by layer and ownership (source: `https://sysdev.microsoft.com`):

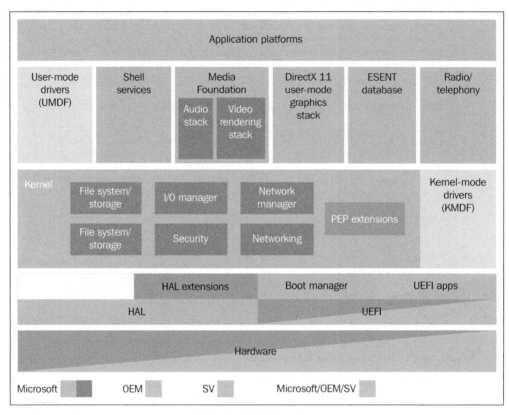

SV refers to SoC vendor

Above the lowest level (hardware level) comes the layer responsible for the boot process. After the phone's **System on Chip (SoC)** bootloaders initialize all the hardware components, they boot the **Unified Extensible Firmware Interface (UEFI)** and hand over the control to the UEFI applications (written by OEMs, SoC vendors, and Microsoft itself) to use UEFI drivers and services. At this point, to deal with all requirements of the Windows Phone boot modes (normal/update/restore/flash), the UEFI environment launches the Boot Manager, which determines the boot mode.

The following diagram describes this high-level process:

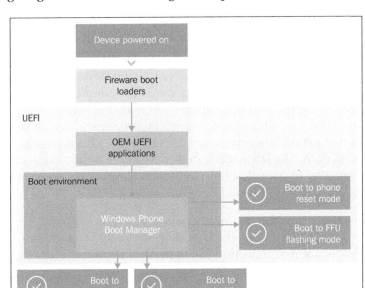

To facilitate interaction between the hardware and the rest of the operating system, Microsoft provides the **Hardware Abstraction Layer** (**HAL**), which offers routines that can be used to abstract the low-level hardware details from drivers and the OS; if the HAL needs any extensions, the SoC vendors add their own HAL as HAL extension.

The Windows Core includes the **Kernel-Mode Drivers Framework** (**KMDF**). This framework is responsible for the Windows Kernel-Mode I/O Manager, which manages communication between applications and the interfaces provided by device drivers, the filesystem, and storage. It is also responsible for the Kernel-Mode Memory Manager, which manages physical memory (Random Access Memory) by handling the allocation/deallocation of memory (virtually and dynamically) and by supporting memory-mapped files, shared memory, and copy-on-write. The KMDF also provides support for the **Human Interface Device** (**HID**) class drivers and the Kernel-Mode Security Reference Monitor (this makes sure that any action taking place on the OS is not violating system policy). The KM Security Reference Monitor provides routines to work with **Access Control List** (**ACL**). The Windows Core also provides low-level network components. All these Kernel-Mode drivers are provided by Microsoft. Another stack is provided by the respective SoC vendors, added to the Windows Core, that is, **Power Management Engine plug-in** (**PEP**) extensions, which are third-party extensions to the Windows power management architecture. The PEP communicates with the power management integrated circuit through some bus to manage power rails and clock resources.

The Mobile Core has the **User-Mode Drivers Framework (UMDF)**, which abstracts hardware functionalities and runs in the user-mode environment. This stack is provided exclusively by Microsoft and includes CoreCLR, Shell Services, Media Foundation APIs (audio and video rendering stacks that offer the possibility to access and sync media files on the device), and the DirectX 11 graphics layer, inheriting several features previously available only on desktops (Direct2D APIs, DirectWrite APIs, Windows Imaging Component APIs, and so on). The Mobile Core also includes the **Extensible Storage Engine (ESENT)** that allows applications to store and retrieve data via indexed and sequential access, and which is optimized for applications that need high-performance and low-overhead storage of structured or semi-structured data. The latest stack in this big layer is the radio/telephony stack, which is an asset to APIs that help in the development of communications applications for Microsoft Windows Phone.

At the top of the Kernel resides the main operating system within the application platforms layer. It is a sub-layered stack made principally of the Windows Phone Shell, System Application, Connection Management, and Platform Services, as seen in the following diagram:

Windows Phone Shell				Windows Phone OS
System Applications				
Connection Management				
Platform Services				
Package Manager	Execution Manager	Navigation Server	Resource Manager	

Let's see the stack:

- **Package Manager**: It handles the application's life cycle. It's responsible for installations and uninstallations and for maintaining the application metadata.

- **Execution Manager**: This is responsible for creating the hosting processes of applications and controls the logical aspects of the application's execution lifetime and background agents.

- **Navigation Server**: It manages all the movement between the foreground applications on the phone. The Navigation Server works with the Execution Manager to orchestrate which application to start or which application to reactivate.

- **Resource Manager**: It is responsible for monitoring the system's resources (CPU and memory usage) by enforcing constraints on the active processes.

Partitions and the filesystem

When it comes to the Windows Phone, the key physical aspects of the data structure in data store are not very well documented. Microsoft divides the architecture of the Windows Phone storage model into five main sections: The **partition** layout describes which partitions are defined on internal storage and what each partition is responsible for. **Expandable storage** refers to how to use an SD card to expand the storage capabilities of the device. The **Folder** layout explains how folders are organized on the device and defines the API you use to access those folders. **Storage utilization** explains how the use of storage is presented to the user and the methods that you can use to clean up the storage. Lastly, the **phone storage service** refers to the service that runs in response to certain storage events. Most of the documentation is exclusively available to OEMs and paid company accounts.

A very interesting research has been conducted by Adrian Leong, aka Cheeky4n6Monkey, on a physical copy of a Windows Phone device (`http://cheeky4n6monkey.blogspot.com/2014/10/awesome-windows-phone-8-stuff.html`) in which 28 partitions have been detected after parsing the JTAG physical image. For example, most of the partitions (26/28) are related to SoC for handling different bootloaders, as seen in the following screenshot:

```
DPP (1) [8MB]
MODEM_FSG (2) [3MB]
SSD (3) [0MB]
SBL1 (4) [1MB]
SBL2 (5) [1MB]
SBL3 (6) [2MB]
UEFI (7) [2MB]
RPM (8) [0MB]
TZ (9) [0MB]
WINSECAPP (10) [0MB]
BACKUP_SBL1 (11) [1MB]
BACKUP_SBL2 (12) [1MB]
BACKUP_SBL3 (13) [2MB]
BACKUP_UEFI (14) [2MB]
BACKUP_RPM (15) [0MB]
BACKUP_TZ (16) [0MB]
BACKUP_WINSECAPP (17) [0MB]
UEFI_BS_NV (18) [0MB]
UEFI_NV (19) [0MB]
PLAT (20) [8MB]
EFIESP (21) [64MB]
MODEM_FS1 (22) [3MB]
MODEM_FS2 (23) [3MB]
UEFI_RT_NV (24) [0MB]
UEFI_RT_NV_RPMB (25) [0MB]
MMOS (26) [78MB]
MainOS (27) [2244MB]
Data (28) [27347MB]
```

Lumia 920 (Windows Phone 8.1) partitions

There are three main partitions on the Windows Phone that are forensically interesting: **MainOS**, **Data**, and **Removable User Data** (not visible in the preceding screenshot since Lumia 920 does not support SD cards). The MainOS partition contains all the Windows Phone operating system components. The Data partition stores all of the user's data, third-party applications, and the state of all applications. The Removable User Data partition is considered by Windows Phone as a separate volume and refers to all the data stored in the SD card (on devices that support SD cards).

Each of the previously described partitions follows a folder layout and can be mapped to their root folders with predefined Access Control Lists. Each ACL is in the form of a list of **Access Control Entries (ACE)**. Each ACE identifies the user account to which it applies (trustee) and specifies the access right allowed, denied, or audited for that trustee.

MainOS volume

The MainOS volume, as mentioned earlier, contains all the operating system components. Just like the desktop-based Windows, its path is `C:\` and it has the environment variable `%SystemDrive%`, which refers to the main operating system partition. Several root folders are generated as part of the OS's image — the following diagram shows the most important ones:

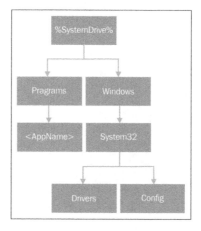

Let's see the folders:

- `%SystemDrive%\Programs`: This root folder contains all the built-in applications; each application is installed in a separated folder, `<AppName>`, as you can see in the following screenshot:

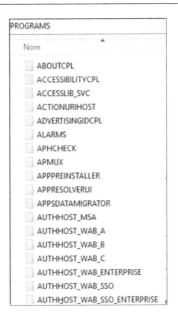

- `%SystemDrive%\Programs\<AppName>`: This folder contains all the installation files of a given application. The `<AppName>` is unique to each application and can be either a GUID or a display name. Each application has Read/Execute ACL applied to its folder. The next screenshot shows the FINDMYPHONE application folder:

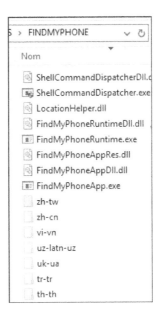

- `%SystemDrive%\Windows`: This root folder holds all the read-only data files that are part of the main operating system; this includes built-in system executables, drivers, and services. The only writable file that this folder contains is the system registry. We can find the following subdirectories in this folder, as seen in the next screenshot:

  ○ `%SystemDrive%\Windows\System32`: Contains system executables and read-only data files

  ○ `%SystemDrive%\Windows\System32\Drivers`: Contains system drivers

  ○ `%SystemDrive%\Windows\System32\Config`: Contains system registry

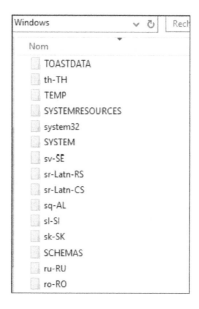

User Data volume

Similarly to the MainOS volume, the User Data volume has its environment path, which refers to the partition as `%DataDrive%`, and the physical path is `C:\Data`. The following diagram shows how Microsoft describes the full User Data partition folder layout:

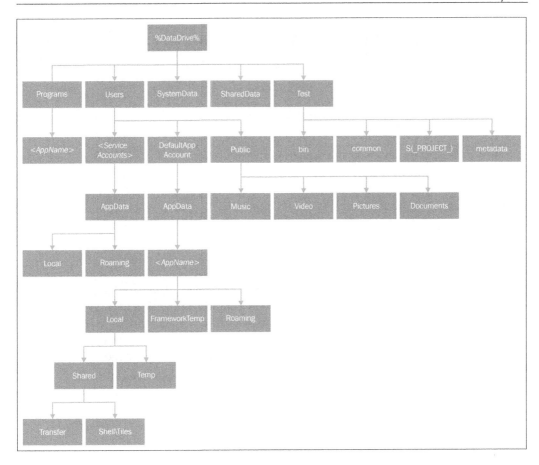

The \Programs folder contains all installed applications that come from the
Windows Store. In the MainOS folders layout, the \programs folder contains as
many \<AppNames> folders as installed applications, where AppNames represents the
application's unique GUID or the application's name. The \Users folder holds the
default user account, built-in services, and public data folders. As subdirectories of
the \Users folder, you can find the following:

- \<Service Accounts>: It contains service application data, including user
  accounts for all services except LocalService and NetworkService system
  services. Services have Full Access except Write DACL (the ability to modify
  the ACL) applied ACL (FA-WDCL).

- \DefaultAppAccount: This contains all applications' data, and there is a single default user account profile for this data, as seen in the following screenshot:

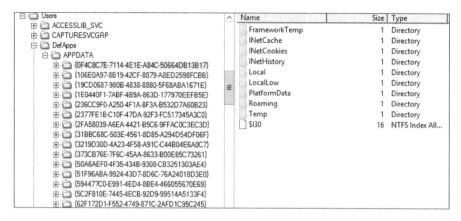

- \Public: This contains all data that does not belong to a single application and data that is stored outside a given isolated application storage. In general, \Public directory contains media files (music, videos, and photos) and Microsoft Office documents. Subdirectories of \Public have self-explanatory names, which are as follows (seen in the next screenshot):

  ° Music

  ° Video

  ° Pictures

  ° Documents

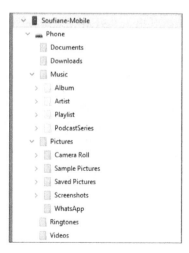

At the same level as the \Users folder are \SystemData, which contains system-wide files, and \SharedData, a directory used by applications to share content (its subdirectories are created by an application's components). The \test folder is aimed at development purposes and does not contain data. It contains the following subdirectories:

- \bin: A test binary deployment folder

- \common: Contains common configuration values

- \ $(_PROJECT_): One directory per build project. Everything required by test is deployed to this directory

- \metadata: Includes metadata for packages and binaries and contains information about test dependencies

Removable User Data

Windows Phone considers **Secure Digital (SD)** cards as a separate volume and supports only one SD card that is mounted as a separate drive assigned to D:\, with %RemovableDataDrive% as the variable environment. The folder layout for SD cards is similar to the %DataDrive% (\Users\Public) data layout in the User Data volume, as seen in the following diagram:

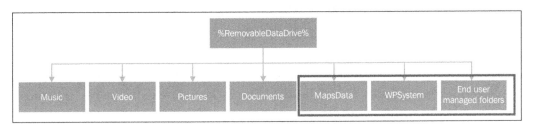

As highlighted in the preceding diagram, the %RemovableDataDrive% directory contains two more folders other than the folders found in \Public in the internal storage: \MapsData, which stores maps data, and \WPSystem, which contains metadata specific to the operating system such as the cache and thumbnails. In addition to this, any content loaded by the user, in any folder layout, is considered as an end user managed folder.

Windows Phone 8.1 supports the following content on SD cards:

- Applications

- Music

- Photos

- Videos

- Map data
- Sideloading application XAPs
- User content in non-system managed locations like eBooks

Even though MainOS and User Data partitions are in the NTFS filesystem, Windows Phone supports only **Secure Digital High Capacity** (**SDHC**) cards in the FAT filesystem format (for cards up to 32 GB) and SD Extended Capacity cards in the exFAT filesystem format (for cards up to 2 TB).

The filesystem adopted in the internal storage is one of the many advantages of opting for the NT Kernel on Windows Phone 8+. The **New Technology File System** (**NTFS**) has improved support for metadata, improved performance and disk space utilization in addition to the "built-in" ACL, and filesystem journaling. The NTFS filesystem has many benefits over the FAT and exFAT filesystems, and a high-level comparison can be found at `http://windows.microsoft.com/en-us/windows-vista/comparing-ntfs-and-fat-file-systems` and `https://support.microsoft.com/en-us/kb/100108`.

Application data storage

Application data refers to data that applications create and manage. Application data, obviously, depends on the application and its life cycle and is only meaningful to that application. The physical storage of application data is managed by the operating system.

Each application is installed in its own isolated storage. In addition to this, each application state separates their data according to the nature of the data in separate folders. All installed applications go to `\AppData`, located at `%DataDrive%\Users\DefaultAppAccount\AppData\`.

This folder contains as many subdirectories as the installed applications. Each subdirectory is created by the application at install time, and is given a GUID equivalent to the application Windows Store ID; all application data must be stored within this subdirectory.

The folders that exist in `%DataDrive%\Users\DefaultAppAccount\AppData\<WindowsStoreID>` are as follows:

- `\< WindowsStoreID >\Local`: Contains all the data that is installed on the device and which will not be synchronized with other devices on which the user has installed the application. The content of this folder can be backed up in the cloud.

- `\< WindowsStoreID >\Roaming`: This folder contains all the data that can be replicated in other devices on which the user has installed the application.

- `\< WindowsStoreID >\Local\Shared`: This folder is used only by Store applications and contains legacy support for the shared content.

- `\< WindowsStoreID >\Local\Shared\Transfer`: This folder is used only by Store applications and holds the data used by the Background Transfer Service to download/upload files for the application.

- `\< WindowsStoreID >\Local\Shared\Shell\Tiles`: Used for live tiles updates.

- `\< WindowsStoreID >\Local\Temp`: Contains temporary files that the application framework can delete in response to a low-storage notification.

Windows phone 8 security models

Windows Phone 8.x is a very closed operating system. Documenting its internals and security model is usually a painful task, but like all other operating systems, WP 8.x provides many key platform security features to protect OS integrity, user's data, and privacy.

To ensure system and user's data integrity, Windows Phone 8 mainly relies on Secure Boot and the application platform security.

Windows Phone 8 Secure Boot

Windows Phone validates firmware images before loading the main operating system using the Secure Boot technology, which is built on a chain of trust extended to hardware and firmware. During manufacturing, a "root of trust" is made by provisioning the hash of the public key used by the SoC vendors and original manufacturers to sign the initial bootloaders. Thus, Secure Boot cryptographically validates all the boot components from the pre-UEFI bootloader to the UEFI environment followed by the main operating system and all the drivers and applications that run on it. The implementation of the UEFI itself respects the UEFI specifications standard available at `http://www.uefi.org/specifications`. The UEFI firmware/hardware level is layered (at its high level) as follows:

	UEFI Secure Boot	Code-signed chain of trust
	Certified hardware	TPM 2.0 – all phones

The integration of cryptographic keys at the hardware level respects standards as described by the second version of the **Trusted Platform Module (TPM)** to ensure platform integrity and to offer (among others) the possibility of full-disk encryption. TPM 2.0 makes use of cryptography algorithms like SHA-1, SHA-256, and RSA. (To learn more about TPM, you can check the whitepaper from SANS at `https://www.sans.org/reading-room/whitepapers/analyst/implementing-hardware-roots-trust-trusted-platform-module-age-35070`.)

The Secure Boot workflow can be outlined as follows:

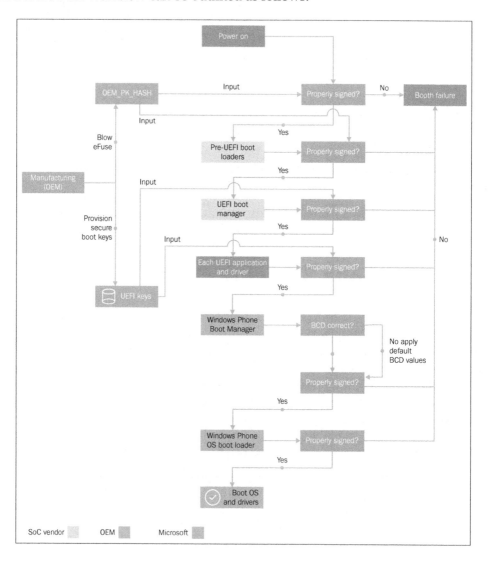

Assuming the scenario in which all verifications succeed, the very first stage of integrity checks start by booting the device, which triggers the process of validating the pre-UEFI bootloaders against the root of trust. This loads (if integrity is verified) the UEFI boot manager. The UEFI boot manager loads, among others, all the UEFI drivers and the Windows Phone boot manager—a UEFI component provided by Microsoft, which ensures that the **Boot Configuration Data (BCD)** settings are correct. If the settings are not right, the Windows Phone Boot Manager will restore the BCD entries to the default value, and will continue by validating the operating system bootloader. At this stage, the Windows Phone OS bootloader checks the integrity of both the boot drivers and the kernel before continuing with the process of validating (or not) all drivers and applications. If the verification fails at any level, the boot process simply aborts.

Windows Phone 8 application security

The application platform and application security model implemented in Windows Phone 8.x is one of the most complete and secure models in the smartphone market. Beyond the fact that Windows Phone is built on top of the desktop version of the Windows's kernel, Windows Phone remains a much more closed environment as compared to Windows.

The very first security mechanism that applies to the Windows Phone application is **Code Signing**; all code must be digitally signed by Microsoft in order to ensure running only trusted code. All applications submitted to the Windows Store (the successor of Windows Marketplace) are subjected to Microsoft's submission process before being signed with a certificate issued by a certificate authority (at the time of writing this chapter, Symantec is the exclusive provider of code signing certificates for the Microsoft App Hub service: `http://www.symantec.com/code-signing/windows-phone/`). In addition to application code signing, OS system files are also digitally signed and verified at runtime; this prevents a file's execution if any data tampering has occurred.

The Windows Phone application security infrastructure also provides WP 8.x with what is called **chambers** or **sandboxes**. The implementation of application sandboxing in Windows Phone 8.x inherits from the NT security primitives meant to control an application's access to system resources and prevents them from acceding other applications' data.

The process-isolation mechanism in Windows Phone 8.x is in the form of
AppContainers (as introduced by Microsoft in their *Understanding Enhanced
Protected Mode* post, which can be found at `https://blogs.msdn.microsoft.com/`
`ieinternals/2012/03/23/understanding-enhanced-protected-mode/`). The
official statement is:

> *Windows 8 introduces a new security sandbox, called AppContainer, that offers
> more fine-grained security permissions and which blocks Write and Read Access
> to most of the system. There's not a lot of documentation specifically about
> AppContainer because all Metro-style applications run in AppContainers, so most
> of the documentation is written from that point of view [...] it's the AppContainer
> that helps ensure that an App does not have access to capabilities that it hasn't
> declared and been granted by the user.*

To define the permissions that can be granted to a given AppContainer, sandboxes in
Windows Phone are influenced by capabilities, requested using the `WPAppManifest.`
`xml` file of the application. The following is a high level abstraction of the Windows
Phone 8.x chambers:

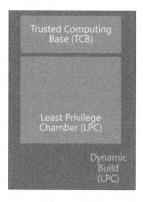

As seen in the preceding diagram, Windows Phone 8.x has two distinct chambers:
Trusted Computing Base (TCB) and **Least Privilege Chamber (LPC)**. The OS's
kernel and all the kernel-mode drivers operate in the TCB chamber, which means
that this is the chamber that has the most rights and privileges. For everything else
(applications developed by Microsoft, OEM, and third-party Windows Store apps),
Windows Phone 8.x applies the principle of *Least Privilege* very strictly by running
apps in the Least Privilege Chamber. By default, few privileges and permissions are
granted to applications, and to be able to grant a "special" privilege like accessing
the camera or using networks features, the application must explicitly request
capabilities at install time.

Capabilities needed in order to carry out different application's tasks must be explicitly specified by the application developer by editing the `WPAppManifest.xml` file. Accessing the camera, microphone, or geolocation are examples of typical capability requests in the Store application. Each capability is an entry in the manifest file that, while installing the app, notifies the user of special software capabilities that the app receives. The following are examples of some capabilities as described by Microsoft:

- `ID_CAP_APPOINTMENTS`: Provides access to appointment data

- `ID_CAP_CONTACTS`: Provides access to contacts data

- `ID_CAP_IDENTITY_DEVICE`: Provides access to device-specific information such as a unique device ID, the manufacturer, or the model name

Once the capabilities are parsed from the manifest file, and explicitly granted by the user at install time, the application's LPC chamber is then provisioned with these capabilities.

The following is an example of the capabilities that are required by WhatsApp:

```
<App xmlns="" ProductID="{218a0ebb-1585-4c7e-a9ec-054cf4569a79}"
Title="WhatsApp" RuntimeType="Silverlight" Version="2.11.312.0"
Genre="apps.normal" Author="WhatsApp Inc." Description=""
Publisher="WhatsApp Inc." PublisherID="{c210c6cb-ed53-478d-a7d8-
86982edf24a1}" IsBeta="false" PublisherId="{bc29b09f-c297-48d6-b6b5-
88c7234f4b6d}">
<IconPath IsRelative="true" IsResource="false">Icon1.png</IconPath>
<Capabilities>
<Capability Name="ID_CAP_OEMPUBLICDIRECTORY" />
<Capability Name="ID_CAP_VOIP" />
<Capability Name="ID_CAP_IDENTITY_DEVICE" />
```

Windows Phone data protection

Windows Phone 8.x addresses data protection by mitigating the risk of unauthorized access to the device's data via two major mechanisms: the first is by controlling device access and applying security policies, and the second is by offering BitLocker technology that lets a user fully encrypt the device's disk.

Device access and security policies

The Windows Phone provides a first stage security mechanism, like most other smartphone operating systems, in the form of a PIN or password. Access to a Windows Phone device can be controlled by setting up a PIN via the settings panel to lock access to the device. The Windows Phone does not provide a built-in pattern lock mechanism.

PINs are set in the **lock screen** option found under the **Settings** menu, as seen in the following screenshot:

Once the lock screen PIN is set, the user can configure a timeout to require it after anywhere between 30 seconds and 30 minutes.

As for most of Microsoft's products, dealing with passwords, passcodes, and dealing with a PIN in the case of Windows Phone, requires storing a hash value in the Windows Phone registry. We will go through a detailed analysis of the Windows Phone PIN in a later section of this chapter.

Windows Phone 8+ also offers the possibility to make use of Exchange ActiveSync v14.1 (a protocol allowing reconciling data between the device and an appropriate Microsoft Exchange server) to synchronize functionalities and policy controls previously set by an IT administrator. This ability to synchronize with a Microsoft Exchange server makes it possible to add password policies for managing password length and complexity. It's also important to note that in the case of syncing with an Exchange Server, the IT administrator can initiate a remote device wipe by using the Exchange Server Management Console.

BitLocker and hardware encryption

Starting with Windows Vista, Microsoft introduced BitLocker as a full disk encryption technology, which is designed to protect users' data by encrypting an entire volume. Windows Phone 8+ uses the same technology to support the encryption of the entire phone's internal data storage.

BitLocker, by default, uses AES with a 128-bit or 256-bit key, depending on the configuration in **Cipher Block Chaining** (**CBC**). (More information on AES-CBC + Elephant diffuser and the white paper is available at `https://www.microsoft.com/en-us/download/details.aspx?id=13866`.) The good news is that there is no "simple" way to turn on device encryption on a Windows Phone device, and the option can only be activated either via the Exchange ActiveSync policy (**Require Device Encryption**) or the Device Management Policy. After being enabled, BitLocker relies on the encryption key protected by TPM 2.0 (as described in the *Windows Phone 8 Secure Boot* section of this chapter), which is a tamper-resistant physical chip bound to the trusted boot chain.

The decryption process is triggered at the very first stage of booting, just after the initialization of the TPM. The interaction with other UEFI-trusted boot components lets the TPM store component measurements in the TPM's **Platform Configuration Registers** (**PCRs**). Once the integrity of the PCR values is checked, the TPM uses the **Storage Root Key** (**SRK**) to decrypt the **Volume Master Key** (**VMK**). The encrypted **Full Volume Encryption Key** (**FVEK**) is then read from the volume and the decrypted VMK is used to decrypt it. The disk sectors are decrypted with the FVEK as they are accessed to deliver plaintext data to applications and processes.

The following figure describes the overall process (source: `https://technet.microsoft.com/en-us/library/cc162804.aspx`):

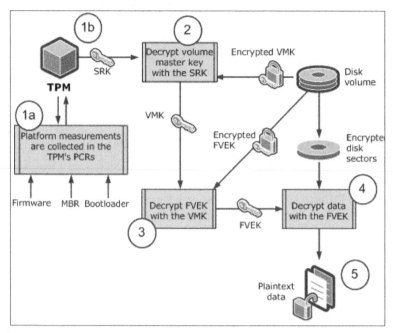

The logical flow of BitLocker decryption process in BitLocker with TPM option

The strength of the AES algorithm and the hardware protection used make decrypting a Windows Phone BitLocker encrypted volume not possible at the time of writing this book. According to Microsoft (`http://blogs.msdn.com/b/si_team/archive/2006/03/02/542590.aspx`), BitLocker is a backdoor free technology, which means that, at the time this chapter is being written, there is no way to recover data from an encrypted device.

Windows Phone logical acquisition

Windows Phone 8.x is one of the most challenging smartphone operating systems in a forensics context. Common acquisition methods are not fully supported and only a few available forensic tools can perform partial logical acquisitions from Windows Phone devices.

Most of the commercial tools offer only very limited data acquisition or only over-the-air (cloud) acquisition, as we will see in the following sections. As most forensic examiners rely on forensic tools, facing a Windows Phone 8.x device remains a relatively big deal, especially when some tools list some devices as supported even if that's not the case. The **Computer Forensic Tool Testing (CFTT)** program of the National Institute of Standards and Technology publicly reports test results for mobile device acquisition tools (`http://www.cftt.nist.gov/mobile_devices.htm`), and almost all tools fail when acquiring data from Windows-based devices. Phone Forensics Express v2.1.2.2761 was not able to connect to a Nokia Lumia 920 device (a test conducted on December 18, 2015. The report is available at `http://www.dhs.gov/sites/default/files/publications/508_Test Report_NIST_Mobile_Phone%20Forensics%20Express%20v2.1.2.2761_December%202015.pdf`). MOBILedit Forensic v7.8.3.6085 was able to successfully connect to an HTC Win 8x, HTC PM2330, and a Nokia Lumia 920 but no data was extracted. When selecting Phonebook from the connected device's pane, the following error occurs: *Requested operation is not implemented in current version (00002AFD)* (the report dates to December 18, 2015 and is available at `https://www.dhs.gov/sites/default/files/publications/508_Test%20Report_NIST_Mobile_MOBILedit%20Forensic%20v7.8.3.6085_December%202015.pdf`) MOBILedit's result remains the same if we try to extract the Phonebook even with the latest version, 8.2.0.8069 (at the time of writing this chapter), but the tool can access public folders (normally accessible via computer explorer).

Windows Phone logical acquisition using MOBILedit! Forensic 8.2

To acquire the \Public data using MOBILedit Forensic, make sure the device is unlocked, then connect it using a USB cable. Once detected, click on the device as seen in the following screenshot:

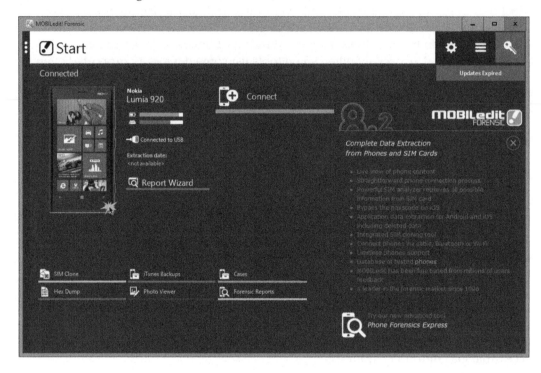

The tool offers two options: acquiring the device's **Phonebook** and exploring **Files**:

The **Phonebook** option results in the previously described error:

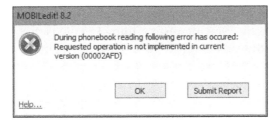

The **File** option acquires data from the `Documents`, `Downloads`, `Music`, `Pictures`, `Ringtones`, and `Videos` folders:

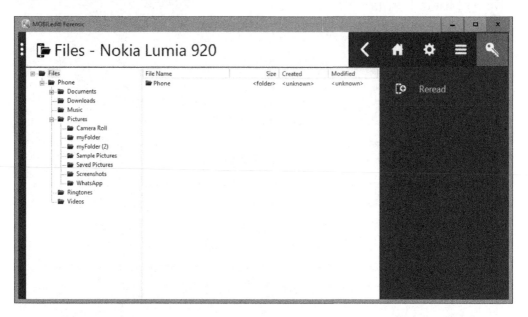

In the preceding screenshot, you can see that all WhatsApp media goes to the `\Pictures\WhatsApp` folder.

The `\Pictures\Saved Pictures` folder contains all the photos saved by the device's user (from the web or from apps), and all screen captures are saved under `\Pictures\Screenshots`. One interesting thing to note is that MOBILedit reveals a subdirectory under the `\WhatsApp` folder, which is not listed via a normal computer's explorer, named `\WhatsApp\PTT`:

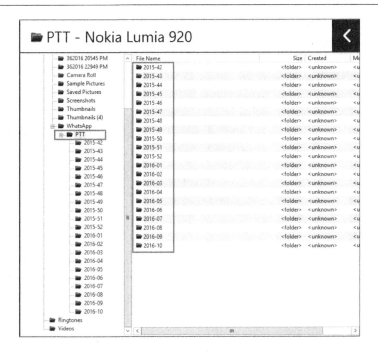

The folders under the \PTT directory seem to follow the naming scheme year-IncrementalInteger. Each of these folders contains one or more .aac.waptt and/or .opus.waptt files, as seen in the following screenshot:

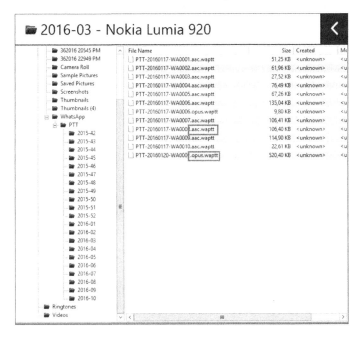

You can extract single or multiple files by selecting the desired file/files and then clicking on the button on the right panel, as shown in the next screenshot:

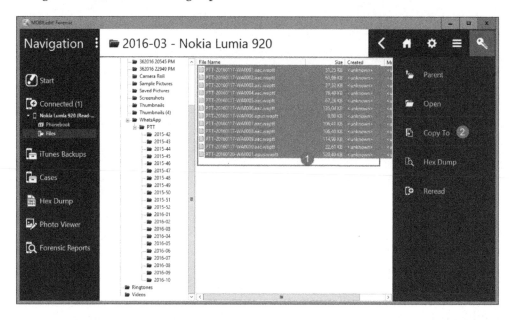

Then, choose the folder in your computer where you want to save extracted files. By removing the `.waptt` from the files' extensions, we get playable AAC and OPUS audio files. Those files represent WhatsApp's sent and received voice notes.

The OPUS file format is a lossy audio coding format designed to efficiently code speech and general audio in a single format while maintaining low-latency enough for real-time interactive communication and low-complexity enough for lower-end ARM3 processors. You can play the OPUS files using Media Player on Windows, but you need to grab the OPUS codec. Links for codecs are at `http://www.free-codecs.com/download/dc-bass_source_mod.htm`.

Windows Phone logical acquisition using Oxygen Forensic Suite 2014

The Oxygen Forensic Suite software is a commercial product that allows a limited logical acquisition of a Windows Phone 8.x device. It allows data to be extracted from the device but offers limited analysis capabilities. To start the extraction, it is necessary to connect the device and to unlock it if it's PIN/passcode-locked.

Then, you need to click on the **Connect device** button from the main screen, as shown in the following screenshot:

This shows Oxygen's **Extractor** utility window, which lets the examiner choose either device data extraction or backup import. Click on the **Live device acquisition** button and then click on **Next**, as highlighted on the following screenshot:

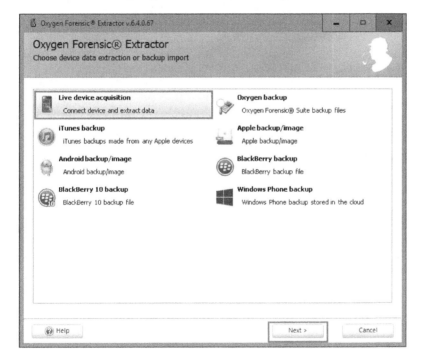

Before the software begins the extraction procedure, you can choose the type of connection you want to start. You can choose between **Auto device connection** and **Manual device selection**, as shown in the following screenshot. For Windows Phone 8.x devices, it is generally sufficient to select **Auto device connection**:

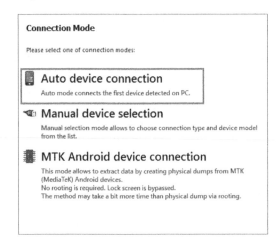

The software will now start searching for a connected Windows Phone device:

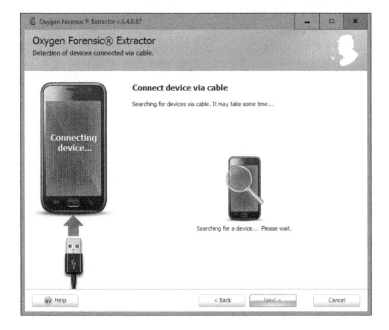

If it succeeds, the detection wizard will show information about the detected device (model, serial number, and hardware and software revisions):

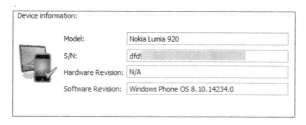

The examiner can then fill in information about the device and the current investigation case, as seen in the next screenshot:

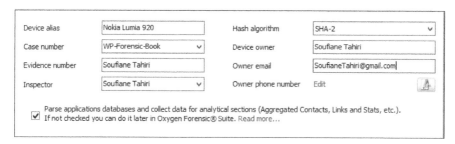

At this point, the examiner can select the data he wants to extract by choosing the ones supported by this method, as shown in the following screenshot:

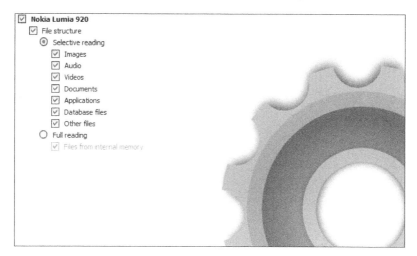

On clicking the **Next** button, the software shows the summary of the case (based on the previously set options), and on clicking the **Extract** button, the acquisition procedure starts and displays a progress bar:

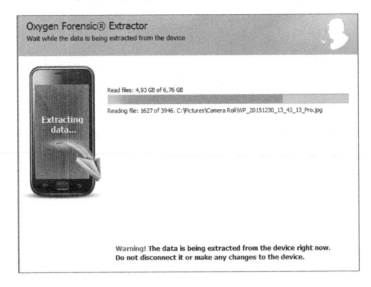

The operation can take several minutes/hours depending on the data size. Once finished, the wizard will invite you to save the extracted data to an archive, to open the device in order to start analyzing data, or to export/print the device data report:

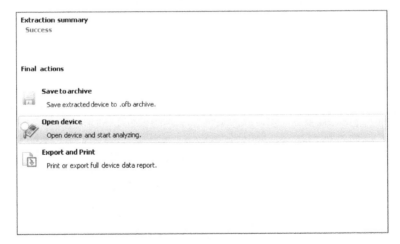

Select the option that suits you the most and click on **Finish**.

The Oxygen Forensic Suite was able to only extract the public folder data; no application data, phonebook, calendar, SMS, or e-mails, and so on were extracted.

Sideloading contacts and appointments acquisition agent

As seen in the previous section, phonebook and calendar entries are not acquired even when using most of the well-known forensic tools. Extracting contacts and appointments are, in many investigation cases, major evidences that help in establishing links between a suspect and others involved in a given case. The technique we are going to explain in this section requires the development and deployment of an agent (or simply application) using Windows Phone SDK, which will be installed on the target device with appropriate capabilities granted to report back the device's phone book and calendar entries.

To extract the phonebook and appointments entries, we will use **WP Logical**, which is a contacts and appointments acquisition tool designed to run under Windows Phone 8.1 (details on how the application was implemented and the link to download it are given in the *WPLogical implementation* section). Once deployed and executed, WP Logical creates a folder with the name `WPLogical_MDY__HMMSS_PM/AM` under the public folder `\Phone\Pictures\`, where M is for month, D is for day, Y is for year, H is for hour, MM is for minutes, and SS is for seconds of the extraction date. Inside the created folder, you can find `appointments__MDY__HMMSS_PM/AM.html` and `contacts_MDY__HMMSS_PM/AM.html`.

WP Logical extracts the following information (if found) related to each appointment, starting from *01/01/CurrentYear* at *00:00:00* to *31/12/CurrentYear* at *00:00:00*:

- Subject
- Location
- Organizer
- Invitees
- Start time (UTC)
- Original start time
- Duration (in hours)
- Sensitivity
- Replay time
- Was it organized by the user?
- Was it canceled?
- More details

It also extracts the following information about each contact found:

- Display name
- First name
- Middle name
- Last name
- Phones (kind—personal, office, or home—and the numbers)
- Important dates
- E-mails (kind—personal, work, and so on—and the e-mail address)
- Websites
- Job info
- Addresses
- Notes
- Thumbnail

WP Logical also allows the extraction of some device-related information such as the phone's time zone, the device's friendly name, **Store Keeping Unit** (**SKU**), and the like.

Windows Phone 8.1 is relatively strict regarding application deployment. WP Logical can be deployed in the following two ways:

- Uploading the compiled agent to the Windows Store and getting it signed by Microsoft, after which it becomes available in the Store for download
- Deploying the agent directly to a developer-unlocked device using the Windows Phone Application Deployment utility

Since it is the quickest way, we will start with the developer unlocking the device. Before we can deploy the agent to a Windows Phone device, we have to register the phone for development. After we register it, we can install, run, and debug the agent that targets Windows Phone 8.1. Before proceeding to the device unlock process, the examiner must have the following:

- Windows Phone SDK 8.1
- A Microsoft account (formerly known as a Windows Live ID. You can sign in for an account at `http://windows.microsoft.com/en-US/windows-live/sign-up-create-account-how.`)

As part of Windows Phone 8.1 SDK, Microsoft offers **Windows Phone Developer Registration 8.1** as a standalone tool, which can be found at `C:\Program Files (x86)\Microsoft SDKs\Windows Phone\v8.1\Tools\Phone Registration.`

Assuming that you've successfully installed the SDK and signed in for a Windows Live account, start by turning on the device and unlocking the phone screen. Then, connect the device to a computer by using a USB cable. On the computer, start Windows Phone Developer Registration 8.1, and you will get a screen that looks like the following screenshot:

Verify that the **Status** message displays **Identified Windows Phone 8 device. Click the Register button to unlock the phone**, as seen in the next screenshot:

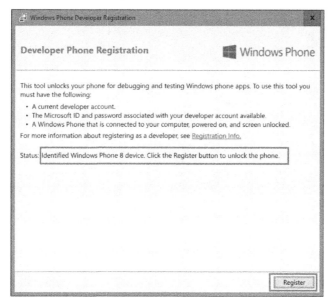

Click on **Register**. In the **Sign In** dialog box for your Microsoft account, enter the e-mail address and password for your Microsoft account. Click on **Sign In**:

Once your phone is successfully registered, the **Status** message displays **Congratulations! You have successfully unlocked your Windows Phone**, as seen in the following screenshot:

Now once the device is registered, we can proceed by deploying the agent. You can grab a packaged agent from `https://github.com/soufianetahiri/Windows-Phonne-Logical-Forensic/blob/master/WindowsPhoneLogical_1.0.0.2_AnyCPU.appx`.

The Windows Phone 8.1 SDK also comes with Windows Phone Application Deployment 8.1, a tool that lets us deploy our agent on the device. Make sure that the device is connected to a computer, and start the deployment tool from `C:\Program Files (x86)\Microsoft SDKs\Windows Phone\v8.1\Tools\AppDeploy\AppDeploy.exe`:

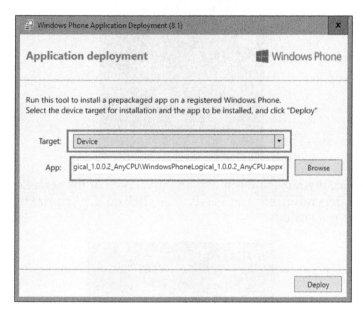

Make sure you select **Device** from the **Target** dropdown list box. In the **App** field, click on **Browse** and select `WindowsPhoneLogical_1.0.0.2_AnyCPU.appx`; then, click on **Deploy**. Once deployed, a success message will be printed as follows:

Now locate **WindowsPhoneLogical** on the device and start it:

The user interface is simple and self-explanatory; check or uncheck **Contacts** and **Appointments** depending on your needs, then click on the **Acquire** button, as seen in the following screenshot:

The log window will print out the acquired data, as shown here:

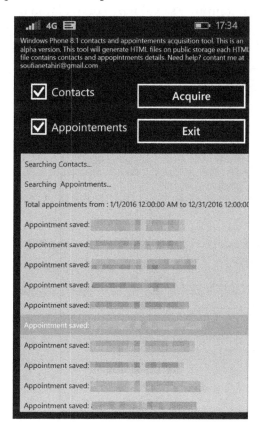

Once each process is done (contact and appointment extractions), close the notification messages:

Close WP Logical, unplug and replug the device, then go to the \Phone\
Pictures\ folder via the computer's explorer. You will find a folder named like
WPLogical_3102016_55138_PM, where contacts and appointments are saved in
two separate HTML files, as you can see in the following screenshot:

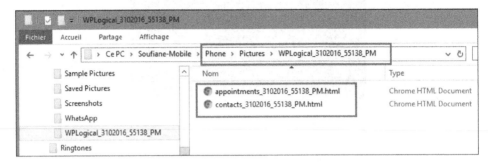

The generated files can be copied to the examiner's computer. Contacts are sorted in
a table like the following:

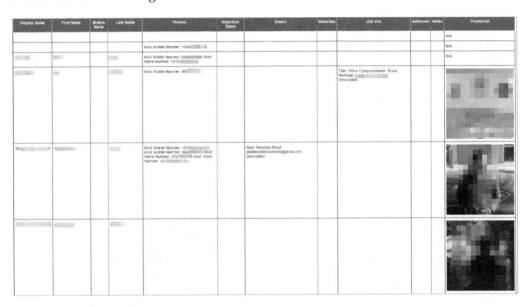

You can click on each thumbnail to save it as a JPEG file. Appointments are sorted as follows:

PBC - Call with Soufiane Tahin	skype: soufianetahin	Address: ...r@gmail.com Name: Gebriel	Address Name: Soufiane Tahin Response: None Role: RequiredAttendee Adress: ...@gmail.com Name: Gebriel Response: Accepted Role: RequiredAttendee	3/1/2016 9:00 00 AM +00 00		0 8	Public	False	False	Hi Soufiane. Here is our Skype call to better understand information on the ... team technology... Strategy	Growth Management	P...	Also the interview ...speak to you shortly. – Gabriel ...around www pr...	On the call I will also provide more regarding the Consulting.
	N/A			3/3/2016 12 00 00 AM +00 00		24	Public	False	False			
	N/A			3/3/2016 12 00 00 AM +00 00	3/3/2016 12 00 00 AM +00 00	24	Public	False	False			
	N/A			3/4/2016 12 00 00 AM +00 00	3/4/2016 12 00 00 AM +00 00	24	Public	False	False			
60° JAZZ TRIO en concert au Boultek // Ven 04 mars 2016	Boultek	Address: Boultek Name: LAC-L'Bouh-art		3/4/2016 8 30 00 PM +00 00		3	Public	False	False	VENDREDI 04 MARS / 20h30 SALLE 36 - Boultek! 30 DHS #JAZZ avec 60° JAZZ TRIO C'est à l'occasion d'un concert en 2014 que Clément Brapman (chant et batterie), réunit Alexis Pivot (piano) et Etienne Renard (contrebasse). Les trois musiciens, faisant alors partie de la même génération montante du jazz français, se découvrent tout un vocabulaire commun et une complicité immédiate. Les concerts qui suivent seront autant d'occasions d'enrichir ce langage, à la fois intime et intuitif. A découvrir. PLUS D'INFOS SUR 60°JAZZ TRIO http...r/clementbrajman com/ https //soundcloud com/cbrajman https //www reverbnation com/aeunspivot EN VIDEO : http //y2u be/XsTcOVJDDik

In addition to this, general details about the device and extraction are reported and sorted as follows:

Acquisition details

Phone Timezone: (UTC) Casablanca
FriendlyName: Soufiane-Mobile
OS: WindowsPhone **Firmware Version:** 3051.50009.1451.1001
Hardware Version: 6.5.0.
Product Name: RM-821_apac_taiwan_341
Store Keeping Unit: NOKIA RM-821_apac_taiwan_341
Total Items Extracted: 840

WP Logical implementation

Contacts and calendar entries reside on the Windows Phone 8.1 device as **Contact** and **Appointment** data type. As described by Microsoft (`https://msdn.microsoft.com/en-us/library/windows/apps/windows.applicationmodel.contacts.contact.aspx`), the Contact class has many properties that can reflect forensically interesting information such as a contact's address(s), e-mails, first and last name, job info, phone number, and so on. The Appointment class also has properties that can be used to correlate some of the user's activities, especially if the user synchronized the device with Facebook or Gmail accounts, since the Windows Phone automatically syncs all events from those services with the device's calendar. All properties are available at `https://msdn.microsoft.com/en-us/library/windows/apps/windows.applicationmodel.appointments.appointment.aspx`.

The developed agent makes use of the APIs provided by the Windows Phone 8.1 SDK (`https://dev.windows.com/en-us/downloads/sdk-archive`) to make the contacts and appointments information readable and ready to be explored from a forensic workstation. The agent app is implemented using C#, and the main steps involved in this implementation are as follows.

We first create objects of type `ContactStore`, which represents a database that contains contacts, and of type `AppointmentStore`, which represents a store that contains appointments. Then we invoke the methods `ContactManager.RequestStoreAsync()`, which retrieves a `ContactStore` object that enables searching or retrieving contacts on the device, and `AppointmentManager.RequestStoreAsync()`, which requests the `AppointmentStore` object associated with the calling application as follows:

```
ContactStore contactStore = await ContactManager.RequestStoreAsync();
AppointmentStore appointmentStore = await AppointmentManager.RequestSt
oreAsync(AppointmentStoreAccessType.AllCalendarsReadOnly);
```

Now we can call the methods `ContactStore.FindContactsAsync()` and `AppointmentStore.FindAppointmentsAsync()` and store the results on read-only collections of elements of types `Contact` and `Appointment` respectively, as follows:

```
IReadOnlyList<Contact> contacts = await contactStore.
FindContactsAsync();
IReadOnlyList<Appointment> appointments = await appointmentStore.FindA
ppointmentsAsync(utcDateTime, TimeSpan.FromDays(365), options);
```

The `FindAppointmentsAsync()` method requires the following parameters:

- `RangeStart`: This is of the type date and represents the start time of the time window for which appointments are retrieved
- `RangeLength`: This is of the type number and represents the length of the time window for which appointments are retrieved
- `Options`: These are of type `FindAppointmentsOptions` and are used to specify more options for this operation in the form of `AppointmentProperties`

At this point, `IReadOnlyLists` contain contacts and appointments data that we can parse, sort, and store in a way that suits our need.

The full source code of the operational agent is publicly released and can be downloaded from `https://github.com/soufianetahiri/Windows-Phonne-Logical-Forensic`.

Windows Phone cloud acquisition

Windows Phone 8.x offers the possibility to back up the data on the device to OneDrive, Microsoft's cloud service, to a user who signs in using a Microsoft account.

Depending on the settings previously set on the device, the Windows Phone cloud backup can contain the following:

- The apps installed on the device along with high scores and progress from the participating apps
- Account passwords
- Call history
- SMS and MMS messages
- Photos and videos
- Start screen layout and theme color
- Accounts previously set up on the device
- Internet Explorer favorites
- Custom words added to the device's dictionary
- Settings from around the device, including photos, messages, e-mails, accounts, lock screen, speech preferences, and so on.

For detailed information on creating Windows Phone backups, you can visit https://www.windowsphone.com/en-US/how-to/wp8/ settings-and-personalization/back-up-my-stuff.

Access to My Windows Phone is available through the Microsoft single sign-in service via the Windows Live! account, which means that the original user credentials for that account are mandatory. Online backups can be acquired by the examiner without having the original Windows Phone device in hands. To date, only a few commercial forensic tools are able to acquire the Windows Phone cloud data. Oxygen Forensic® Suite, Elcomsoft Phone Breaker, and Passware Password Recovery Kit Forensic 2016 support this option.

Assuming that the user's Windows Live! credentials are known, the following section demonstrates how to perform a cloud acquisition using Elcomsoft Phone Breaker v5.20 and Passware Password Recovery Kit Forensic 2016.

Cloud acquisition using Elcomsoft Phone Breaker

The following description is given at the Elcomsoft website:

> *EPB allows you to download Windows Phone data provided you know the credentials to the Microsoft account that was used for creating a backup of the data.*

EPB can access the following data for the Windows Phone:

- Contacts
- Notes
- SMS messages

Downloaded data is saved in an archive containing databases with backup information and a `Manifest.xml` file containing information about every device from the account and the file name for every database file.

After starting EPB, select the **Microsoft** tab in the **Tools** menu and click on **Download Windows Phone data**:

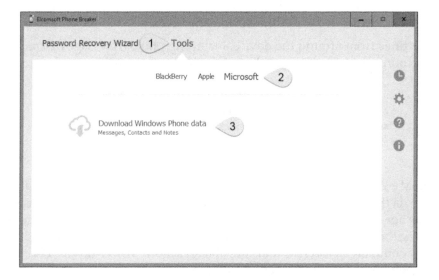

In the window that is displayed, provide the username and password of the Microsoft account that was used for taking backup of the data and click on **Sign in**:

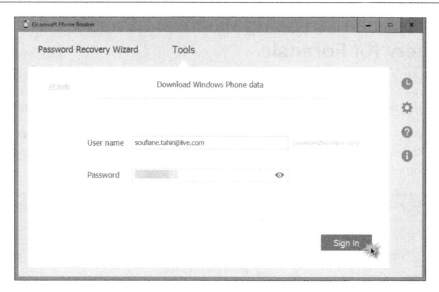

Select the location for saving the data downloaded from the Microsoft account in the next window. Note that you can change the Microsoft user whose backup data you want to download by clicking on **Change user**:

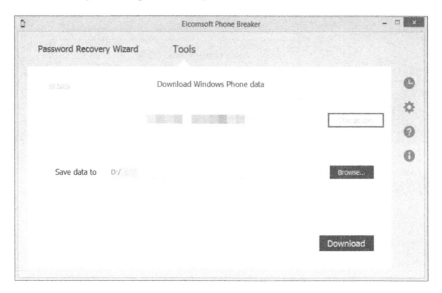

Click on **Download** to start downloading the backup data. When downloading is finished, you can view the downloaded data at the location on the local computer where it was saved by clicking on the View button (the little icon representing an eye). Click on **Finish** to close the **Download Windows Phone data** window.

Cloud acquisition using Passware Password Recovery Kit Forensic

On Passware's official website (`https://www.passware.com/kit-forensic`), the developers of this tool affirm that a cloud acquisition is possible by downloading backups and data from cloud services: Apple iCloud, MS OneDrive, and Dropbox.

To acquire the Microsoft OneDrive backup, start Passware Password Recovery Kit Forensic and select **Mobile & Cloud Forensics** from the main window, as shown in the following screenshot:

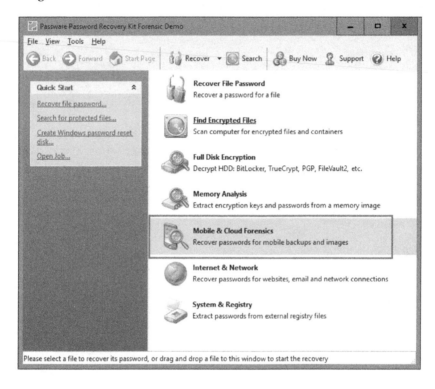

Then click on **OneDrive** to acquire the backup from Microsoft's cloud:

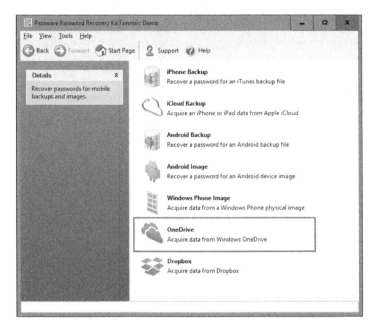

Using the known account's credentials, fill in the **Login** and **Password** fields, then choose the path to save the downloaded data and click on **Next**, as seen in the next screenshot:

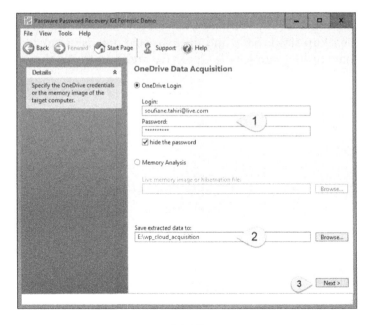

Once the backup gets downloaded, you get a confirmation window like the following screenshot:

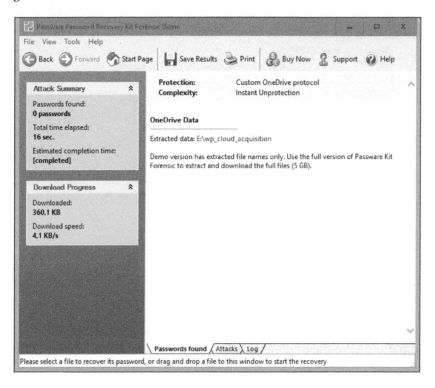

The demo version extracts only filenames, as you can see from the preceding screenshot. The backup size is 5 GB and the extracted data is organized on the computer in a manner that mimics the OneDrive architecture, as shown here:

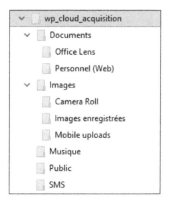

JTAG and physical acquisition

Currently, the Windows Phone 8+ devices are physical acquisition resistant and most (if not all) forensic tools cannot achieve it. However, **Cellebrite** claims on their website that their **UFED** is the first in the industry to support the physical extraction and decoding of Windows Phone devices running OS versions 8.0 and 8.1, including HTC Pro, HTC HD2 T9193, Xperia X1, Nokia Lumia 520, and LG GM750 (`http://www.cellebrite.com/Pages/windows-phone-forensics-physical-extraction-and-decoding-from-windows-phone-devices`). This said, the test (conducted by the Computer Forensic Tool Testing Program of the National Institute of Standards and Technology) results of data acquisition using **UFED 4PC v4.2.6.5** and **Physical Analyzer v4.2.6.4** for Nokia Lumia 920 and HTC PM23300 running Windows Phone 8.0 show that only extremely limited data was acquired: no SMS messages, application data, Internet data, or social media data (including Facebook, Twitter, and LinkedIn) were extracted, and no deleted file was recovered. The test was conducted in January 2016 and can be viewed at `https://www.dhs.gov/sites/default/files/publications/508_Test_Report_NIST_Mobile_UFED4PC_v4.2.6.5_January_2016.pdf`.

If the target device is not encrypted, Windows Phone devices and Nokia Lumia can be subjects of physical acquisition by NAND. This is made feasible using **JTAG**, which is a nondestructive approach that can bypass all security measures and access the memory of the device. As described in the previous chapter, the JTAG technique requires disassembling the device, reading the NAND by soldering the connecting wires to the JTAG TAPs, and then acquiring the physical image using the RIFF JTAG software. The soldering step can be skipped if the device jigs are available.

The following image shows a disassembled Nokia Lumia 620 with highlighted JTAG TAPs located under an EMI shield above the SD card slot:

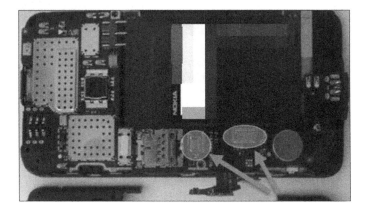

The shield can be removed using a hot air rework station at a temperature of approximately 350 centigrade, and the result will be as seen in the following image (source: `http://forensicswiki.org/wiki/File:6-Lumia620-EMI.jpg`):

Now the examiner solders wires to the JTAG TAPs, as shown in the following image (source: `http://forensicswiki.org/`):

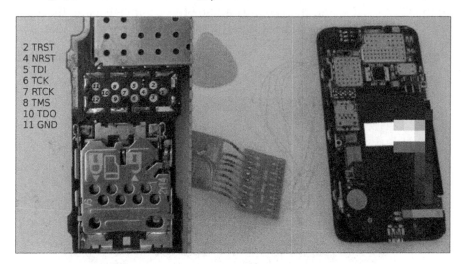

At this point, the device is connected to the RIFF box and physical acquisition can be started using the RIFF JTAG software:

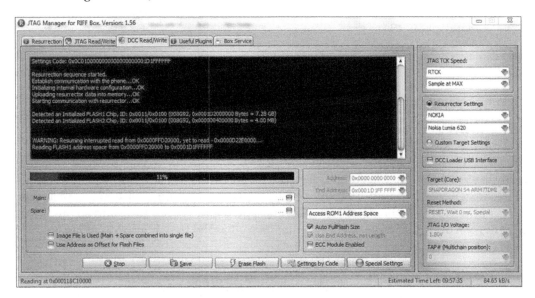

In some cases, the soldering process can be avoided and a cleaner way could be used if the device's jig is available; in such a case, a Dolphin clip is used along with the adequate jig. As you can see, the following image shows a disassembled Nokia Lumia 520 connected to a RIFF box using a Dolphin clip and the Lumia jig:

The Nokia Lumia JTAG set for Dolphin clip (7-in-1 jigs) has been developed for Nokia Lumia 520, 620, 720, 820, 920, 925, and 928 mobile phones and can be found at `http://www.fonefunshop.co.uk/cable_picker/98235_Nokia_Lumia_JTAG_Jigs_For_Dolphin_Clip.html`.

You can also get a Dolphin clip with the main cable set from `http://gsmserver.com/item/cables-and-adapters/dolphin-clip-with-main-cable-set/`.

The physical image acquired can be parsed using **Belkasoft Evidence Center**.

Belkasoft Evidence Center is a digital forensic solution enabling security experts and forensic specialists to collect and analyze digital evidence from computers and mobile devices. Belkasoft Evidence Center can automatically locate, process, and analyze evidence stored inside hard drives, forensic images, and dumps. Hundreds of evidence types are supported out of the box, such as documents, e-mails, pictures and videos, chats and browser histories, encrypted and system files, and so on. Information on Belkasoft Evidence Center as well as the free demo download are available at `http://belkasoft.com/trial`.

First, run the tool and then create a new case by filling in the case information by giving a case name, specifying a folder to store the data, adding the investigator's name, specifying the local time zone, and filling in the description of the case, as shown in the following screenshot:

On clicking the **OK** button, the tool will invite you to add evidence to the created case:

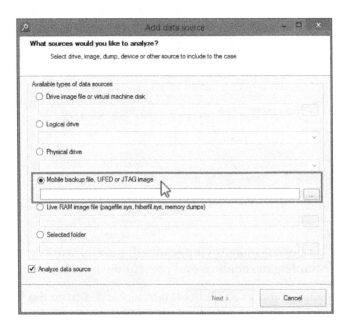

Select the **Mobile backup file, UFED or JTAG image** option. Click on **Next** and the tool will show the types of data it can handle, as seen in the following screenshot:

Once you click on **Next** and **Finish**, the tool starts searching and extracting important types of evidence essential for an investigation, such as contacts and address books, call logs, Skype chats and communication histories in third-party messengers, browsing history, and cached social network conversations. The Task Manager shows you the extraction progress (as seen in the following screenshot), and the sorted evidence will be displayed on the left panel hosting the Case Explorer:

Depending on the size of the image being scanned, the tool will take a few minutes or a few hours to complete the analysis and present the findings.

The following screenshot shows a SQLite database, carved from the JTAG physical dump of a Nokia Lumia 520 shown in the built-in SQLite Viewer:

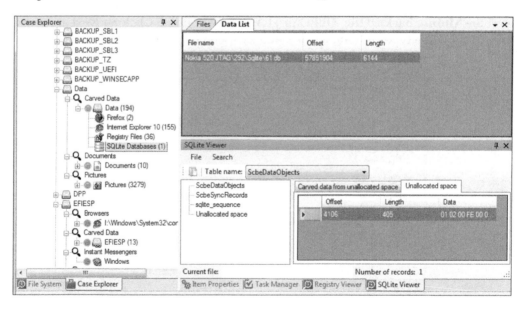

Belkasoft offers an interesting feature when it comes to Windows Phone 8 dumps, that is, the possibility of parsing `Pagefile.sys`, which is a file created by the operating system (as for the desktop version of Windows OS) in order to overcome the lack of RAM on a device. Thus, `Pagefile.sys` usually contains information used by some applications running in the background such as opened Internet Explorer tabs or chat sessions of social applications. The tool offers quite effective parsing capabilities, and can carve the Windows Phone's `Pagefile.sys` file to extract pictures, cached webpages, and data from social application.

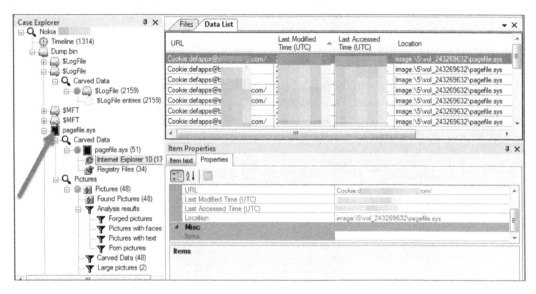

Artifact location and user PIN study

In this section, we will look for the location of some of the evidence generated by a Windows Phone 8+ device. Usually, in a forensics investigation process, SMS/MMS messages are some of the most looked-for evidence. Windows Phone 8.x stores MMS data at `%DataDrive%:\SharedData\Comms\Unistore\data\` as `.dat` files under subdirectories named `0` to `+99` with more subdirectories named `a` to `p`.

The following is a picture contained within a received MMS:

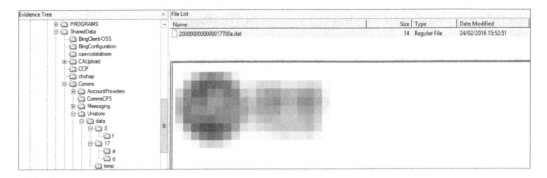

The SMS and contact information (including synced contacts from LinkedIn, Facebook, and Twitter) data is stored under the `%DataDrive%:\Users\WPCOMMSERVICES\APPDATA\Local\Unistore\` directory as a `store.vol` file, which is an ESE database:

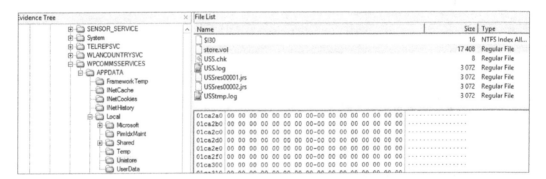

The database is simply a huge repository of evidence and contains more than 54 tables (`Activity`, `Appointment`, `EmailMetadata`, `EmailRecipientInfo`, and so on). You can explore it using the **ESEDatabaseView** downloadable from `http://www.nirsoft.net/utils/ese_database_view.html`. This utility can convert, on the fly, the date/time from the MS Format to a readable format from the **Options** menu. The following is the activity feed of the device owner and synced contacts from Twitter and LinkedIn (from the table `Activity`):

27/03/...	Reuters Top News	https://t.co/kW7XQcj1yk
Twitter	WikiLeaks	https://t.co/eWYhEhKnlp
Twitter	RT	https://t.co/dLJ3V7zQin
Twitter	SANS Institute, EMEA	https://t.co/3kk1xPF5wl
Twitter	RT	https://t.co/ky0orjDeul
Twitter	WikiLeaks	https://t.co/eWYhEhKnlp
Twitter	Virus Bulletin	https://t.co/JFymH2EHWr
Twitter	Morgan Marquis-Boire	https://t.co/x9gFQiq27l
Twitter	WikiLeaks	https://t.co/eWYhEhKnlp
Twitter	RT	https://t.co/wojSe5FJim
LinkedIn	Ashish	http://image-store.slidesharecdn.
LinkedIn	William	?f-4ff8-9bb5-eb1a04ca0950-original.jpeg
LinkedIn	Remo	
LinkedIn	Remc	http://flip
LinkedIn	Soufiane Tahiri	https://www.linkedin.com/pulse/digital-forensics-models-1-soufiane-tahiri
LinkedIn	Shahriar	http://buff.ly/1pb3MHt
LinkedIn	Shahriar	http://buff.ly/1pb3MHt

Table names are stored in the Table `MSysObjects` under the column `Name`, and the ID associated with each name is used as the name of other tables' columns. You can use this table to correlate names. The `\Unistore\` folder also contains a `USS.log` file, which is an ESE database transaction rollback file. Examining this file can be useful, since you can recover deleted SMS/MMS messages from it.

Windows Phone 8+ stores call history in an ESE database, also named `Phone` with no extension, which can be found under `%DataDrive%:\Users\WPCOMMSERVICES\APPDATA\Local\UserData\`. The database contains one interesting table named `CallHistory` holding all call details (start time, end time, caller location, resolved numbers, and so on). The following screenshot shows the information that you can gather regarding each call:

The Windows Phone, like all Microsoft operating systems, uses Internet Explorer as its default navigator. Internet Explorer stores cached history and cookies. The cached history is stored in the `WebCacheV01.dat` database under `%DataDrive%:\Users\DefApps\APPDATA\Local\Microsoft\Windows\`. This database contains 42 tables with 34 tables of the name `Container_X`, where `x` goes from 1 to 34 and represents the container ID. Each table seems to be related to an application (Skype, weather app, Facebook, and the like) and each container table contains cached URL, access count, creation time, and access time. In the following screenshot, `Container_31` seems to hold the cached contact data from Skype and `Container_25` holds the data cached from Facebook. `Container_31` seems to hold various browser cached URLs:

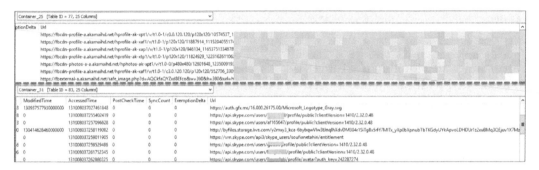

Navigation history and cookies are stored under `%DataDrive%:\Users\DefApps\APPDATA\INERNETEXPLORER\INetCache\` and `%DataDrive%:\Users\DefApps\APPDATA\INERNETEXPLORER\INetCookies\` respectively, as seen in the following screenshot:

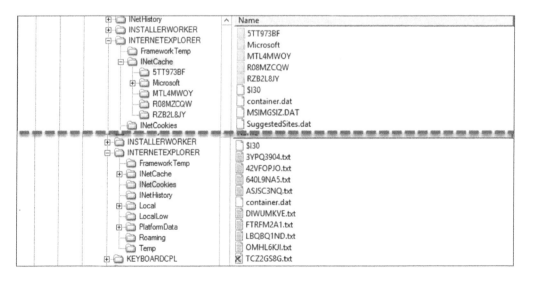

In order to take cloud backups, Windows Phone 8 must be configured using a Windows Live! account. The configured account is stored in the `CommsBackup.xml` file under `%DataDrive%:\Users\DefApps\APPDATA\Local\BackupVols\`:

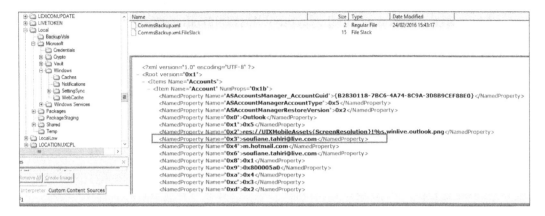

As mentioned earlier in this chapter, in contrast to all kinds of evidences stored in the form of ESE databases or XML files, the user's pass code is stored in the Windows Phone registry, which is extremely similar to the desktop Windows registry. All registry hives are stored under `%SystemDrive%:\Windows\System32\config`, as you can see in the next screenshot:

The most relevant hives are Software and System, as per research conducted by forensic experts Adrian Leong (http://cheeky4n6monkey.blogspot.com/2014/10/awesome-windows-phone-8-stuff.html) and Francesco Picasso (http://blog.digital-forensics.it/2015/07/windows-phone-pin-cracking.html). My own findings point to the fact that the PIN hash is stored in the Software hive registry key \Microsoft\Comms\Security\DeviceLock\ObjectXX, where XX could be 21 or 31. In my case, in a physical dump of a Lumia 920 running Windows Phone 8.10.14234.375, the XX was equal to 21:

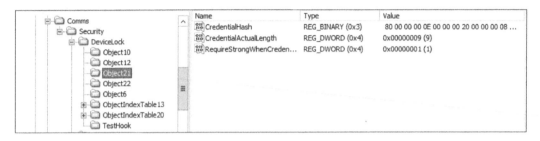

The Object21 registry key contains three values: CredentialHash, CredentialActualLength, and RequireStrongWhenCredentialSet that hold, respectively, the hash value of the PIN set by the user, the PIN length, and a flag set to 1 or 0 to require a string PIN or not when it is set up by the user. The PIN set on my Lumia 920 is 9 digits in length, as suggested by the CredentialActualLength value seen in the preceding screenshot. The bytes blob of the hashed PIN is as follows:

```
Offset      0  1  2  3  4  5  6  7   8  9  A  B  C  D  E  F
00000000   80 00 00 00 0E 00 00 00  20 00 00 00 08 29 F2 52   ▌         )òR
00000010   17 A3 87 34 45 B6 5D 4F  14 69 2E 4C BC 2C CC AF   £▌4E¶]O i.L¼,Ì‾
00000020   36 85 9D C4 2E DD 6A D8  6A 98 2E 79 93 DD CA A3   6▌ Ä.Ýj_Øj▌.y▌ÝÊ£
00000030   8D D1 9F 8C 80 D4 8D 03  16 EE A2 34 57 03 22 D5   Ñ▌▌▌Ô  î¢4W "Õ
00000040   D0 B1 BD 9D 6F 8C BC 5E  EB 14 85 8B 5E 68 88 DF   Ð±½ o▌¼^ë ▌▌^h▌ß
00000050   D4 DE 33 97 25 91 9D 75  89 E1 50 F3 8B 87 69 57   ÔÞ3▌%´ u▌áPó▌▌iW
00000060   57 FE 27 6F 00 0D CF 5F  5A 2F EF A4 EC 80 46 05   Wþ'o  Ï_Z⁄ï¤ì▌F
00000070   57 41 A3 D2 1E 78 5D 85  4C AA 6D A9 7A 2A A4 79   WA£Ò x]▌Lªm©z*¤y
00000080   04 9E 3B 7A 0C FB CA 31  51 3C 1C 7A 53 00 48 00   ▌;z ûÊ1Q< zS H
00000090   41 00 32 00 35 00 36 00  00 00 BB 4A 50 44 4E 30   A 2 5 6   »JPDN0
000000A0   A6 C8 62 5B 83 50 58 FE  82 9B 2A 23 70 72 AC 40   ¦Èb[▌PXþ▌▌*#pr¬@
000000B0   63 93 23 56 95 C7 31 61  4B 89                     c▌#V▌Ç1aK▌
```

The data size equal is to 0xBA (186 bytes). Francesco Picasso on his blog post described very well how this data is arranged: the first two double-words represent the length of the three following byte arrays, the second one is the Unicode (UCS-2LE) string SHA-256, and the last array represents the SHA-256 hashed PIN, which is exactly equal to the length of a SHA-256 hash (32 bytes):

00000070	57	41	A3	D2	1E	78	5D	85	4C	AA	6D	A9	7A	2A	A4	79
00000080	04	9E	3B	7A	0C	FB	CA	31	51	3C	1C	7A	53	00	48	00
00000090	41	00	32	00	35	00	36	00	00	00	BB	4A	50	44	4E	30
000000A0	A6	C8	62	5B	83	50	58	FE	82	9B	2A	23	70	72	AC	40
000000B0	63	93	23	56	95	C7	31	61	4B	89						

As with most of the newly implemented hashes, the PIN hash is produced using a 128 bytes pseudo randomly generated salt.

Offset	0	1	2	3	4	5	6	7	8	9	A	B	C	D	E	F
00000000	80	00	00	00	0E	00	00	00	20	00	00	00	08	29	F2	52
00000010	17	A3	87	34	45	B6	5D	4F	14	69	2E	4C	BC	2C	CC	AF
00000020	36	85	9D	C4	2E	DD	6A	D8	6A	98	2E	79	93	DD	CA	A3
00000030	8D	D1	9F	8C	80	D4	8D	03	16	EE	A2	34	57	03	22	D5
00000040	D0	B1	BD	9D	6F	8C	BC	5E	EB	14	85	8B	5E	68	88	DF
00000050	D4	DE	33	97	25	91	9D	75	89	E1	50	F3	8B	87	69	57
00000060	57	FE	27	6F	00	0D	CF	5F	5A	2F	EF	A4	EC	80	46	05
00000070	57	41	A3	D2	1E	78	5D	85	4C	AA	6D	A9	7A	2A	A4	79
00000080	04	9E	3B	7A	0C	FB	CA	31	51	3C	1C	7A	53	00	48	00
00000090	41	00	32	00	35	00	36	00	00	00	BB	4A	50	44	4E	30
000000A0	A6	C8	62	5B	83	50	58	FE	82	9B	2A	23	70	72	AC	40
000000B0	63	93	23	56	95	C7	31	61	4B	89						

Using the salt, the PIN hash, and the PIN length, we can try to recover the plain text PIN using the `wp8-sha256-pin-finder.py` script available at `https://github.com/cheeky4n6monkey/4n6-scripts/blob/master/wp8-sha256-pin-finder.py`.

To execute this script, you must provide it with the salt, PIN hash, and PIN length as follows:

```
python wp8-sha256-pin-finder.py salt hash length
```

As you can see in the next screenshot, the plain text PIN in my case was 662135560:

```
C:\Users\Soufiane>python c:\wp8-pin.py 0829F25217A3873445B65D4F14692E4CBC2CCCAF36859DC42EDD6AD86A982E7993DDCAA38DD
19F8C80D48D0316EEA234570322D5D0B18D9D6F8C8C5EEB14858B5E6888DFD4DE339725919D7589E150F38B87695757FE276F000DCF5F5A2FE
FA4EC8046055741A3D21E785D854CAA6DA97A2AA479049E3B7A0CFBCA31513C1C7A B84A50444E30A6C8625B835058FE829B2A237072AC4063
93235695C731614B89 9

Running wp8-sha256-pin-finder.py v2015-07-30

PIN code is 662135560

C:\Users\Soufiane>
```

In addition to this, we can find out when this PIN was set by viewing the value of `CredentialSetupTime` in the registry key `Object22`, as follows:

Name	Type	Value
VUFailureCount	REG_DWORD (0x4)	0x00000000 (0)
AuthResetFailureCount	REG_DWORD (0x4)	0x00000000 (0)
ActiveLAPGUID	REG_BINARY (0x3)	B5 A5 B5 A7 35 56 41 42 A7 FD 27 2E 0C 1F EA A6
CurrentCredentialHash	REG_BINARY (0x3)	80 00 00 00 0E 00 00 00 20 00 00 00 23 C8 16 EF 9A 74 9
CredentialSetupTime	REG_BINARY (0x3)	D0 2C 74 0C 1D 6F D1 01

The value `0xD02C740C1D6FD101` is 8 bytes in length and represents Microsoft Filetime, which is defined as a 64-bit value that represents the number of 100-nanosecond intervals that have elapsed since 12:00 AM. January 1, 1601 Coordinated Universal Time (UTC) (`https://msdn.microsoft.com/en-us/library/ms724290(vs.85,loband).aspx`). Microsoft uses little endian to store integers, which means that the given value must be written like `0x01D16F1D0C742CD0` before converting it to the decimal value:

1D1 6F1D 0C74 2CD0

HEX	1D1 6F1D 0C74 2CD0
DEC	131 008 034 724 130 000
OCT	7 213 361 641 435 026 320
BIN	0001 1101 0001 0110 1111 0001 1101 0000 1100 0111 0100 0010 1100 1101 0000

This results in the value `131008034724130000`, which can be converted to UTC time using free online converters like `http://www.silisoftware.com/tools/date.php`.

Once converted to UTC, we can see that the PIN was set on the device on Sunday, March 13, 2016 at 7:15:35 PM.

Summary

In this chapter, we went through different approaches towards Windows Phone 8.x forensic analysis. In contrast to most mobile OSs, the Windows Phone forensic acquisition and analysis requires manual effort in addition to automated tools. We saw that most of the available forensic tools cannot fully acquire data from a Windows Phone device, which makes it a very challenging platform for forensic examiners. There is no easy way to gain full access to a user's data in a Windows Phone device, and in many cases, many tools and approaches must be used in order to acquire evidence. With the introduction of full disk encryption, even extracting the full memory dump using advanced techniques like JTAG is useless. This makes it more painful for examiners dealing with this OS. As we discussed in this chapter, by adopting the Windows NT kernel, Windows Phone 8.x inherited many of its security enhancement features, making it harder to explore. We also explained the sideloading technique to logically acquire some of the device's data. This technique may not be forensically sound, but in most cases, it's the only available way to extract some kind of data and should produce forensically sound evidences if the examiner follows the standard best practices, which we will discuss in the next chapter.

6
Mobile Forensics – Best Practices

The purpose of this chapter is to go beyond the technical aspects of smartphone device forensics and introduce you to some of the best practices of recovering digital evidence from a mobile device under forensically sound conditions. This chapter will describe the methodology of the forensic process used for mobile devices and will present guidelines for specific activities in the handling of digital evidence.

This chapter will cover the following topics:

- Mobile forensics process
- Mobile device identification
    - Physical characteristics
    - Device info
    - Service provider

Presenting a mobile forensics process

The first chapter of this book introduced an abstraction of different forensic frameworks. Smartphone forensics is an evolving field of digital forensics; it was described by **Digital Forensics Research Workshop** in 2001 as follows:

> *The use of scientifically derived and proven methods toward the preservation, collection, validation, identification, analysis, interpretation, documentation, and preservation of digital evidence derived from digital sources, for the purpose of facilitating or furthering the reconstruction of events found to be criminal, or helping to anticipate unauthorized actions shown to be disruptive to planned operations.*

In real world challenges and actual circumstances, conducting a forensic examination is subject to the local legal system and its rules of evidence and different constraints related to the device itself (OS, device model, technical challenges, and so on), as well as the case being investigated. A forensics examination dealing with a smartphone can be extremely difficult and requires us to write to the target device, side load an agent, install a bootloader, or remove a chip in many, if not all, cases; thus, smartphone forensics is not always subject to a single model or framework and the examiner will, in general, adopt and adapt different stages from different models in order to acquire evidence that is acceptable in a court of law. Since standard read-only protection does not always work during an investigation, every procedure must be subject to a prior test, validation, and documentation. Following a well-established methodology is very crucial, especially when dealing with mobiles, as not following the proper guidelines during evidence gathering can result in loss or damage to the evidence or render evidences inadmissible in court of law.

It's important to note that there is no standard smartphone forensic model. However, in order to ensure that the result of each device examination is consistent and defendable, every smartphone forensic process should follow specific steps to produce potential digital evidence that can be of evidential value.

The investigation is generally trigged by an **evidence intake** phase, which is a determinant phase in which the examiner develops the specific objectives of each case. This initial phase entails paperwork to **document** a custody chain, ownership information, the type of incident the mobile device was involved in, and the type of data and information the requester is seeking. The documentation phase is an omnipresent phase that will last the whole process and before starting the identification, most of the examiners (whether representing agencies or organizations) use forms to document the intake of devices.

The very first stage of the investigation is **identification**; this step can dramatically influence the overall investigation process and can lead to an efficient management of the overall time and effort spent on the examination. Before proceeding in an investigation case, the examiner must always keep in mind to identify at least four major points:

- **Legal authorities**: It's important to be aware of the local legislation before starting to look into the data within a device. Prior to any device examination, the examiner must start by determining and documenting the legal authorities that exist for the search of the device, in order to define the scope, breadth, and depth of the **Electronically Stored Information** (ESI) which he is authorized to examine. If an examination is requested pursuant to a warrant, the examination must be limited to the scope of that warrant, and in the case of the examination is pursuant to consent, the examiner must not go beyond the limitations of the consent (for example, consent to examine messages within a particular date range). Being aware of legal restrictions can be very limitative in terms of the scope of the examination and can save the examiner valuable time and effort while extracting and documenting data.

- **Goals of the examination**: Depending on the data requested, identifying the goals of the examination determines how deep the examiner must go in order to extract desired evidence. Each case, is unique and having a clear understanding of this fact helps to determine the goals of the examination, helping the examiner decide the level or levels of examination. In some cases, the examination includes recovering deleted data, which depends on the device and is usually only feasible if particular tools are available. The goals of the examination have a consequent impact on selecting the tools and techniques required when examining a device and increase the efficiency of the examination process.

- **Identifying the device**: Identifying the make and model of the device, as well as its information, is a step that every examiner must follow and document properly as a part of an examination. The information regarding the identification of the device should be well documented, since it can assist the examiner in the determination of the tools he will need. We will discuss more about device identification in the next section.

- **Removable and external data storage**: Identifying if the device offers the option to extend its memory using an SD card is important. Finding out the slots of these small-scale storage modules is difficult, but once identified it's wise to remove it to preserve the data that it contains, document the serial number and any other identifying detail, activate the write protection switch if present, and then create a forensic duplicate of the content. This media storage can be handled in a traditional forensic manner, in the same way as any other storage media. Today's smartphones also allow external storage of data "over the air", using cloud based-storage similar to iCloud, Google, or OneDrive. The examiner should consider this even when accessing the stored data on the cloud is subject to further legal authority. In addition to this, most modern (and even less modern) smartphones are designed to synchronize their content with a trusted computer, which is, in general, the user's computer. The examiner must consider the potential existence of a full or partial backup of the device's data on the device owner's computer.

In addition to this, the examiner must identify any other source of potential evidence, especially biological evidence, as most smartphones can be considered an interesting repository of fingerprints and sources of DNA; thus, prior to the device examination, and in order to avoid any unwanted contaminations, considerations should be made as to whether or not the other evidence collection issues exist and the examiner is invited to wear gloves when handling the evidence.

The identification process is a great facilitator of the **preparation** phase, while identifying the case needs the examiner to start the preparation for the examination of the device. The forensic workstation, cables, and software relative to the device being examined are prepared; depending on the previously identified and documented make and model of the device, the examiner can start gathering information regarding the available tools that can extract data from the desired device. Choosing the appropriate tool depends on many factors; in addition to the resources available to the examiner or to the organization/agency responsible for the investigation, the goals of examination and the type of the device are determinant in choosing the appropriate tools.

Given the hardware and software difference between computers and smartphones and in contrast to the available computer forensics tools, smartphone forensics tools are considerably different due to the fact that most smartphone operating systems are typically closed, which makes interpreting their internals very hard. The examiner has a variety of software that he can use, including commercial, open source forensic tools, and even non-forensic tools designed to manage a device's content. On the other hand, the examiner should be aware of the fact that non-forensics tools may allow the flow of information from both the computer to the device and from the device to the computer, which is not forensically sound and is not designed to include integrity hashes.

Many smartphone forensic tools use the same protocols and techniques as non-forensic tools in order to communicate with the device, but they are designed in a manner to extract and calculate integrity hashes of data from a device.

Forensic hash validation

A forensic hash is used to maintain the integrity of an acquisition by computing a cryptographically strong and non-reversible value over the acquired data. After acquisition, any changes made to the data can be detected, since the new hash value computed over the data will be inconsistent with the old value. For non-forensic tools, hash values should be created using a tool, such as **sha1sum**, and retained for integrity verification. Even tools labeled as forensic tools may not compute a cryptographic hash, and in these cases an integrity hash should be computed separately.

Note that mobile devices are constantly active and update information (for example, the device clock) continuously. Therefore, back-to-back acquisitions of a device will be slightly different and produce different hash values when computed over all the data. However, hash values computed over selected data items, such as individual files and directories, generally remain consistent. If hash inconsistencies occur, they may require the examiner to perform an element-by-element verification, thus ensuring data integrity. Hash validation across multiple tools is challenging due to proprietary reporting formats (source: NIST Guidelines on Mobile Device Forensics).

Preparing the appropriate tools is not always an easy task and understanding the different types of mobile acquisition tools and the data they are capable of recovering is important for the examiner. The **National Institute of Standards and Technology (NIST)** has developed a Mobile Device Tool Classification System (http://nvlpubs.nist.gov/nistpubs/SpecialPublications/NIST.SP.800-101r1.pdf), which provides a framework for forensic examiners to compare the extraction methods used by different tools to acquire data and to let an examiner easily classify and compare the extraction methods of different tools. The tools listed on the NIST guidelines are grouped by the tool-levelling system developed by the Sam Brothers and designed to categorize forensic tools by the depth to which they are capable of accessing data on a device. The tool classification system is displayed in the following diagram:

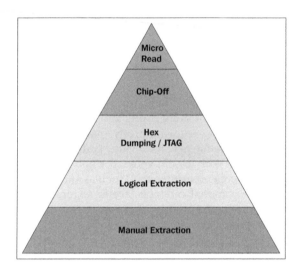

As you move up the pyramid (from the bottom, level 1, to the top, level 5), the methods and methodologies involved in acquisition become more technical, invasive, time consuming, and tools get more expensive. Depending on the goals of the examination and circumstances, and before picking the appropriate level, the examiner must be aware of the fact that once a level is used, alternating the levels might not be possible. Using each level can permanently modify or destroy data if the methodology or tools are not utilized properly. Proper training and mentoring is critical in obtaining the highest success rate for data extraction and the analysis of the data contained within mobile devices.

A Micro Read involves recording the physical observation of the gates on a NAND or NOR chip with the use of an electron microscope. Due to the extreme technicalities involved when performing a Micro Read, this level of acquisition would only be attempted for high profile cases equivalent to a national security crisis after all other acquisition techniques have been exhausted. Successful acquisition at this level would require a team of experts, proper equipment, time, and an in-depth knowledge of proprietary information. There are no known law enforcement agencies performing acquisitions at this level. Currently, there are no commercially available Micro Read tools (source: NIST Guidelines on Mobile Device Forensics).

The following table provides a non-exhaustive classification of some tools currently used in mobile device forensics and the facilities they provide: acquisition, analysis, or reporting:

Tool	Acquisition level	Network type			Analysis	Reporting
		GSM	CDMA	iDEN/ TDMA		
BlackLight	2	X	X		X	X
MOBILedit! Forensic	2	X	X		X	X
UFED Classic (and Touch) Logical	2	X	X	X	X	X
XRY Logical	2	X	X	X	X	X
Device Seizure	2/3	X	X	X	X	X
EnCase Smartphone Examiner	2/3	X	X		X	X
XRY Complete	2/3	X	X	X	X	X
CDMA Workshop	3	X	X			
Oxygen Forensic Suite (Analyst)	2	X	X		X	X
UFED Touch Ultimate	2/3	X	X	X	X	X
Lantern	2/3	X	X		X	X

Headings contained within the table are as follows:

- **Tool**: Contains tool name.

- **Acquisition level**: Contains level(s) at which the tool performs data extractions: 1 is manual extraction, 2 is logical extraction, 3 is physical extraction, 4 is chip-off, and 5 is Micro Read.

- **Network type**: This specifies the acquisition of devices operating over which networks is possible.

- **Analysis**: Indicates whether the tool provides the examiner with the ability to perform an examination or analysis of the acquired data or not.

- **Reporting**: Indicates whether the tool provides the examiner with the ability to generate reports or not.

You can find more about forensic tools at `http://toolcatalog.nist.gov/taxonomy/index.php`. Additionally, the examiner must remember that a single tool will be sufficient to acquire all the data from all devices; various mobile forensic tools offer different capabilities for processing different devices, and this variation of tools from one software vendor to another may lead to the use of different definitions for mobile data extraction techniques. Therefore, the examiners have to pay attention to understand how the vendor is using definitions with regards to the capabilities of its tool (some examples of differences in semantics include: object extraction, container extraction, logical extraction, logical acquisition, filesystem extraction, physical extraction, physical acquisition, physical memory dump, device profile, and so on.)

After being prepared enough to go further on the investigation, the first step in recovering digital evidence starts by **securing and preserving** it. In order to exploit the eventually extracted evidence correctly, the examiner must secure and evaluate the scene and must be familiar with mobile devices and with tangential equipment, such as media, cables, and power adapters. The overall scene should be roughly searched for associated peripherals (such as removable media, **Universal Integrated Circuit Card (UICCs)**, or personal computers), thus ensuring that related evidence is not overlooked. The examiner must consider interviewing the owner or user of the device and is invited to request any security codes, passwords, or gestures needed to gain access to the device content. If the device is found in a damaged state, it does not mean that an eventual exploitation is impossible; the damaged equipment should be taken back to the lab in order to try a restore it to the working state. The **Scientific Working Group on Digital Evidence (SWGDE)** has developed guidance regarding the best practices for the collection of damaged mobile devices available at `https://www.swgde.org/documents/Current%20Documents/2016-02-08%20SWGDE%20Best%20Practices%20for%20Collection%20of%20Damaged%20Mobile%20Devices_v1-1`.

During the whole process, the examiner must be as vigilant as possible while documenting the scene; attention must be paid to everything and not only the device itself. The evidence must be accurately accounted for and identified, and even non-electronic materials, such as invoices, manuals, and packaging, may provide useful information about the capabilities of the device, the network used, account information, and, in some cases, unlocking codes. A record of all visible data should be created. All digital devices, including mobile devices, which can store data, should be photographed along with all the peripherals, such as cables, power connectors, removable media, and connections.

By definition, a mobile device is intended to communicate via cellular phone networks, Bluetooth, Infrared, and wireless (Wi-Fi), which brings us to the importance of *isolating it from the network* as a step of securing the evidence. The examiner must be aware that some mobiles can be remotely locked or wiped by simply receiving a command (a text message, for example); isolating the device from communication sources helps to keep the integrity of the evidence by disabling capabilities, such as receiving incoming calls or text messages that may alter the current state of data stored on the sized device. In addition to the incoming data, isolating the device also prevents the altering of current stats via outgoing data, such as GPS location, that may be delivered to an adversary providing the geographic location of the forensic examiner. In the situation where a device is found connected to a personal computer, the examiner should make a capture of this personal computer's memory before unplugging the device and then stopping synchronization.

The NIST Special Publication 800-101 regarding *Guidelines on Mobile Device Forensics* provides some key implications for proper device isolation that are summarized here:

- Enabling the Airplane mode requires interaction with the mobile device using the keypad, which poses some risk; however, this risk can be reduced if the technician is familiar with the device in question and also documents the actions taken (on paper or on video). Remember that the Airplane mode does not prevent the system from using other services such as GPS in all cases.

- Turning off the mobile device may activate authentication codes (for example, UICC PIN and/or handset security codes), which are then required to gain access to the device, thus complicating acquisition and delaying examination.

- Keeping the mobile device on but radio isolated (for example, Wi-Fi, cellular and Bluetooth), shortens battery life due to increased power consumption, as devices that are unable to connect to a network raise their signal strength to maximum. After some time, the failure to connect to a network may cause certain mobile devices to reset or clear network data that otherwise would be useful if recovered. Faraday containers may attenuate the radio signal but not necessarily eliminate it completely, thus allowing the possibility of communications to be established with a cell tower, if in its immediate vicinity. The risk of improper sealing of the Faraday container (for example, a bag improperly sealed or exposed cables connected to the forensic workstation may act as an antenna) and unknowingly allowing access to the cell network also exists.

The examiner has to be aware of the fact that even if a device is totally isolated, user data can still be affected if the device is programmed to send an alert for appointments or if alarms are set previously. For example, in many devices the alarm is capable of turning on and establishing network connectivity on an inactive device. Another example to be considered is key remapping; some users remap hardware keys to perform a different action other than the default. If a non-desired situation arises, the examiner should document it.

Once the device is ready to be analyzed, the examiner should seal this in a container and label it according to the agency or organization specifications to begin the device processing. Depending on the sensitivity of the case being examined, the examiner should also bear in mind the organization's or agency's backlogs of digital forensics casework and can envisage an on-site triage if possible, which involves a manual or logical on-scene acquisition, followed immediately by an initial analysis of the data extracted. Special attention must be paid to devices that offer full disk encryptions and they must be processed immediately if found in an unlocked state. The NIST Special Publication 800-101 presents a **Generic On-Site Decision Tree** that can be used as a general guide for organizations and agencies to help with the prioritization of on-site triage examinations via the description of some of the actions and decision points.

The examiner will have to answer some basic questions, such as:

- Is the device in an unlocked state and functional, thus permitting a manual or logical data extraction?
- Is the extraction urgent?
- Can the mobile device be transported to a forensics laboratory in less than 2 hours?
- Is the device supported by the tool and has the examiner received proper training?
- Does the device show that it has more than 50% remaining battery power?

Have a look at the following diagram:

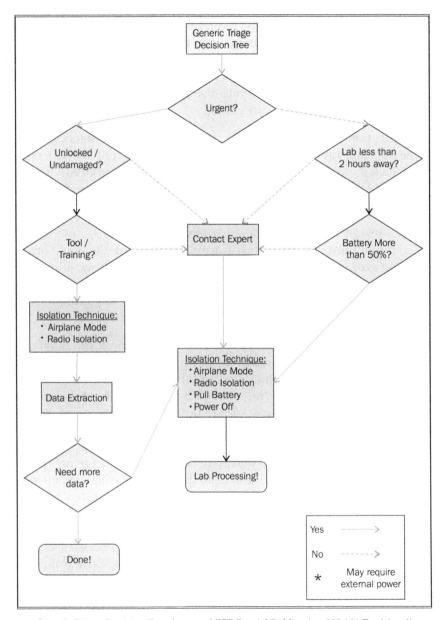

Generic Triage Decision Tree (source: NIST Special Publication 800-101 Revision 1)

Whether it's an on-site extraction or in a forensic laboratory, the previously identified tools to work with should be used to process only specific items requested for recovery. If any concern exists about the requested data, the examiner is advised to contact the submitter for clarification before any processing. In the cases involving a limited scope search warrant, the examiner should take care to only report items covered by the warrant. The examiner is recommended to document the version of the tools being used with a consideration to also document the order of software and hardware used during the device's processing.

During the acquisition phase, the examiner is advised to use a reference clock and to document the date and time from the device and then determine the differences from the reference clock if any. The date and time on the device is important information that can be affected during acquisition. It's very important to document differences of date and time if detected.

If the device has installed any data storage extension (for example, microSD card), the examiner should remove it prior to any acquisition in order to avoid any data alteration during acquisition processes. Memory cards should be acquired separately using traditional forensics processes. If, for one reason or another, the examiner is not able to process the data storage extension separately, documenting the date and time of both the device and card acquisition is especially important.

In this process, the examiner intends to extract digital evidences and must pay attention to separate relevant information from irrelevant information. This process must be followed by a careful documentation of the stats and the content of every piece of extracted data. Having enough information about the case being investigated helps in setting a starting point of potential evidences and provides a clear idea about the type of data, keyword or phrase the examiner can target when analyzing the extracted data. The set of capabilities and features that modern smartphones offer, including e-mails, personal information management, social media, or messaging, can point the examiner to different potential evidences that a device can hold, including contact information (phonebook), calendar and appointments, outgoing, incoming, and missed phone calls, photos, videos and different media files, web browsing activities, social media related data, geolocation data, electronic mails and documents, and more. During the process of acquisition, the examiner should prepare a basic background about the incident or the case being investigated by answering five important questions about the case: *Who?* (who is involved), *What?* (what is the nature of the occurred events?), *When?* (establishing a timeline of events), *Why?* (the examiner should have enough information about the motivations behind the events) and *How?* (devices, application, or whatever tools were used by individuals involved).

Once extracted, the data is effectively processed. The examiner should be aware of the fact that forensic tools can report incomplete, erroneous, and sometimes conflicted data. This engages the examiner in a **verification and validation** process in which he must verify the accuracy of the extracted evidence. The examiner has several methods to make sure that the extracted data is accurate. If the examiner has the possibility to handle the device itself (if it's not locked or if the unlock code is known), he can proceed by comparing the extracted data to the data displayed on the device. Manually scrutinizing the device can make irreversible changes to some evidence (such as missed calls or unread messages), so the examiner must be extremely careful when handling the device directly and is invited to video record the process of manually navigating the device's content via its interface menu. The most common verification technique is using hash values. If the examiner was successful in extracting the filesystem, forensic tools can be used to hash the extracted files (as mentioned earlier in this chapter) and any extracted file can be then checked against the original file in order to verify its integrity. Extracting files and hashing them twice (maybe using different tools) can be another option to confirm a file's integrity. It's important to note that there are cases where data extraction alters files, as explained in *Hashing Techniques for Mobile Device Forensics* by Shira Danker, Rick Ayers and Richard P. Mislan (`http://citeseerx.ist.psu.edu/viewdoc/download?doi=10.1.1.437.3256&rep=rep1&type=pdf`).

If level 3 or 4 acquisitions (physical acquisitions) were supported, the examiner can check manually the underlying hex code using different techniques (as explained in *Chapter 2*, *Do It Yourself – Low-Level Techniques*) to decode data and correlate/confirm results reported by forensic tools; this method is quite challenging, time consuming, and requires a certain level of expertise and experience with file formats and encoding methods, but it is still efficient and should not be ignored in the evidence validation process. The examiner may need more than one technique to validate his finding.

To recapitulate the verification options, the examiner can:

- Compare extracted data with data on the device
- Use hash values to determine file integrity
- Manually carve physical dump

After being sure of the integrity of the acquired data, the examiner will **document and report** his findings. As described in this section, documentation is a task that follows the examiner during the whole investigation process and the examiner should note what was done or noticed during the acquisition and examination while respecting the eventual represented organization or agency's policies. Maintaining a careful record of what was done and what was observed during the previous stages of the overall investigation process will be of great value when writing the final report. To facilitate documentation and reporting, the examiner can use examination worksheets in order to be sure that all the basic information is reported. The examiner must remember that a good report relies on good documentation (including notes, photographs, and generated contents using forensic tools).

The **National Institute of Justice (NIJ)** provides samples of worksheets on their publication *Forensic Examination of Digital Evidence: A Guide for Law Enforcement* (https://www.ncjrs.gov/pdffiles1/nij/199408.pdf) that can be adapted to the examiner's need. The following is sample of a removable media worksheet:

Removable Media Worksheet

Case Number: _____   Exhibit Number: _____

Laboratory Number: _____   Control Number: _____

Media Type / Quantity

Diskette [ ]	LS-120 [ ]	100 MB Zip [ ]	250 MB Zip [ ]
1 GB Jaz [ ]	2 GB Jaz [ ]	Magneto-Optical [ ]	Tape [ ]
CD [ ]	DVD [ ]	Other [ ]	

Examination

Exhibit # Sub-Exhibit #	Triage	Duplicated	Browse	Unerase	Keyword Search

Examiner _____   Date _____   Supervisor Review _____   Date _____

Digital Evidence Removable Media Worksheet	Page 1 of 2

The reporting is done when all the relevant data is bookmarked and the search has been done. Most modern forensic tools provide a built-in reporting feature that follows a predefined template that can be customized by the examiner in order to include the organization (or agency) logo and report header. Most generated reports include the examiner's name, a case number, the device type and category, the case's title, date, and categories of evidences found. In addition to this, the automatically generated reports can be usually customized to either include the relevant evidence found, extracted data, or let the examiner choose whether data is to be included or not in the final report in order to minimize its size and to facilitate its readability. The examiner should not consider a generated report as the final report; in addition to the forensic tool generated report, the final report should include a summary of all actions taken, conducted analysis, and the relevance of the evidence acquired. Obviously, the type of data that needs to be presented determines the support that will be used, so evidentiary data, such as video or audio, should be included in the final report on removable media.

It's mandatory that the final report includes every piece of information capable of identifying the case. The examiner should be sure that his final report outlines the test results and findings and has his signature.

The report is an important part of the forensic investigation and will definitely be scrutinized once presented to the concerned party. The examiner should make sure that his final report:

- Summarizes the incident or the case being investigated.
- Is technically sound and includes a glossary explaining the acronyms and technical terms.
- Is understandable. Knowing to whom the report will be presented will help the examiner in writing it using "appropriate words".
- Is clearly formatted and structured and has a logical progression of evidence.
- Includes conclusions, recommendations, and opinions. In addition to evidence, the examiner should include where the evidence leads to and is encouraged to include his opinion based on facts, his own experiences, and expertise.
- Adheres to laws as appropriate (a report of a Homeland Security case is not redacted as a report of a gambling case).

While redacting his final report, the examiner should keep in mind the decision maker's requirements, and obviously the final report must meet those requirements.

According to The National Institute of Standards and Technology in *Guidelines on Mobile Device Forensics*, the report must include the following information:

- Identity of the reporting agency
- Case identifier or submission number
- Case investigator
- Identity of the submitter
- Date of evidence receipt
- Date of report
- Descriptive list of items submitted for examination, including the serial number, make, and model
- Identity and signature of the examiner
- The equipment and setup used in the examination
- Brief description of steps taken during examination, such as string searches, graphics image searches, and recovering erased files
- Supporting materials, such as printouts of particular items of evidence, digital copies of evidence, and chain of custody documentation
- Details of findings:
  - Specific files related to the request
  - Other files, including deleted files that support the findings
  - String searches, keyword searches, and text string searches
  - Internet-related evidence, such as website traffic analysis, chat logs, cache files, e-mail, and news group activity
  - Graphic image analysis
  - Indicators of ownership, which could include program registration data
  - Data analysis
  - Description of relevant programs on the examined items
  - Techniques used to hide or mask data, such as encryption, steganography, hidden attributes, hidden partitions, and file name anomalies
- Report conclusions

In addition to this list of information that a report could include, the Scientific Working Group on Digital Evidence in their second version of *Best Practices for Mobile Phone Forensics* suggest the following elements to be included as well:

- Copy of legal authority
- Chain of custody
- Photographs or documentation of any visible damage
- Information regarding the packaging and condition of the phone
- Sufficient detail to enable another examiner, competent in the same area of expertise, to repeat the findings independently
- Documentation of any anomalies in the data acquisition (for example, acquisition disruptions, faulty cables, and incoming data)
- Substantive communication notes regarding the case
- Supplement reports related to the examination

The full list of elements can be found at `https://www.swgde.org/documents/` `Current%20Documents/2013-02-11%20SWGDE%20Best%20Practices%20for%20` `Mobile%20Phone%20Forensics%20V2-0`.

The report written is meant to be presented. The examiner should consider how its final reports will eventually be **presented** clearly to a wide variety of audiences, who will decide whether to use the evidence acquired in court or not. The audience can vary depending on the nature of the case (legal and technical experts, law enforcement officers or corporate managers, and so on). In most cases, it's preferable to present the final report in both paper and electronic format as the extracted data could be important to supported forensic tools for further analysis if required. Pictures of call history logs or text messages can be visually compelling to a non-technical person (like a jury). The examiner can use Mind Map or the Timeline software to present his findings so that the progression and the correlation of events can be shown clearly to the audience.

MindView-Law Enforcement (`http://www.matchware.com/`) is a great tool for creating professional timelines of accidents and crime scene data and enables examiners to quickly brainstorm and input data and then present this data as a timeline or export it to PowerPoint, Word, or an HTML website.

The following is a sample of a criminal profiling mind-map template from the MindView tool:

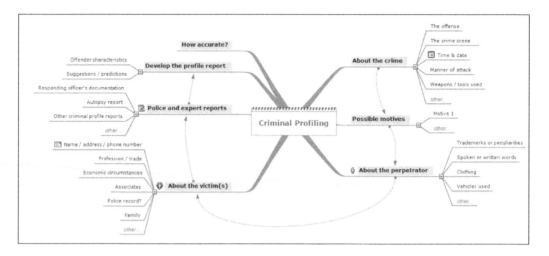

The following is a sample of a Timeline template:

The overall forensics process ends with **archiving** acquisition case files in adequacy to the organization or agency policies and applicable laws. Archiving is an important step of the process in which all the retained documentation and data should be stored in useable, proprietary, and non-proprietary formats. The examiner should also think about retaining a copy of tools used to facilitate viewing data at a later date.

Similar to any forensic investigation, several approaches and techniques can be used to acquire, examine, and analyze data from a mobile device; this section provided a proposed process in which guidelines from different standards and models (SWGDE's *Best Practices for Mobile Phone Forensics*, NIST's *Guidelines on Mobile Device Forensics*, *Developing Process for Mobile Device Forensics* by Det. Cynthia A. Murphy) were summarized. As a recapitulation of what was said, the following flowchart schematizes the overall process:

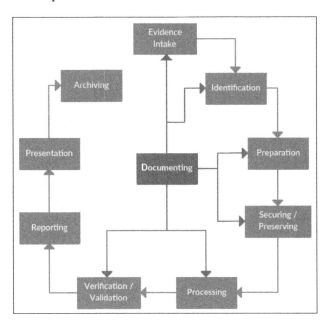

Here's the process in detail:

- **Evidence intake**: Triggers the examination process. This step should be documented.

- **Identification**: The examiner needs to identify the device's capabilities and specifications. The examiner should document almost everything during the whole process of identification.

- **Preparation**: The examiner should prepare tools and methods to use and must document them.

- **Securing and preserving evidences**: The examiner is invited to protect the evidences and to secure the scene as well as isolate the device from all the networks. The examiner should be vigilant when documenting the scene.

- **Processing**: At this stage, the examiner should start performing the actual (and technical) data acquisition and analysis and document steps, tools used, and all his findings.

- **Verification and validation**: The examiner should be sure of the integrity of his findings and must validate acquired data and evidences. This step should be documented as well.

- **Reporting**: The examiner produces a final report in which he documents process and finding.

- **Presentation**: This stage is meant to exhibit and present finding.

- **Archiving**: At the end of the forensic process, the examiner should preserve data, report, tools, and all his findings in common formats for an eventual later use.

There have been many worldwide efforts to produce a solid framework and to standardize digital forensics in order to help lead a mobile forensic investigation successfully, and many organizations and states are publishing standards and best practices guidelines that the examiners can visit to expand their knowledge of digital forensics. The following is an example of the references:

- ISO/IEC 27037:2012, Information technology – Security techniques – Guidelines for identification, collection, acquisition, and preservation of digital evidence

- ASTM E3046 – 15, Standard Guide for Core Competencies for Mobile Phone Forensics

- **Internet Engineering Task Force (IETF)** RFC 3227, Guidelines for Evidence Collection and Archiving

- **European Network of Forensic Science Institution (ENFSI)**, Guidelines for Best Practice in the Forensic Examination of Digital Technology

- **Association of Chief Police Officers (ACPO)**, Good Practice Guide for Digital Evidence

- **Scientific Working Group on Digital Evidence (SWGDE)**, SWGDE Proposed Techniques for Advanced Data Recovery from Security Digital Video Recorders Containing H 264 Data

- **Scientific Working Group on Digital Evidence (SWGDE)**, Scientific Working Group on Digital Evidence Bylaws

Mobile device identification

Device identification is an interesting and important part of any investigation process that allows an examiner to choose an appropriate forensic tool to identify a particular device at a later time. A mobile device is identified by its make, model, and service provider. In the most recent devices, the manufacturer's label is visible in the device's battery compartment but the examiner should be aware of the fact that removing the battery may affect the state of the device's volatile memory even if the device is found in an inactive/turned off state.

There are many "tips" that the examiner can use to identify a mobile device including the following:

Physical characteristics

The examiner can rely on the device's physical characteristics to identify its make and model. The dimensions, weight, shape, and unique design of some particular devices can help the examiner to either immediately identify a device or to query available online repositories (`http://www.gsmarena.com/search.php3`, `http://mobile.softpedia.com/phoneFinder`, and `http://www.phonescoop.com/phones/finder.php`) based on the selected attributes to get the device's specifications. In order to be sure of the match, the examiner is invited to use more than one source.

Depending on the examiner's experience, identifying some manufacturers of mobile devices is easy and the correlation between the size, number of contacts, and shape of the device's data cable and the manufacturer of the device may be helpful in identification.

Device info

Information regarding the device can be found on the battery cavity; most mobile device manufacturers print their logos and list the make, model number, and some of (or all) the device's unique identifiers, such as the **Electronic Serial Number (ESN)**, the **Mobile Equipment Identifier (MEID)**, the **Federal Communications Commission Identification Number (FCC ID)**, and the **International Mobile Identifier (IMEI)**. The following photo shows the manufacturer logo, make, model, IMEI, and FCC ID of a Nokia Lumia 720:

The ESN and MEID are specific to **Code-Division Multiple Access (CDMA)** mobile devices, with CDMA being a digital cellular technology that uses spread-spectrum techniques.

The ESN is a unique 32-bit ID that identifies the device on the CDMA network, and the examiner must be aware that the ESN can be listed either as 11 digits in decimal format or as eight hexadecimal digits, which are not numeric conversions of each other, and the examiner can use services such as http://www.elfqrin.com/esndhconv.php to convert values. The first 8-14 bits of the ESN identify the manufacturer and the remaining bits represent the assigned serial number.

The MEID is a substitute of the ESN due to its 32-bit limitation. The examiner is more likely to find only the MEID, since there has been a shortage of ESN since November 2008. The MEID is 56-bits and is listed in hexadecimal as: eight bits representing the regional code, 24 bits representing the manufacturer code, and 24 bits representing the manufacturer's assigned serial number.

Just like MEID, the IMEI identifies all mobile devices on the **Global System for Mobile Communications (GSM)** and the **Universal Mobile Telecommunications System (UMTS)** networks. The IMEI has a total of 15 numeric digits, 14 digits plus a check digit, and can be decoded to identify the device's manufacturer, brand, power class, band, and more. The initial eight digits are the **Type Allocation Code (TAC)** and represent the device's model and revision. Services such as `http://www.nobbi.com/tacquery.php` can be used to identify phone and manufacturer by TAC. The next six digits represent the device's serial number and the last digit represents the check digit calculated using the **Luhn algorithm**.

A database lookup service is available at `https://imeidata.net/` and can return detailed information about the IMEI being looked for, as you can see from the following screenshot:

The FCC ID is independent of the network and is found in almost every hardware that generates a radio signal. On mobile devices, the FCCID can help the examiner find the device's manufacturer and retrieve the device user manual, device photos, radio frequency test results, and in some cases JTAG taps. The first three characters of the FCC ID represent the manufacturer code and the remaining 14 characters/digits are the product code. The FCC provides a database lookup service available at the FCC website at `https://www.fcc.gov/general/fcc-id-search-page`.

The examiner should make sure that any research he does regarding codes and unique device identifiers is properly documented too.

Service provider

The service provider or the carrier for a mobile device can be identified by its printed logo on the device; in some cases, the carrier prints its logo as a branding and advertising effort and this could help the examiner to identify the carrier on which the device operates. The examiner is advised to keep in mind that mobile devices are subject to unlocking technology in order to operate under a different carrier, so the examiner should examine the **Subscriber Identity Module** or **Subscriber Identification Module** (SIM) if present.

The SIMs is shipped in three different formats with different sizes: Mini SIM (2FF), Micro SIM (3FF), and Nano SIM (4FF):

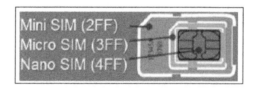

The SIM circuit is a part of the function of a UICC and one appellation could be used to refer to the other. Each UICC is imprinted with a unique identifier called the **Integrated Circuit Card Identification** (ICCID), which may be 19 to 20 digits long and respects ITU-T recommendation (`http://www.itu.int/en/ITU-T/publications/Pages/recs.aspx`). It consists of two digits representing the major industry identifier as defined by ISO/IEC 7812, one to three digits representing the country code, one to four digits representing the issuer identifier, 12 to 14 digits representing the account ID, one digit for checksum using the Luhn algorithm, and an extra digit (the 20th) returned by the `AT#CCID` command.

Variable identification numbers (country code, issuer identifier, and account ID) are a fixed number of digits within a country, world zone, or for each particular issuer identifier number. You can learn more from **E.118** at `http://www.itu.int/rec/` `dologin_pub.asp?lang=e&id=T-REC-E.118-200605-I!!PDF-E&type=items`.

The International Numbering Plans website (`http://www.numberingplans.` `com/?page=analysis&sub=simnr`) supports ICCID queries for this information.

Summary

This chapter covers the essential best practices for performing a mobile device investigation process accurately; we covered the important mobile forensics phases, starting from evidence intake to the archiving stage. The process described was based on the NIST guidelines for mobile device forensics. Even if it's true that technical examination may one differ from device to another, the examiner is always invited to adopt and roughly follow a consistent framework in order to produce repeatable, presentable, and defensible results.

In the upcoming appendix, we will present a step-by-step guide for preparing a forensic workstation based on Santoku Linux.

Preparing a Mobile Forensic Workstation

Mobile incident response is a little different from computer incident response, especially if we point out some unique properties of mobile devices, such as the introduction of application stores models, lack of administrative access to smartphones, and mobile's explosive growth. The dramatic growth of annual smartphone unit sales has left the forensic community a lack of time to mature (source for the following graph: `http://ben-evans.com/benedictevans/2015/11/7/mobile-ecosystems-and-the-death-of-pcs`):

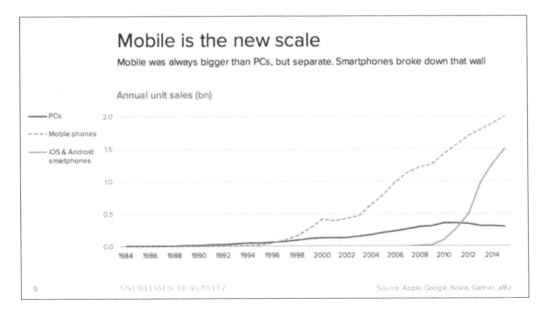

This growth gave birth to many common scenarios in which an examiner would be solicited to respond to a mobile incident, such as malware infection, suspicious device behavior, stolen or lost device, e-discovery, legal hold, or data breach. Thus, setting up an appropriate environment is a key component of mobile incident response. The community is continuously trying to keep pace with this unstoppable growth of technology. The easiest way to set up a mobile forensic workstation is by adopting one of the freely available open source Linux distributions, specially crafted to let the mobile forensic examiners acquire and analyze data from most smartphones by including most of the useful tools and utilities related to mobile forensics. This section will describe how to set up Santoku Linux on a virtual environment. The examiner can also decide to install the operating system directly on a computer, but it's recommended to use virtual environments.

Before setting up Santoku, the following is required:

- Santoku Linux .ISO file (`https://santoku-linux.com/download/`).
- VirtualBox or VMWare Player (in this section, the latest version of Oracle VM VirtualBox version 5.0.16 was used. It can be downloaded from `https://www.virtualbox.org/wiki/Downloads`).
- A host machine with a dual-core processor (minimum), 8 GB RAM, and 40 GB (or larger) free hard drive space.

After installing and running VirtualBox (the default installation path is `C:\Program Files\Oracle\VirtualBox\`), click on **New** to create a new virtual machine. A wizard will show up to guide you through different parameters. The first screen is to choose the name and the virtual machine's operating system:

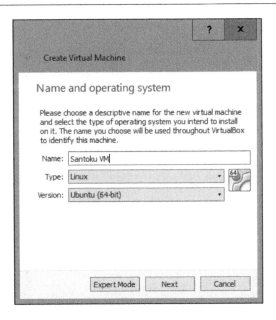

Click on **Next** and select the appropriate amount of memory for the virtual machine; it's recommended to select at least 4 GB:

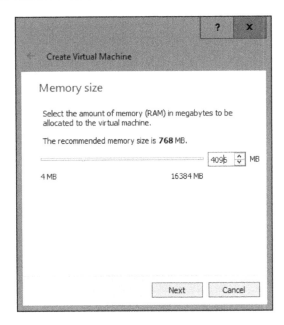

Click on **Next** and choose **Create a virtual hard disk now** on the screen that follows:

Click on **Create** and select the **VDI (VirtualBox Disk Image)** option on the following screen:

Click on **Next**; on the **Storage and physical hard disk** screen leave the **Dynamically allocated** option selected and click on **Next**. On the **File location and size** screen, you can click on the folder icon to choose the location where the virtual hard disk drive will be stored and then select the size of it either by adjusting the slider or by typing the value in gigabytes depending on your needs; however, it's recommended that you allocate around 40 GB:

Click on the **Create** button, and from the VirtualBox's main window, select the newly created virtual machine and click on **Settings**:

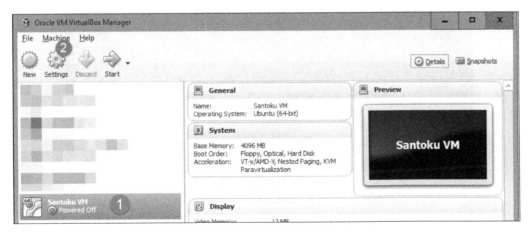

Select the **Storage** option on the left of the **Settings** screen and then click on the CD icon next to **Controller: IDE**. To add an optical drive, a question box will pop up; select **Choose disk**:

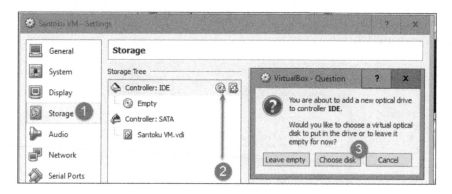

Navigate to your downloaded santoku_0.5.iso file, click on **Open** and then on **Ok**, which will bring you back to the main VirtualBox menu.

The virtual machine is now ready and we can proceed with the Santoku installation; select the newly created virtual machine from the main menu and click on **Start**.

To begin an installation process, choose **install – start the installer directly** and hit *Enter*:

Choose your language and click on **Continue**; on the **Installation type** screen, select
Erase disk and install Santoku, and click on **Install Now** as follows:

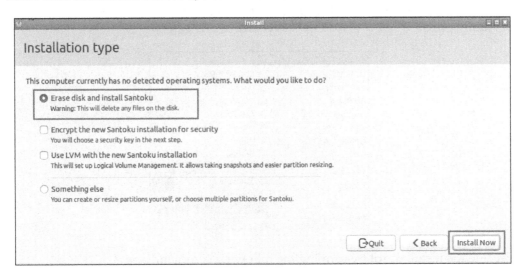

Choose your time zone and keyboard layout, user name and password settings, and
click on **Continue**. After the installation is complete, reboot when prompted and then
log in using the username and password you created during the installation process.

The last step that remains is installing VirtualBox Guest Additions; this is an optional
step that will improve the VM graphic, shared folders, and offers other features.
Click on **Devices | Insert Guest Additions CD image...**:

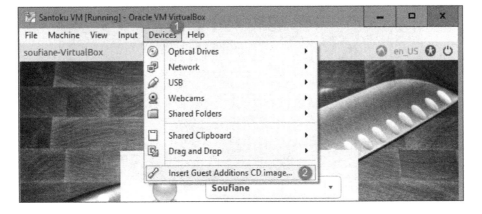

If asked for authentication, type in the password you created during the installation process, click on **OK**, and close the **Removable media detection** window that appears. Next, open a terminal window by navigating to **Accessories | LXTerminal** or simply press *Ctrl + Alt + T* on the keyboard:

Execute the install script by running the following command:

```
sudo sh /media/username/VBOXADDITIONS_5.0.16_105871/VBoxLinuxAdditions.run
```

You will need to enter the administrator password, which you set up during installation. In the preceding command, swap `username` with the username you are logged in with, and in `VBOXADDITIONS_5.0.16_105871` the version following `VBOXADDITIONS` may be different:

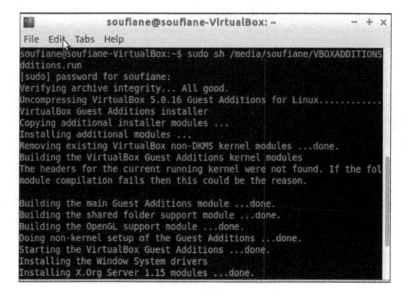

Optionally, you can update local packages index by typing the following command:

```
sudo apt-get update
```

After the command is completed, upgrade the packages by typing the following command:

```
Sudo apt-get upgrade
```

If asked to continue, type y and hit *Enter*.

The Santoku Linux VM is now operational; if you want to connect a mobile device to it, click on **Devices | USB** and select a detected device, as you can see from the following screenshot:

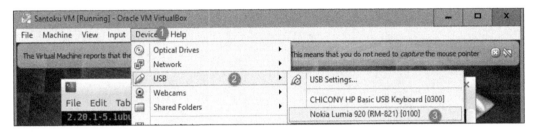

Do not hesitate to visit https://santoku-linux.com/howtos/ to get familiar with the environment and tools it offers.

Obviously, Santoku is not the only option. SANS Institute published a white paper entitled *Building a Low Cost Forensics Workstation* (https://www.sans.org/reading-room/whitepapers/incident/building-cost-forensics-workstation-895), which describes the requirements for a low cost forensics workstation that can be used in electronic investigations, and they offer a free Linux distribution dedicated to incident response and digital forensics called **SANS Investigative Forensic Toolkit (SIFT)** Workstation Version 3 (https://digital-forensics.sans.org/community/downloads). SIFT is a very respectable and well-maintained distribution that includes a collection of various tools to aid you in performing forensics analysis tasks. You can find the whole documentation, user manual, tools, commands, and scripts at https://sift.readthedocs.org/en/latest/.

In addition to Santoku and SIFT, **CAINE (Computer Aided INvestigative Environment)** is another Linux-based distribution that offers an interesting forensic environment and is available at http://www.caine-live.net/.

Index

B

Bag Grid Array (BGA) type 180
Belkasoft Evidence Center
  about 244
  URL 244
BitLocker 214
Board Support Package (BSP) 195
Boot Configuration Data (BCD) settings 209
bypassing security
  about 137, 138
  Android device, rooting 143-146
  bootloader/recovery mode 139-142
  lock pattern, cracking 146-148
  PIN/password, cracking 149-156

C

CAINE (Computer Aided INvestigative
    Environment)
  URL 291
Cellebrite 241
chambers 209
Chaos Computer Club (CCC) 117
Cipher Block Chaining (CBC) 213
Code-Division Multiple Access (CDMA)
    mobile devices 278
Code Signing 209
command parameters
  -all 164
  -apk 164
  -f 164
  -noapk 164
  -noshared 164
  -nosystem 164
  <packages> 164
  -shared 164
  -system 164
Common Language Runtime (CLR) 57
Component Object Model (COM) 194
Computer Forensic Investigation Process
    (CFIP)
  about 5
  Acquisition 5
  Admitting 5
  Evaluation 5
  Identification 5

Computer Forensic Tool Testing (CFTT)
    program 215
Content Providers 129
Cortana 194
crypto footer 152
CryptoTool
  about 47
  URL 47

D

Data 200
data protection
  Complete Data Protection 69
  Data Protected Until First User
    Authentication 69
  Data Protection Unless Open 69
  No Protection 69
DB Browser for SQLite
  reference 119
DE4DOT
  URL 62
decompiler 57
decompiling 57-62
Deployment phases, IDIP
  about 8
  confirmation and authorization 8
  detection and notification 8
device backup 85
Device Firmware Upgrade (DFU) mode 76
dex2jar
  about 60
  reference 60
dex2oat utility 128
Digital Crime Scene Investigation Phases,
    IDIP
  Digital Crime Scene Reconstruction 10
  Document Evidence and Scene 10
  Presentation of Digital Scene Theory 10
  Preservation of digital scene 10
  Search for Digital Evidence 10
  Survey For Digital Evidence 10
Digital Forensic Research
    Workshop (DFRWS)
  about 6, 20
  Analysis 6
  Collection 6

JPEG format
  carving 20
JTAG 241
JTAG TAPs 178
just-in-time (JIT) compilation 127

K

Kernel-Mode Drivers
        Framework (KMDF) 197
KeyChain API 130
Keychain Data Protection 70
keyguards 138
KingRoot 143

L

Least Privilege Chamber (LPC) 210
Lempel-Ziv-Markov chain algorithm
        (LZMA) 25
Linux Kernel 127
Linux United Key Setup (LUKS) 152
Location Manager 129
logical acquisition 84-90
Low-Level Bootloader (LLB) 76
Luhn algorithm 279

M

MainOS volume
  %SystemDrive%\Programs 200
  %SystemDrive%\Programs\
        <AppName> 201
  %SystemDrive%\Windows 202
  about 200
mandatory access control (MAC)
        implementation 136
Manifest.mbdb 102
Manifest.plist 103
markers 20
MD5 algorithm
  URL 56
Media Framework 127
Message-Digest Algorithm (MD5) 55
metadata
  about 27

administrative 27
  descriptive 27
  extracting 28-39
  structural 27
mobile device identification
  about 277
  device info 278, 279
  physical characteristics 277
  service provider 280
MOBILedit backup 85
MOBILedit! Forensic
  about 110
  used, for artifact recovery 110-115
MOBILedit! Forensic 8.2
  about 85
  for Windows Phone logical
        acquisition 216-220
Mobile Equipment Identifier (MEID) 278
mobile forensics
  about 2
  features 2-4
mobile forensics process
  evidence intake phase 258
  preparation phase 260
  presenting 258-276
mobile forensic workstation
  preparing 283-291
Motorola type byte 28

N

National Institute of Justice (NIJ)
  reference 270
National Institute of Standards and
        Technology (NIST) 45, 262
National Software Reference Library
        (NSRL) 56
Navigation Server 198
NetCat 171
New Technology File System (NTFS) 206
Nmap 171
normal/direct acquisition 83
Notification Manager 129
NT filesystem (NTFS) 194

Made in the USA
Middletown, DE
12 December 2018